D1237803

WILLIAM F. MAAG LIBRARY
YOUNGSTOWN STATE UNIVERSITY

Selected Plays of

ALEKSEI ARBUZOV

WITHDRAWN

Other Titles of Interest

English Texts

Aleksei Arbuzov London, 1980

Selected Plays of
ALEKSEI ARBUZOV

Translated by
ARIADNE NICOLAEFF

PERGAMON PRESS

OXFORD · NEW YORK · TORONTO · SYDNEY · PARIS · FRANKFURT

U.K.	Pergamon Press Ltd., Headington Hill Hall, Oxford OX3 0BW, England
U.S.A.	Pergamon Press Inc., Maxwell House, Fairview Park, Elmsford, New York 10523, U.S.A.
CANADA	Pergamon Press Canada Ltd., Suite 104, 150 Consumers Rd., Willowdale, Ontario M2J 1P9, Canada
AUSTRALIA	Pergamon Press (Aust.) Pty. Ltd., P.O. Box 544, Potts Point, N.S.W. 2011, Australia
FRANCE	Pergamon Press SARL, 24 rue des Ecoles, 75240 Paris, Cedex 05, France
FEDERAL REPUBLIC OF GERMANY	Pergamon Press GmbH, 6242 Kronberg-Taunus, Hammerweg 6, Federal Republic of Germany

Copyright this edition © 1982 Pergamon Press Ltd.
Copyright for individual plays © Ariadne Nicolaeff
The Promise was first published in 1967 by the Oxford University Press.

All Rights Reserved. No part of this publication may be reproduced, stored in a retrieval system or transmitted in any form or by any means: electronic, electrostatic, magnetic tape, mechanical, photocopying, recording or otherwise, without permission in writing from the publishers.

First edition 1982

Application for permission to perform the plays must be made in advance, before rehearsals begin, by both professional and amateur companies, in the United States of America and Canada to Harold Freedman, Brandt & Brandt Dramatic Department, Inc., 1501 Broadway, New York, NY 10036, and for all other territories to John Cadell Ltd, 2 Southwood Lane, London N6 5EE.

Library of Congress Cataloging in Publication Data
Arbuzov, Aleksei Nikolayevich
Selected plays of Aleksei Arbuzov.
I. Nicolaeff, Ariadne. II. Title.
PG3476.A633A25   1982   891.72'42   82-364

British Library Cataloguing in Publication Data
Arbuzov, Aleksei
Selected plays of Aleksei Arbuzov.
I. Title
891.72'42   PG3476.A633
ISBN 0-08-024548-X

Printed in Great Britain by A. Wheaton & Co. Ltd., Exeter

PG
3476
.A633 A25
1982

TO DEAR FRANK HAUSER

WHO IS AN INTEGRAL PART

OF THIS ADVENTURE

WILLIAM F. MAAG LIBRARY
YOUNGSTOWN STATE UNIVERSITY

CONTENTS

FOREWORD

I first met Aleksei Nikolayevich in 1968: he was in England for the première of *Confession at Night* at Nottingham and he and Ariadne Nicolaeff stopped off at Leicester on the way back to see a production of *The Promise* which I had directed.

In the course of a riotous supper, at which he told a number of very funny stories with a deadpan face and lethal comic timing, he told us about the Nottingham production. At the end of the first act, after a tremendous battle, the stage empties, a bird sings and the curtain falls. When Arbuzov saw a dress rehearsal there was no birdsong. "Where is my bird?", he demanded indignantly and the director, confident in the logic of naturalism, said it was impossible because all the birds would have been frightened away by the gunfire. "Ah yes," said Aleksei Nikolayevich, "but this is a very wise bird who knows he's in a theatre."

My next very clear impression of him was in 1970 when he was again in England and asked Ariadne if I would like to take him to the theatre. I felt greatly honoured but insisted that Ariadne join us for supper as my Russian was certainly not up to a whole evening tête-à-tête. He had chosen *The Ruling Class* which opens with an elderly general dressing up in a tutu, ascending a step ladder and hanging himself. Arbuzov leaned over to me and whispered "Why did he do that?" "A sexual deviation" I answered. He paused, then grunted and five minutes later leaned over and said "See you at the end. I'm going to explore the deviations of Soho."

In 1976, when I was director of the Bristol Old Vic, we decided to stage, simultaneously, an Arbuzov play in each of our three theatres. We did *The Promise* and the English premières of *Once Upon a Time* and *Evening Light*. Arbuzov and his wife Rita, a wonderful and ebullient lady, arrived for the last week of rehearsals loaded with gifts for every single actor in the company. He came to a run through of *Evening Light*, the play I directed, and at the end I went on stage for the moral support of my colleagues, turned to the stalls and said: "Aleksei Nikolayevich, is there anything you would like to say to us?" There was dead silence. We turned collectively white. "Ariadne", I asked at length, "is he very displeased?" "Oh, quite the contrary", she said cheerfully, "he is weeping".

So, I love Arbuzov and I love his work. The critics have mostly been rather snobbish about his plays, disappointed at the absence of protest, criticism, repression, and angst but this is why I love them. He writes about people in the Soviet Union governed by a system under which very few of us would wish to

live. We find that these people worry about their salaries and chances of promotion, their children, and their dogs, that they like picnics and fairgrounds,
look forward to holidays, fall in love with other mens' wives, and find life and
their relations with their fellows often difficult. While, in Auden's phrase, "the
living nations wait, each sequestered in their hate", the importance of Arbuzov,
one of the most popular and successful living dramatists in his own country, for
an international public is that he tells us that behind that iron curtain are people
just like ourselves.

We're not supposed to write about eternal verities, it's considered pretentious
and arty-crafty but sometimes only big words will do. In the Bristol programme
for the Arbuzov season I wrote "the universal message of the brotherhood of
man which all peoples acknowledge in their hearts remains constant whatever
politicians and diplomats and generals try to make us think of each other". I
believe that still.

RICHARD COTTRELL

TRANSLATOR'S NOTE

I think the translation of any play for the stage is about actors, audiences, and time; as well as language and meaning. It is not only a question of what words will convey the meaning. There are several questions. How long will it take an English actor to say in English what the Russian actor says in Russian? How quickly will an English audience react to something meant for a Russian audience? How Russian is the play supposed to feel?

Aleksei Nikolayevich Arbuzov, a man of the theatre and an expert in audience reaction, always had something to say about this: "Your production here takes two hours and twenty-five minutes. Our Moscow production takes over three and a half hours". It invariably startled the cast, the director and me. Fortunately Aleksei Nikolayevich always came back to have a look at another production of yet another one of his plays.

They could be described as explorations of sensibility. They are about ordinary people who find or lose themselves in their involvements. Sometimes they refuse to get involved. Sometimes they get involved in a course of action but mostly with each other. Through their subjective experience, the life of their emotions, these ordinary people are extraordinary.

Obviously any translation is different from the original and it is second best. I should first like to say something about the Russian language. It is good at defining relationships. The concept is built into its grammar and ways of addressing people. In a Russian sentence, who is or does what, for how long with or to whom, when, where, how, and why, is always clear. With its declensions and conjugations that define the start, duration, direction, violence, and end of an action, the grammar automatically conveys the meaning and it can be modified with great subtlety.

Who feels what about whom and what is defined by suffixes tacked on to nouns. The result is a variety of names and nicknames, derogatory and affectionate. In the same way feelings are expressed about objects. Largely through Chekhov's plays English audiences are used to the Russian name-with-patronymic form of address. But nowadays it can be respectful or sneering. Then there is the Russian *thou*. What can I do about it? Mostly nothing; sometimes I slip *dear* into the English sentence.

I stake my boundaries. I know an English sentence has to be *made* to make sense; and a succession of sentences are strung together for the overall meaning. The result is precise, logical and concise, sometimes at the cost of shades of feeling. The feeling can be the meaning. If I modify the sentence, I may weaken

1

the statement. It is fascinating to try and get really close to the original. But another translation danger is getting trapped in the Russian grammar. Its echoes sound awkward in English. Then if I turn everything around, which I may have to for a strong dramatic statement, I could fail to return to the original soon enough. Obviously I have tried everything to keep the balance between the play as a compelling piece of theatre and its interest as a contemporary Russian play by Aleksei Arbuzov. These are only some of the hazards. What about problems of obscurity, not to mention style? Positive social and historical references may turn negative from culture to culture. They may not be known. There are also obscure experiences, like famine, seige, and invasion.

As for style, I can only say, the rhythm and tunes of the two languages are different. Anatoly Efros, the Russian director, on the problem of staging Aleksei Arbuzov's recent plays in Russian, indirectly warns the translator: "The problem facing the director is to find a way of staging what is elusive and unreal, partly a tale of fantasy and infinitely poetical, which on the stage invariably and imperceptibly turns into a sugary-sentimental and false melodrama." To counteract this, Anatoly Efros seeks the "slight haze" of Aleksei Arbuzov's plays, which is their essence. I have the same problem — possibly it is the reverse problem: how precisely does one define the meaning. Translating press reviews and interviews in the notes, I have often summarized and simplified.

I must now mention transliteration, the method of writing Russian names and words in the Latin alphabet. There are some differences in the transliteration of the names in the play texts and the same names in the cast lists. Over the years the plays were translated for the stage. In certain contexts I used English or French names and phonetic transliteration to help the actors. I propose to leave them as they are. This book may lead to further stage productions. But in the reference sections I have used the Cambridge University system of transliteration with a few Pergamon Press modifications.

The information about the plays mostly comes from the archives of VTO (Vserossiyskoye Teatral'noye Obshchestvo/Theatre Society of All-Russia), the editorial department of Iskusstvo and the Lenin Library. I thank their staff for being so generous with their time and knowledge. I have done my best to avoid errors but the paper-work of a book based on two languages is horrendous. I thank Beryl Dyson for her unfailing help.

ARIADNE NICOLAEFF

ALEXSEI ARBUZOV – Chronology of His Life and Work

1908 Born in Moscow; orphaned and in the aftermath of the Revolution wandered about homeless until taken in by his aunt.

1925 Studied acting at drama school, his only formal education.

1928 Began directing in Leningrad. Organized touring theatre groups and wrote agitprop for them.

1930 Wrote *Class*, his first play.

1933 Ran the literary section of the first Kolkhoz Theatre.

1934 Wrote *Six Loves*, his first comedy.

1938   *Tanya.*

1939 Founded in Moscow the Studio Theatre with the director Pluchek, in which the actors created the plays, e.g. *A Town At Dawn* in 1941. Toured shows for frontline troops. The Studio Theatre closed at the end of the war.

1943 Wrote *A Little House On The Outskirts.*

1946   *A Meeting With Youth.*

1954   *Years Of Wandering.*

1958   *The Twelfth Hour.*

1959   *It Happened In Irkutsk.*

1964   *The Promise/My Poor Marat.*

1966   *Confession At Night.*

1967   *The Happy Days Of An Unhappy Man.*

1969   *Lovely To Look At!*

1970   *Once Upon A Time/Tales Of Old Arbat.*

1971   *The Choice.*

1972   *In This Nice Old House.*

1973   *Evening Light.*

1975   *Old-World/Do You Turn Somersaults?/Old-World Comedy.*

1978   *Cruel Games.*

4

THE PROMISE

The Promise was first performed at the Oxford Playhouse on 29 November 1966 by the Meadow Players Ltd. with the following cast:

Lika	Judi Dench
Marat	Ian McShane
Leonidik	Ian McKellen

The play was directed by Frank Hauser and designed by Alix Stone.

Peter Bridge presented the Oxford Playhouse Production at the Fortune Theatre in London on 17 January 1967 with the same cast.

The Promise was first performed in New York on 14 November 1967 at the Henry Miller Theater with the following cast:

Lika	Eileen Atkins
Marat	Ian McShane
Leonidik	Ian McKellen

The play was again directed by Frank Hauser. The scenery was by William Ritman and the lighting by Tharon Musser. The play was presented by Helen Bonfils, Morton Gottlieb and Peter Bridge.

Moy Bedny Marat (The Promise) was first performed in Moscow on 26 January 1965 at the Leninsky Komsomol Theatre with the following cast:

Lika	Olga Yakovleva
Marat	A. Zbruyev
Leonidik	L. Krugly

It was directed by A. Efros and designed by V. Lalevich and N. Sosunov.

A second Moscow production opened the same year and ran concurrently at the Central Theatre of the Soviet Army with:

Lika	A. Pokrovskaya
Marat	G. Krynkin
Leonidik	A. Mayorov

It was directed by L. Heifets and designed by M. Mukoseyeva.

Moy Bedny Marat was first performed in Leningrad on 23 March 1965 at the Lensovet Theatre with:

Lika	Alisa Freindlikh
Marat	D. Barkov
Leonidik	A. Pustokhin

It was produced by I. Vladimirov, directed by V. Fialkovsky and designed by A. Medkov.

7

WILLIAM F. MAAG LIBRARY
YOUNGSTOWN STATE UNIVERSITY

CHARACTERS

MARAT

LIKA

LEONIDIK

Act One   March to May 1942

Act Two   March to May 1946

Act Three   December 1959

The action takes place in Leningrad

WILLIAM F. MAAG LIBRARY
YOUNGSTOWN STATE UNIVERSITY

ACT ONE

30 March 1942

One of the few habitable flats in a semi-derelict house on Fontanka. The room is almost bare, the furniture having been used for fire-wood. Only a bulky sideboard and a large wide divan remain.

LIKA, wrapped in any old thing, is on the divan. The spring twilight of Leningrad fills the room. It will soon be evening.

The door opens quietly. MARAT appears on the threshold, looks round the room in some surprise and sees LIKA. It is a long time before they speak.

LIKA [*worried*]. Who are you?

MARAT. And who are you? [*Slight pause.*] No, really . . . What are you doing here?

LIKA. Living.

MARAT. Who let you in?

LIKA. The caretaker. There weren't any corpses in this flat. The glass wasn't broken in the window – the only one that wasn't on this floor. Simply a miracle. [*Quietly.*] Do you want to throw me out?

[*MARAT doesn't answer.*]

Don't. I've been here nearly a month. I'm getting used to it.

MARAT [*after looking round the room*]. There were some things here . . . Well, furniture, and so on . . . Where's everything?

LIKA. I burnt it.

MARAT. The lot?

LIKA. The lot.

[*MARAT sits down on the window sill in silence.*]

Who are you?

MARAT. I used to live here. It's our flat.

LIKA [*slight pause*]. Where have you been?

9

MARAT. That's my business. [*Pause.*] Look, there was a photograph on the wall here between the windows – a naval officer – in a frame . . . Have you seen it?

LIKA. I burnt it.

MARAT [*viciously*]. Well, that's cool of you. Did it provide you a lot of heat . . . that piece of cardboard?

LIKA. It wasn't the only one I burnt. There were a lot of photographs . . . [*Excusing herself, as it were.*] All together it was quite something. A picture frame burns awfully well, you know. It's very good firewood.

MARAT. What a mess you've made of the sideboard.

LIKA. Why? It's standing there all in one piece. I've only taken a splinter here and there.

MARAT. You are businesslike. [*Not loudly.*] You burned my childhood.

LIKA [*cheering up for some reason*]. I recognize you now. You are the boy in the rowing boat, the boy on the bicycle! And in the launch with the officer. I didn't burn everything at once, you know, I had a good look at them first.

MARAT. How was I? Did I burn well?

LIKA. Why are you making fun of me?

MARAT [*serious*]. I could weep. Shall I?

LIKA [*quietly*]. I'm sorry.

MARAT [*turning round*]. Why are you lying down? Have you given up?

LIKA. No, I just came in. I wanted to get warm, that's all.

MARAT [*with a laugh*]. It's one way . . . [*Serious.*] Why didn't you burn the sideboard?

LIKA. I couldn't manage. It's very bulky.

MARAT [*after looking about*]. Are you here alone?

LIKA. Quite alone.

MARAT. Aren't you afraid?

LIKA. Of course I'm afraid, I'm not such a fool. It isn't so bad when there's gunfire. It's a form of life after all . . . But when there's a sudden silence I feel afraid. [*Puzzled.*] I don't know what I'm afraid of. No one's going to break in. The house is supposed to be derelict. The stairs are very rickety. Strangers wouldn't risk it . . . They're sound, really – it's just how they look.

Only two flats on our staircase are inhabited, you know. Actually in the other flat they've stopped going out. I get them their bread and I tidy up . . . In return they promised me their furniture when they don't need it any more. [*Falls silent.*] Yes. It's frightening.

MARAT. What about Flat 5? No one?

LIKA. Empty. [*Slight pause.*] Your friends?

MARAT. There was a girl there, Lelya. She was going to Tbilisi in the autumn.

LIKA. She must have gone.

MARAT. Where did you live?

LIKA. In number 6, down the road.

MARAT. I don't remember you, somehow.

LIKA. Before the war I was a little girl.

MARAT. Number 6 . . . Yes, you were unlucky.

LIKA. No walls left.

MARAT [*pause*]. Was there anyone in?

LIKA. Nanny. My mother's an army doctor at the front. I stayed with Nanny. She'd been with us for twelve years, part of the family . . . The house was hit when I went to get the bread. I came running back, but there was just nothing. Only your house was standing. It was on the first of March. The day after tomorrow it will be a month.

MARAT. What about you — not too weak?

LIKA. I feel well enough on the whole. I had three parcels from mother during the winter, you know, brought by airmen. [*Slight pause.*] Now there won't be any more parcels. They won't find me.

MARAT. They will, if they want to. You're obviously lucky.

LIKA. How unkind you are.

MARAT. How old are you?

LIKA. I might be sixteen in a fortnight.

MARAT. Why might be?

LIKA. Anything might happen.

MARAT. Oh, go on, you and your pessimism! I shall be eighteen next year. I don't get neurotic about it. I'm sure I'll be eighteen.

LIKA. When I was quite small, I used to dream about how I'd be sixteen. I used to imagine what would happen to me. Do you remember — "children under sixteen not allowed". It applied to all the best films. It was so humiliating . . . Of course, I always got in — I looked very much older, you know. [*Falls silent.*] It would be a pity not to live till then.

MARAT. You will now.

LIKA. I expect so. I've been living on two lots of bread coupons, you know. A whole month! Nanny was killed on the first.

MARAT. Just the job.

LIKA [*slight pause*]. Why do you make these jokes?

MARAT. I have a sense of humour. But I'm not as lucky as you. [*Takes from his pocket two ration cards for bread, looks at them.*] I have two lots of bread coupons too. That's for one day only. The thirty-first. Tomorrow.

LIKA. Don't. Don't cry.

MARAT. I'm not crying. I've got used to everything now.

LIKA [*after looking at the ration card*]. Your mother?

MARAT. My sister. [*Quietly.*] You see this button on my jacket? She sewed it on this morning. Today.

LIKA. You were staying with her?

MARAT. On Kamenny Island. I went to stay with her as soon as the war started. It was a small, timber house, only two floors. Bombing it was a fat lot of use. [*Slight pause.*] Her husband joined the Home Guard in August, and she was alone, silly little fool . . . I kept telling her, let's go back, let's go home. But she didn't want to. "Better here on the island," she said. "And then, supposing Kolenka comes back! No, I must be here." [*Falls silent.*] If she'd listened to me, she'd be sitting here now. [*Quietly.*] Alive.

LIKA. How can anyone know. [*Looks at* MARAT *carefully.*] And where are your parents?

MARAT. Father was in the navy. He hasn't written for five months. [*Slight pause.*] And there's nothing left . . . Not a single photograph. I should have taken it down . . .

[*He looks at* LIKA.]

LIKA [*quietly*]. I didn't know.

[*A shell explodes somewhere near.*]

Quite close.

MARAT. Aha.

LIKA. Shall I go?

MARAT. Where will you go?

LIKA [*cautiously*]. You haven't anywhere to go either.

MARAT. Me too.

LIKA. There used to be a small sofa in that corner.

MARAT. It would come in handy now.

LIKA. How was I to know.

MARAT [*slight pause*]. What's your name?

LIKA. Lidya Vasilyevna . . . Lika. And yours?

MARAT. Marat Yevstigneyev. They used to call me Marik.

LIKA. If we had a small mattress . . .

MARAT. All right. It's a big divan.

LIKA. What are you? . . .

MARAT. We'll fit in. You with your head to the wall, and mine towards the door.

LIKA [*pause*]. We mustn't.

MARAT. Why not?

LIKA. Well . . .

MARAT. You're just a girl.

LIKA [*doubtfully*]. Well. [*Thinking it over.*] What about sawing it in half?

MARAT. It has springs, you little fool.

LIKA. We'll try it tomorrow.

MARAT. We must go and have a look at the other flats, perhaps we'll find something.

LIKA. People have looked.

MARAT [*sitting on the corner of the divan*]. We'll make out.

LIKA [*quietly*]. It's good there are two pillows left. [*Holds out one of the pillows to him.*] But keep away.

MARAT [*casually*]. Now that's enough.

[*Silence.*]

What are you? . . . Are you laughing?

LIKA [*surprised and delighted*]. You're breathing.

MARAT. Of course I'm breathing.

LIKA [*just audible*]. No more silence.

MARAT. Stop mumbling.

4 April

An old mattress has appeared. MARAT *is asleep on it. A neat pile of firewood in the corner is all that's left of the sideboard. It's after five in the morning. Distant gunfire.*

LIKA [*just awake*]. Marik! . . . Marik! . . .

MARAT [*waking up*]. Oh? . . . What do you want? . . .

LIKA. It's an air raid, Marat . . .

MARAT. Idiotic . . . What's the time?

LIKA. After five . . .

MARAT [*losing his temper suddenly*]. Why did you wake me?

LIKA. You've only been here five days. I don't know what you feel about air raids.

MARAT. What, what . . . I loathe them.

LIKA [*after pause*]. Well, what shall we do?

MARAT. Let's go on the roof.

LIKA. There hasn't been anyone on duty for ages.

MARAT. Why not?

LIKA. We're derelict. Uninhabited. That's how we rate.

MARAT. If we're derelict, why did you wake me up?

[*A land mine falls close.*]

LIKA. Phew!

MARAT. Go down into the basement — that's the thing.

LIKA. I don't want to . . . It's warm here.

MARAT. I still haven't the slightest idea why you woke me.

LIKA. Oh, all right, let's go to sleep again.

MARAT. It's no good now. [*Sighs.*] And I was given such a dream!

LIKA. What?

MARAT. Toasted tea-cake with raisins . . . Then the music started and I was kissing a girl I know . . .

LIKA. I don't understand why you're telling me this.

[*A land mine explodes somewhere close.*]

MARAT. Right, we're going into the basement.

LIKA. He agrees. Look how noble he is! Or perhaps you're just a coward?

MARAT. Well, you know . . . I spent six months on the roof. Do you know how many incendiaries I threw off that roof?

LIKA. I don't know . . . Is she in your form at school?

MARAT. Who?

LIKA. The girl you were kissing?

MARAT. What's it got to do with you?

LIKA. The girl in Flat 5? Lelya?

MARAT. Maybe.

LIKA. I can just imagine . . . I bet she gets around in Tbilisi as well.

MARAT. Look . . . Hell! There's the gunfire.

LIKA. There are plenty of vacant flats. You can move tomorrow — and that's that.

MARAT. I'm not moving from here.

LIKA. Why not?

MARAT. You won't survive without me.

LIKA. I've survived so far — I'll survive all right.

MARAT. Spit over your left shoulder — tfoo! tfoo!

LIKA. I'm not going — tfoo! tfoo! I'm lucky.

MARAT [*furious*]. What saved you? Mummy's little parcels. Nanny — her extra coupons! There won't be any more . . . Unless I go up in flames somewhere and you inherit my coupons. But I shouldn't count on it, because I'm lucky too . . . tfoo . . . tfoo . . . If you must know, your whole way of life is wrong! You cut yourself off. Like a small wild animal. You made your lair here.

LIKA [*indignant*]. Just a moment, what lair?

MARAT. Of course! You retreated into yourself and cut yourself off. Utterly! Is that worthy of a Soviet child?

[*This time a land mine explodes nearer still.*]

LIKA. Heavens, what is all this . . . [*Bursts into tears.*]

MARAT [*gets off his mattress, goes to the window*]. It fell near the bridge, I expect . . . Now, why are you bawling?

LIKA. You're a fool! I'm not a child!

MARAT. Well — a young lady . . . A fat lot of difference! All the same your way of life is quite wrong. You cut yourself off but utterly from the common battle of the people. Loneliness leads to dystrophia . . .

LIKA. Clever, aren't you? Did you think that up by yourself?

MARAT [*flaring up*]. If you must know, I had half of what you had to eat, in spite of which my morale is almost satisfactory. And that's because I did everything a Leningrader should. And perhaps rather more.

LIKA. You're just showing off.

MARAT. No, I'm not showing off.

LIKA [*wiping her eyes*]. Then you're telling lies.

MARAT. That's different.

LIKA. These five days you've been telling me lies non-stop. Do you deny it?

MARAT. Of course not.

LIKA [*with sudden interest*]. Why do you tell lies?

MARAT. It's more fun. [*Sharply.*] And look here, no more isolation. I'm taking you to the service centre today and you're going to start being useful. You're perfectly fit. It's quite embarrassing to look at you. You must help people who aren't.

LIKA. I have been helping.

MARAT. The neighbours? Not enough. Just nothing! You must be of service to others all day and every day. Unceasingly. Understand?

LIKA. All right.

MARAT. What's all right?

LIKA. I agree.

MARAT. But you sit and read Turgenev all day. What a thing to do. You burnt the whole library, and kept Turgenev.

LIKA. But I like him!

MARAT. How can you — the chronicler of the country house! He can't mobilize anyone!

LIKA. He mobilizes me.

MARAT. Splendid! So we'll go to the centre today and you'll put your name down.

LIKA. All right, I've said so already. [*Slight pause.*] What are we going to do now?

MARAT [*vicious*]. No one knows.

LIKA [*cautious*]. Marik . . .

MARAT. Well?

LIKA. Let's light the stove.

MARAT. We mustn't. We must keep the sideboard.

LIKA. There's a lot of it left.

MARAT. Not much.

LIKA. And perhaps we'll get the neighbour's furniture.

MARAT [*flaring up*]. Aren't you ashamed? Waiting for people to die, so as to get their furniture?

LIKA. It's awful . . . awful . . . [*She bursts into tears.*]

MARAT [*goes up to her, sits on the divan*]. Look, that's enough . . . You mustn't go on like that. You're always crying.

LIKA. I never cried when I was alone . . .

MARAT. Is it my fault again?

LIKA. No . . . But you mustn't think . . . I don't want their death at all, not for anything . . . I simply thought that if they . . . No, no — really it's awful . . . [*Sobs quietly.*]

MARAT. You're a silly little fool . . . Just a silly little fool.

[*Cautiously strokes her hair.*]

LIKA [*frightened*]. What are you doing?

MARAT. Nothing . . . I'm calming you down.

LIKA. Oh – oh . . .

MARAT. Mustn't I?

LIKA [*slight pause*]. You may.

MARAT. Don't cry. The neighbours will go on living and we'll get some more wood.

LIKA. Promise?

MARAT. Of course.

LIKA. Then let's light the fire. [*Whispers, fondly forgiving.*] Let's light the fire. The spring will be here soon.

[MARAT *strokes her hair again.*]

Let's light it . . . Do you hear [*smiles*], Marat Yevstigneyev? [*Suddenly anxious.*] No . . . Don't calm me down any more.

MARAT. I won't. [*Snatches his hand away, moves away.*]

[*A land mine explosion somewhere far off.*]

LIKA. That's the other side of the station. [*Pause.*] Marik . . . Why do you look like that?

MARAT. All right.

14 April

Towards evening. LIKA *is standing by the table, with food tins shaken out of a small wooden case spread out in front of her.* MARAT *enters.*

LIKA [*rushes towards him*]. Marik!

MARAT. Stop! The distribution of presents comes first . . . [*Holds out a red rose made of paper.*] You now spit on all cinema managers from the highest tree.

LIKA. Where did you get it?

MARAT. It was a swop. Extraordinary thing – I immediately think of Easter eggs. And there's more – a lump of sugar.

LIKA. Thank you ... And now close your eyes. Come on. [*Leads him to the table.*] Now open. Celebration! Well?

MARAT [*quietly*]. The parcel ...

LIKA. Why, aren't you glad?

MARAT. My sugar's dwindled.

LIKA. Never! If you like, I'll eat it right now, this very moment. [*Places the lump of sugar in her mouth.*] What bliss! Oh, this Marat Yevstigneyev! We'll give him a bit too. We'll bite it off. Can't be helped.

MARAT. How did this find you?

LIKA. It's a cunning-clever parcel ... Just look ... Condensed milk, stew ... even jam! And a letter. Mother's well. She's got a medal.

MARAT. You're happy.

LIKA. Marik — it'll be the same for you ... You'll see. Don't be sad. After all I have achieved what I wanted. I'm sixteen! We'll have a party at once.

MARAT. She sent it to you.

LIKA [*seriously*]. Marat, you're a pig.

MARAT [*quietly*]. We'll have a party.

LIKA [*not loud*]. I should think so ...

MARAT [*looking at her*]. Once upon a time there lived an old man with his old woman ...

LIKA. What's that about?

MARAT. You wouldn't understand.

LIKA. Am I such a fool?

MARAT. No, you aren't a fool. [*Unsmiling, slowly.*] I could tell you what you are. But I shan't.

LIKA. Then to hell with you! The kettle's boiling. Open the tins.

[*A shell explodes near by.*]

It's started.

MARAT. Twenty-one gun salute in your honour.

LIKA [*after pause*]. That's a silly joke.

MARAT. Today I am the fool. Poor fool. I could tell you why. But I shan't.

LIKA. Oh, good. Have you opened the tin?

MARAT. Almost. We're going to eat half of it. No more. Do you understand?

LIKA. Yes, sir.

MARAT. What did you do at the centre today?

LIKA. We inspected number 17, down the road. We went through all the flats. [*Slightly surprised.*] You know, I'm not a bit afraid of dead bodies any more, I'm used to them. Is that a good thing?

MARAT. Probably.

LIKA. You're wise.

MARAT. Very wise.

LIKA. What did you do today, oh, wise one?

MARAT. I worked on the water main. It'll be easier when we get the water supply going. Spring's coming. In a fortnight it's the first of May. [*Thoughtful.*] Do you remember . . . May Day?

LIKA. Rather . . . Mother and I were on the rostrum once.

MARAT [*obstinate*]. It will be just the same again. It will, it will be!

LIKA. No, it won't be the same.

MARAT. What's it going to be like?

LIKA. I don't know. Different.

MARAT. Better?

LIKA. Perhaps. But different, you know.

MARAT. But I don't want it different. I want everything to be the same.

LIKA. Poor Marik.

MARAT. Possibly. We'll see.

[Silence.]

LIKA. The smell's driving me mad. Can you smell it?

MARAT. Rather. [*He breathes it in.*]

LIKA. Darling stew . . .

MARAT [*by the stove*]. It's so beautiful in the frying-pan.

LIKA. Let's hurry up and eat.

MARAT [*holding his plate out*]. Share it out equally. No, that's dishonest!

LIKA. But then I get the frying pan. Break the crust off.

MARAT. Heavens, talk of living it up . . .

[*They eat in silence.*]

LIKA [*pushing away the plate*]. It was magnificent.

MARAT [*licking his lips*]. But it's finished.

LIKA. And now – the condensed milk. Hand me the glasses.

MARAT. One spoonful per glass.

LIKA. Two, today.

MARAT. All right, one and a half.

LIKA. And biscuits.

MARAT. Two, each.

LIKA. Three, today.

MARAT. Who's quarter-master?

LIKA. I wouldn't have survived without you. We know that.

MARAT. Attention please – I shall now make a speech, a toast that is.

LIKA. A toast that is – that's funny . . . [*Laughs.*]

MARAT. Control yourself. [*Gets up and raises his glass of milk.*] My congratulations, Lika. A year ago I was also sixteen. In short, I have an idea of what it's like. Be happy, Lika. Lika . . . [*Thoughtfully.*] But what is this Lika? I could tell you. But I shan't.

LIKA. What an orator! Bravo!

MARAT. May Hitler drop dead. But [*in French*] passerons. Long live Lika! [*They touch glasses.*] Now I shall kiss your hand. You've grown up – it's the done thing. [*Kisses her hand.*] Are you pleased?

LIKA. The great Yevstigneyev kissed my hand. Unforgettable.

MARAT. How about you . . . Have you ever kissed anyone?

LIKA [*slight pause*]. I love my mother and I'd never do anything to upset her.

MARAT. I expect you had full marks for conduct.

LIKA. Yes, believe it or not. Did you?

MARAT. Not more than three out of five.

LIKA. That's obvious.

MARAT. So you haven't kissed anyone?

LIKA. Well, I have . . . once.

MARAT [*somehow astounded*]. Whatever for?

LIKA. It happened. [*Pause.*] The mistakes of one's youth.

MARAT [*grown sad*]. Obviously.

LIKA. Mother writes that I should be evacuated to Moscow. When she finds out our flat doesn't exist and Nanny is dead, she's bound to think of something.

MARAT [*after pause*]. Well then, go . . .

LIKA. Do you want me to go?

[*Silence.*]

MARAT [*in a squeaky voice*]. Oh, do not leave me alone, Lydia Vasilyevna. Do not go, take pity on our little ones.

LIKA. You're a fool.

MARAT. Of course. You don't know what a fool I am. I could tell you. But I shan't.

LIKA. It's dark. Open the door of the stove.

MARAT. We'll lose the heat.

LIKA. I want you to. It's my day today.

[MARAT *partly opens the stove. The room is lit with a flickering golden light.*]

[*Not loud.*] Shall we dance?

MARAT. There's no music.

LIKA. We don't need it. We have our own. Slow waltz — this one . . . [*Sings softly.*] Know it?

MARAT. Yes.

[*Humming the waltz, they slowly circle about the room. Very distant gunfire.*]

LIKA. Marik . . .

[*They stop.*]

It's awful, there's so much sorrow about — and we . . .

MARAT [*quietly*]. It isn't our fault.

[*Again they slowly circle about the room. Then they stop humming. They stand still and say nothing for a long time, their arms around each other.*]

LIKA [*breathless with excitement*]. Marik . . . Marik . . .

[**MARAT** *kisses her.*]

God . . . What's going to happen?

MARAT [*quietly*]. I could tell you . . . [*Whispering.*] But I shan't.

LIKA [*smiles, happy*]. Poor darling Marik.

[*The door opens.* **LEONIDIK** *staggers in. Without taking anything in, he takes a step towards the fire and falls heavily.* **LIKA** *and* **MARAT** *rush towards him without saying anything.*]

LEONIDIK [*incoherently*]. Firewood . . . Good firewood . . .

21 April

A week later. A home-made camp bed has appeared in the room for **LEONIDIK**. *It is the end of yet another April day — sunset outside the window.*

LIKA [*on the threshold*]. Is he asleep?

MARAT [*sitting beside* **LEONIDIK**]. Mmm . . . Why are you so late?

LIKA. I was held up at the centre. Have you fed him?

MARAT. I heated up the porridge as soon as I got back. He's sort of peculiar — he's terrified of hospitals. Nobody knows why. He's an eccentric.

LIKA. Eccentric?

MARAT. Well, yes — odd. It really is a shame, he ate the whole of your parcel. Still, he's recovering.

LIKA. You know, at first I was sure he had pneumonia. Now it's obvious he only had a chill. He'd have died of pneumonia.

MARAT. Yes, I was awfully sorry for him. I've seen plenty of people die. But he's nice.

LIKA. The whole point is that he doesn't look like anyone. Everyone looks like someone. But he doesn't.

MARAT. Who do I look like?

LIKA [*after thinking it over*]. You look like everyone all together.

MARAT. Good for me!

LIKA. All the same it does help my being a doctor's daughter. I cured him in a week. True, you were a wonderful help.

MARAT. I am a wonderful person. I look like everyone all together. It isn't that easy.

LIKA. I wonder, why does he have that funny name — Leonidik?

LEONIDIK [*opens his eyes*]. He also sometimes wonders why.

LIKA. Weren't you asleep?

LEONIDIK. Actually, it is funny — Leonidik. [*With a laugh.*] Mothers are capable of anything. [*He is silent.*] Marat, is your mother alive?

MARAT. No . . . [*He laughs.*] I've never seen her.

LIKA. It's simply awful the way you both talk.

LEONIDIK. Why? Marat is a man and he loves his father.

LIKA. You're both quite potty.

LEONIDIK. We aren't potty. It's just that we've seen it all. All of it.

MARAT. Look, why don't you relax? You aren't fit enough to get all worked up.

LEONIDIK. Leonidik . . . There's no denying it. It is funny. [*Slight pause.*] Don't talk for a bit, I'll tell you a thing or two. Besides he ate your parcel, as Marat sadly said, so now you're his nearest and dearest. I have to tell someone what happened . . . It isn't funny keeping it to myself. [*Pause.*] I loved my mother very much. Unutterably. My father was a busy man, never there, always at work, and they were always singing his praises. I think I was the only one who didn't know what was so good about him. It's true, every Sunday from two to four he used to try hard to talk to me, but he always thought I was three years younger . . . [*Thinks it over.*] He died five years ago on my birthday — I was twelve that day . . . Lots of people went to the cemetery and they all said he was a remarkable man. Perhaps. I don't deny it. But he died and for me nothing had changed. Only the meals were more frugal. [*Smiles suddenly.*] For me mumma was everything — gay, funny, kind. We were always together — like Siamese twins. Then a man appeared . . . A man . . . And she simply forgot me — do you understand that? Well, why? He wasn't all that young and quite ugly. He used to sing to her quietly the whole time . . . In the evening I used to hear them dancing in the next room — the two of them! When war broke out, they wouldn't have him in the army . . . I should think not, he was so short-sighted, he couldn't tell a cat from a dog. Just as well he wasn't too much of a bore and he never panicked much during the raids. The famine started . . . I watched them both getting weaker and weaker. They were quite emaciated by the New Year. [*Sharply.*] Listen to what I'm going to tell you. I was sorry for them, but I couldn't forget . . . [*Hurriedly.*] Once, when things were going very badly, I noticed that she gave him part of her bread. He didn't notice anything and he ate it. Every day she grew weaker. You know, he was short-sighted and he never noticed the difference in the portions. I did! Even when she was dying, she looked at him. Although she did say her last words to me: "Leonidik, look after him . . ." [*Pause.*] Before, he'd never paid much attention to me but now everything was suddenly changed. He began telling me about his life, and how unhappy he'd been before he met her. Sometimes he even sang quietly to me the same songs he'd sung to her. He told me that as a young man he was the moving spirit in something or other, and that he was given an award of some kind. Once he stared at me for a long time and suddenly said: "Leonidik, you're extraordinarily like her." From that day he began helping me to his bread. Of course, I didn't take it, but he went on fussing and worrying about it, and he was delighted when he managed to palm it off on me. I know I should have forgiven him everything. I should have got to like him. But I couldn't! And it was only just before he died that he suddenly understood and asked me to forgive him . . . I wept after he died, though I still remembered what he'd done . . . I couldn't forget. I can't.

LIKA [*quietly*]. But you know that was real love. Perfect love.

LEONIDIK. I'm the only person who'll never see that.

MARAT. You're a strange person. Why tell us all this?

LEONIDIK. I don't know. Sometimes he's afraid. But now you know what happened. [*Smiles.*] Perhaps he'll feel easier.

LIKA [*thoughtfully*]. A person must always sacrifice everything for the other.

MARAT. That is not a fact.

LEONIDIK [*to* **LIKA**]. Why don't you say something?

LIKA [*quietly*]. I keep thinking of what you told us.

MARAT. Cock-crow! [*He crows like a cock.*]

LIKA [*as though coming to*]. What?

MARAT. Over!

[*Pause.*]

LIKA. Leonidik, what would you like to be?

LEONIDIK [*smiles*]. A writer of verse.

LIKA. A poet?

LEONIDIK. Well, it sounds too grand.

LIKA. Marik, how about you?

MARAT. A lion-tamer.

LIKA [*surprised*] . You're joking!

MARAT. Now watch . . . [*He places two large logs on the floor and a plank on top of them.*] Building bridges! [*Flaring.*] Joining river banks, you know. It's interesting, isn't it?

LIKA. Perhaps . . . [*To* **LEONIDIK**.] Mother always wanted me to be a doctor. So I decided as a child — I shall be a doctor! But not just an ordinary doctor — he comes in a white coat and galoshes and sticks a thermometer into every mouth. No! A research doctor! The first to discover . . . well, you know . . .

LEONIDIK. Of course.

MARAT [*in a squeaky voice*] . Do what your mummy tells you. Little girls who don't are naughty.

LEONIDIK. You know what — do please keep quiet.

MARAT [*with a nasal twang*] . Mummy, I want potty . . .

LIKA [*going up to* **MARAT**] . Do you want me to slap your face?

MARAT [*unexpectedly humble*] . Time to go to bed. [*Lies down on his sofa.*] Don't talk too loudly. I have to go to work early tomorrow.

LEONIDIK [*thoughtfully*] . All the same the most difficult thing of all is to understand oneself.

LIKA [*interested*] . Do you think so?

[*Distant shell explosion.*]

29 April

An overcast, windy, spring day. **LIKA** *and* **LEONIDIK** *enter from the street.*

LEONIDIK. Tired?

LIKA. Awfully tired. [*Looking round the room.*] Marat hasn't been in.

LEONIDIK. He'll be back. Did you listen to the news today? I think in the south we're preparing . . . something.

LIKA. If only it were here. To raise the siege! You know how often I dream about it?

LEONIDIK [*very affectionately*]. Get some rest . . . You had a hard day today.

LIKA. Sad – to be more exact. [*Lies down on her divan.*] There's just one thing that frightens me – we've got used to everything . . . every single thing.

LEONIDIK. Why not . . . It will help us.

LIKA. With what?

LEONIDIK. The war.

LIKA [*suddenly surprised*]. Will you go and fight?

LEONIDIK. We'll be called up in the autumn, I expect. I'm the same age as Marat, you know.

LIKA [*with a laugh*]. Supposing there is no autumn, ever?

LEONIDIK [*thoughtfully*]. We can do without.

LIKA [*looking at him*]. What are you up to?

LEONIDIK. Nothing. I'm making use of my distressed condition and I don't think about anything. It's only the second day that he's been out. He sat on a bench that had survived and watched how you cleaned up the forecourt and brought out the dead. [*Pause.*] Are we taking the furniture from the next-door flat?

LIKA. I don't want it. We'll manage without. [*Suddenly exclaiming.*] Where's Marat?

LEONIDIK. Yesterday evening they shelled the centre. He might have stayed the night with someone.

LIKA [*worried*]. But who?

LEONIDIK. He isn't repairing the water main alone. He has friends there. Do you remember, he told us about some quite extraordinary, legendary friends of his, a boy called Yura and a girl called Sveta.

LIKA. Sveta – Svetlana, looks like a banana!

LEONIDIK [*smiles*]. Why are you making fun of her?

LIKA [*jumping off the divan*]. Stayed the night, you know . . . I can just imagine! You don't know this man Marat! Besides he's a liar. He tells lies, tells lies! One a second! Once he brought six pounds of millet home. I asked him – where did you get that? He told me: "A little girl fell through a hole in the ice, I fished her out and her parents gave it to me in thanks." I found out later he hadn't saved any little girls, but simply swopped his fur hat for the grain . . . And that isn't all – you'll be horrified.

LEONIDIK. Fine, I'm sure I will be, but not now . . . Some other time. All right?

LIKA [*losing her temper*]. Why, aren't you interested in Marat?

LEONIDIK. Yes, but not all the time.

LIKA [*disapproving*]. You're sort of buttoned up . . . [*Rather interested.*] Look, do you really write verse?

LEONIDIK [*smiles*]. I have tries at it.

LIKA. Read it.

LEONIDIK. It's bad. No bloody good!

LIKA [*doubtfully*]. You're just showing off.

LEONIDIK. No.

LIKA [*surprised*]. Then why do you write it?

LEONIDIK. I live in hope — supposing I did write something good.

LIKA [*snorts with laughter*]. You are funny . . .

LEONIDIK. You'll die laughing.

LIKA. What's the smear on your cheek? Let me rub it off . . . A bit of spit on my hanky. [*She laughs.*] It's always the way with infants . . .

[MARAT *enters.*]

What blue eyes you have, as blue as blue!

MARAT [*in a squeaky voice*]. Bluer than blue!

LIKA. Marik!

MARAT. The same.

LEONIDIK [*cheerfully*]. Didn't I tell you he'd be back.

LIKA. What have you done to your arm? [*Exclaiming.*] Are you wounded?

MARAT [*carelessly*]. There was an incident.

LIKA. What?

MARAT. All right, let's forget it.

LEONIDIK. You don't have to be so rude. Lika was worrying about you all day.

MARAT. I'm honoured. She's a sensitive young woman. Salaam aleikum.

LIKA. What's all this chatter?

MARAT. It isn't chatter . . . [*Turns towards them, speaking sharply.*] I took a German parachutist prisoner.

LEONIDIK. You did?

MARAT. Yesterday, instead of the waterworks, we were sent to the defence works in the Kirov factory area. There was a bit of a do. We duly took up our stations towards evening and that's when they began shelling. We spent the night under cover. I woke up at night, and I thought I'd go and have a look-see what's what. I went out. It was pitch black, drizzling . . . And suddenly I saw, it wasn't at all clear — there was a man crawling towards a derelict house. I went after him. He fought back — slashed my arm with a knife. That didn't help him. I disarmed him and after a brief struggle handed him over to the soldiers who hurried to the scene.

LIKA [*stroking his bandaged arm*]. You are a real man, Marat.

LEONIDIK. Well done! What can I say? Except that I envy you, Marat.

[*Looks at them attentively and slowly walks out.*]

LIKA [*quietly*]. I've been so worried about you.

MARAT [*suddenly affectionate*]. Really?

LIKA. You've completely changed, not at all as you were. You're going away from me. Don't go. Remember how good it was together?

MARAT. I haven't forgotten. [*Long silence.*] It's you who are going away, not me. Sometimes I even think you have gone completely.

LIKA [*quietly*]. No. [*Very affectionately.*] I'm here, Marik. [*Looking at him.*] What's wrong? Are you crying?

MARAT [*fiercely*]. I hate myself . . . pitiful object.

LIKA [*astounded*]. Why?

MARAT. All right, to hell with it! [*Walks up and down the room.*] Now listen to me! You must say goodbye to your Service Centre. You're capable of more. I talked about you at the hospital. You're going there as a probationer.

LIKA. When did they put your bandage on?

MARAT. At daybreak.

LIKA. I'll change it.

MARAT. There's no point. You know that the hospital work will make you weep your eyes out. But it has to be done. It has to be — do you see?

LIKA. All the same I am going to change your bandage. I have my first aid pack. They gave them to us at the centre.

MARAT. I don't want it. Got that? You'll work as probationer for a couple of months, pass some exams. You'll be doing good and you won't lose anything. Do you agree?

LIKA. Yes. The wound must be cleaned. Marik, it's essential . . .

[*Takes him by the arm.*]

MARAT. Don't you dare!

LIKA. But I know how to do it. At the centre they taught us everything. I'll do it just beautifully, you'll see.

MARAT [*suddenly deflated*]. All right . . .

[LEONIDIK *returns and stands in the doorway.*]

LIKA. Now don't move. Sit very quietly. [*Carefully starts undoing the bandage.*] Was the German strong?

MARAT. Yes.

LIKA. Very big?

MARAT. Ordinary.

[LIKA *removes the bandage and looks at the arm for a long time.*]

[*Uncertain.*] The German was — Hullo!

[LIKA *turns and sees* LEONIDIK.]

LIKA. What a deep wound . . . I'm going to clean it up. That's right . . . [*Meets* MARAT'*s eyes and stares at him.*] Does it hurt?

MARAT [*quietly*]. Very.

LIKA [*begins bandaging*]. It will pass.

LEONIDIK [*goes up to* MARAT *and hits him lightly on the shoulder*]. You have to put up with it, old thing . . .

LIKA [*sharply*]. Don't touch him.

4 May

A bright sunny day. LIKA *is alone. She's been doing her smalls.* MARAT *enters. There is an uncomfortable pause.*

MARAT [*both cheeky and shy*]. Greetings!

LIKA. We met this morning.

MARAT. Nicely put. [*Pause.*] Where's Leonidik?

LIKA. He went for a walk. The doctor said he can start work tomorrow.

MARAT. Good for the doctor! Good for Leonidik! Good for us. He owes it to us.

[**LIKA** *gives a weary sigh.*]

Shall I shut up?

LIKA. As you like.

MARAT. Have you been to the hospital?

LIKA. I don't need your advice. [*Indifferent almost.*] Why are you back so early?

MARAT. We all stopped for elevenses.

LIKA. Haven't you had enough play-acting?

MARAT [*shyly*]. Look at me.

LIKA [*continues with her job*]. Why?

MARAT [*quietly*]. You haven't looked at me for six days.

LIKA. Have you saved another little girl from drowning? Or caught another parachutist?

MARAT [*sharply*]. Four others! [*He clenches his fists and drops his head.*]

LIKA. How can you play the fool! There's so much grief, children dying next door, but you ... [*Sharply.*] Tell me the truth. What is the scratch on your arm?

MARAT [*after a slight pause*]. I slipped and fell on a roll of barbed wire.

LIKA [*suddenly relaxed*]. They have taught me something at the centre. Barbed wire. I guessed at once. [*Slight pause.*] It's good they put iodine on the cut, it might have got infected. [*Looks at him with slightly exaggerated concern.*] Poor little boy ...

MARAT. Lika ...

LIKA. Shut up! I was ashamed for you and I told Leonidik a lie: "What a deep wound ... " It makes me sick to think of it! And you didn't say anything. You were still hoping I would believe you. [*Suddenly speaks quietly, almost plaintively.*] You wouldn't have done it, if you had the slightest feeling for me ... Why are you laughing?

MARAT [*fiercely*]. Who told you I was laughing?

LIKA. Move away! You haven't the slightest idea how I despise you.

MARAT [*quietly*] . Despise me?

LIKA. Yes. It's all over now. For ever!

MARAT [*almost to himself*] . You're right there.

LIKA [*turning round*] . What did you say?

MARAT. Over!

[LIKA *takes the bowl in which she was doing the laundry and goes out.* MARAT *gets his suitcase and quickly packs a few uncomplicated bits and pieces. He looks round, places a piece of paper on top of the suitcase and writes quickly.*]

LEONIDIK [*coming in and seeing* MARAT] . Why are you back so early? [*Goes to him.*] Two more tram-lines are running.

MARAT [*continuing to write*] . There's plenty of room.

LEONIDIK. And the water's on in the house next door. Your doing?

MARAT. Now then, come over into the sunlight. Let me have a look at you. Oh, Leonidik, you blue-eyed boy . . . [*In a squeaky voice.*] The blue, blue, very green red globe . . . [*Hugs him unexpectedly, goes to* LIKA*'s divan and places the note on her pillow.*] See that she gets it!

[*Takes his suitcase and almost runs to the door.*]

LEONIDIK [*anxious*] . Marat, where are you going?

MARAT [*cheerfully*] . The baths!

[LIKA *comes back.* MARAT *has gone.*]

LIKA. Where has he run off?

LEONIDIK. He really is peculiar . . . The baths . . . He was lying, of course.

[LIKA *is silent and then weeps bitterly.*]

LEONIDIK. Lika, what is it? . . . You mustn't . . . Darling, you mustn't . . .

LIKA. [*Takes his hand.*] Listen, Leonidik, listen . . . [*Quietly.*] I may love him.

LEONIDIK [*after slight pause*] . There was no need to tell me that.

LIKA. He's always telling lies . . . You know he made up that story about the parachutist. He only has a scratch. I covered up for him. I was ashamed for him, but I can't any more! Talk to him. You are the person who's closest to us.

LEONIDIK [*unexpectedly*] . You're fools! [*Uncertainly.*] With the sheer tragedy going on all round . . . [*Angry with himself.*] In any case all this isn't serious. You're still children.

LIKA [*exclaiming*]. Children? Who told you that?

LEONIDIK [*after slight pause*]. He left a note . . . Here.

LIKA [*wipes her tears*]. What else has that wretched liar made up? "To you and to Leonidik". It's to both of us. [*Giving him the note*.] You read it.

LEONIDIK. "Well now, it's true, I didn't catch the parachutist. But I did meet Major Artemov, and we had a good talk that night. A fat lot of use waiting for the autumn and the call up. It's all agreed and this is goodbye. Vengeance, vengeance is mine. I promise you'll hear of me. Lika, all the best, and don't lose heart, Leonidik. Be at the hospital tomorrow, Lika! Tomorrow as ever is! That's all."

LIKA. Marik . . . [*Takes the note and looks at it*.] No, he's lying . . . He's always lying! I don't believe it — he'll be back . . .

LEONIDIK. He isn't lying this time.

LIKA. How do you know?

LEONIDIK. He's grown up. [*Smiles*.] It happens to everyone.

LIKA. Do you want to go too?

LEONIDIK. He went. [*Mildly*.] You see, that's the only thing I can do now. He hasn't given me an alternative.

[*Very distant gunfire*.]

LIKA. Oh God!

LEONIDIK. Why are you frightened? It's a long way off.

LIKA. Every single shot will be aimed at him now . . . only him.

LEONIDIK. He's lucky.

CURTAIN

ACT TWO

27 March 1946

It is still the same room but unrecognizable, since the war is over and life is back to normal. Evening. **LIKA,** *now twenty years old, an independent young woman, is comfortably ensconced on the divan with textbooks and lecture notes spread out all around her.*
The wireless is on low giving the weather forecast.
Telephone rings. **LIKA** *turns off the wireless and lifts the receiver.*

LIKA. Yes, hullo . . . *[After a pause.]* Oh, what an impressive silence. I wonder if it's going to be broken? Won't you answer? . . . *[Exclaiming.]* What? . . . You? . . . At last . . . When did you arrive? . . . Of course, I'm waiting. I got the wire yesterday . . . Afraid? What mustn't surprise me? . . . We haven't seen each other for four years, you've arrived from the next world and you're standing downstairs, why I don't know, while we talk on the phone! . . . Come upstairs at once. The lift's working now . . .

[Puts down the receiver, jumps off the divan, excitedly paces up and down the room. Suddenly laughs and grows sad and looks at herself in the small mirror. Tries to tidy the room up but hears the bell. Quickly goes out and is back in a flash and says, looking at the door.]

Well, come in . . .

[Wearing a private's greatcoat, **LEONIDIK** *enters the room. He has matured and is very altered.]*

LEONIDIK. Wait . . . *[Walks to the armchair in silence, sits, put his hand over his eyes.]*

LIKA. Say something.

LEONIDIK *[opens his eyes, smiles]*. I've dreamed about this moment for four years. *[Gets up.]* May I kiss you?

*[***LIKA*** kisses him impetuously.]*

[Looks round.] It's all so different here . . . This is where my camp bed was, and our stove was here . . .

LIKA. Why don't you take your coat off?

LEONIDIK. You see . . . He doesn't manage it awfully well.

34

[*He takes the coat off with some difficulty and* LIKA *sees that he has an artificial left arm.*]

There it is.

LIKA [*smiles for some reason*]. All right. The war. It's as it should be.

LEONIDIK. Of course. [*Also smiles.*] Actually that's why he mumbled something on the phone to you . . . Didn't want to frighten you.

LIKA. Good Heavens, I've seen worse. You were just lucky.

LEONIDIK. Not entirely. I lost it in Hailar a week before the surrender. It was rather a pity. [*Excusing himself, as it were.*] You know, I wrote I was wounded. I wrote from Manchuria and from Khabarovsk . . . [*Embarrassed.*] Well, I didn't want to go into details.

LIKA. I know.

LEONIDIK [*laughs suddenly*]. Look, am I really back? Have I come back just like that? . . .

LIKA [*also laughs*]. You have, I promise you! . . .

LEONIDIK. When he saw the Nevsky Prospect this morning and over there in the distance the Admiralty Needle . . . and this sky that's unique in the world over Leningrad . . . [*Confused.*] Do I sound funny?

LIKA. Not at all . . . [*Quietly.*] I understand it all.

LEONIDIK [*thrusts a parcel at her*]. That's for you.

LIKA. Slippers?

LEONIDIK. From Japan . . . Funny, aren't they? And quite an amazing comb.

LIKA [*trying it on in front of the mirror*]. Oh, you . . . the image of Carmen! You're attentive, you're wonderful, you're amazing. Want some tea?

LEONIDIK. I'd love some.

LIKA [*plugging in the electric kettle*]. Then wait for it.

[*They sit and look at each other.*]

LEONIDIK. Well, talk . . .

LIKA. What about?

LEONIDIK. How you lived. What happened.

LIKA. Sometimes I think – there's nothing that hasn't happened. Everything's happened, I think. [*Pause.*] You know it all from my letters . . . After you both joined up, I heard mother had died . . . There was no question of my leaving Leningrad then. I went to work at the hospital . . . Besides where would I go? So I went on living here — studying, working . . . The shelling was a great nuisance, of course. [*Smiles.*] That's how I lived.

LEONIDIK. And now?

LIKA. In my second year at medical school.

LEONIDIK. All your wishes realized in fact?

LIKA [*slowly*]. Not all.

LEONIDIK [*uncertain*]. Keep trying.

LIKA [*with a laugh*]. Not everything depends on oneself.

LEONIDIK. No. Everything will be all right.

LIKA. You think so?

LEONIDIK. I'm sure of it. [*Strokes her hand a little longer than necessary.*]

LIKA. Kettle's boiled.

LEONIDIK. Well done!

LIKA. Who?

LEONIDIK. The kettle. Boiled in the nick of time.

[*Silence.*]

LIKA [*busy with the tea things*]. Where are you staying?

LEONIDIK. My cousin's. He was evacuated but he came back in the spring. What's this jam?

LIKA. Quince.

LEONIDIK. My cousin isn't a bit like me. I don't expect we'll get on. [*Cheerfully.*] Actually you're the only person left. In the whole world, the only one.

LIKA. Only me?

LEONIDIK. You and Marat. The three of us. You don't forget what happened that winter in '42. True, isn't it?

LIKA. True enough.

[*They're silent, both sunk in their memories.*]

LEONIDIK. Nice jam.

LIKA. Shall I give you some more?

LEONIDIK. Yes, do . . . Do you remember I ate the honey your mother sent you?

LIKA [*smiles*]. Marat was terribly hurt.

LEONIDIK. He was only pretending. He was feeding me up all the time . . . Funny Marat. [*He looks at her.*]

LIKA. Yes. [*Not immediately.*] What do you intend to do?

LEONIDIK. He isn't absolutely clear yet.

LIKA. But still?

LEONIDIK. There's a possibility of working on a newspaper. Three years of frontline journalism is something. But the newspaper is only a springboard. You see, he has with him a suitcase of poems.

LIKA. Are there any good ones these days?

LEONIDIK. No good ones as yet. Possibles are beginning to appear.

LIKA. That's something.

LEONIDIK. I'm eating all your jam.

LIKA. We don't begrudge it. Eat, you news hound.

LEONIDIK. Oh, no, he was with the advanced troops the first year. Amazing how the war spared him, then. Amazing! He even had friends then, but the only one to stay alive . . . Yes, he was always wonderfully lucky, even when he walked into this room, saw you and ate your parcel.

LIKA. Aren't you still lucky?

LEONIDIK. I suppose I am. You see, I've eaten all your food as usual. [*Points at the artificial arm.*] His luck ran out just the once.

LIKA [*quietly*]. How did it happen?

LEONIDIK. I caught a parachutist.

LIKA. You're joking!

LEONIDIK. Honestly.

LIKA [*with a laugh*]. Funny, if it's true.

LEONIDIK [*slight pause*]. He still doesn't write?

LIKA. No. In all these years I got three greetings telegrams from him. He sent them on my birthday. In '43, '44 and '45 . . .

LEONIDIK. Were they just greetings? Didn't he give you his address?

LIKA. No. [*A note of despair breaks through.*] No! [*Pause.*] More tea?

LEONIDIK. He's finished the quince.

LIKA. Try the shortbread.

LEONIDIK. All right, fill it up . . . [*Tries the shortbread.*] All the same . . . [*Knocks on the table with the shortbread.*] Well, well.

LIKA. They go down with the tea all right. [*Impulsively takes his hand.*] Leonidik! . . . [*Hopefully.*] Do you think he's alive?

LEONIDIK [*smiles*]. I expect we'll find that out on your birthday . . . In a fortnight. When his greeting should arrive.

LIKA. He couldn't forget us, could he?

LEONIDIK [*firmly*]. He wouldn't dare.

LIKA [*suddenly calm, with a kind of conviction*]. He's been killed.

LEONIDIK. He's just eccentric. [*Slight pause.*] This shortbread is utterly inedible.

LIKA. So you don't like your cousin?

LEONIDIK. I don't. He has no self-respect.

LIKA. Is that very bad?

LEONIDIK. It is rather, as I see it.

LIKA. Stay with me, for old time's sake. We'll put up some kind of partition.

LEONIDIK [*laughs, goes to her, kisses her temple*]. Thanks . . . the times have changed.

LIKA. You aren't going?

LEONIDIK. I've drunk the tea, I've eaten the quince and the shortbread is inedible.

LIKA [*serious*]. Are you a fool?

LEONIDIK [*after some thought*]. Yes.

LIKA. Will you come tomorrow?

LEONIDIK. If necessary.

LIKA. It is, for me.

LEONIDIK. Then I'll come. [*Decides to put on his greatcoat, but isn't immediately successful.*]

LIKA. Let me help.

LEONIDIK [*sharply*] . No.

LIKA. Why not?

LEONIDIK. He must do everything himself. [*Smiles.*] Or else he's had it.

LIKA. Oh!

LEONIDIK. Victory! The coat is on. [*Moves to door.*]

LIKA. Strange, isn't it? We haven't told each other anything.

LEONIDIK. You think so?

[*They are again silent.*]

See you tomorrow. [*He goes quickly.*]

17 April

The end of the day, but the room is still full of spring sunshine.
LEONIDIK is cosily settled on the window sill, reading a book.

LIKA [*entering*] . Hullo!

LEONIDIK. Hullo to you! You're forty minutes late!

LIKA. There was a general meeting. [*Cheerfully surprised.*] How did you get in?

LEONIDIK. I've grown extraordinarily popular in this flat during the last three weeks. Please note the neighbours will now let me in at night even.

LIKA. You're quite a lad.

LEONIDIK. Beloved by my public! I have won over all your old ladies. One of them even asked if I was settling here soon.

LIKA [*stops smiling*] . What did you answer?

LEONIDIK [*slight pause*] . I referred her to you for information on that particular subject.

LIKA. Not one of your better jokes.

LEONIDIK [*gloomy*] . Sorry.

LIKA. Did you collect the cinema tickets?

LEONIDIK. For the nine o'clock house — "Titan" as agreed.

LIKA. Clever!

LEONIDIK. I'm not sure about that.

LIKA [*quietly*] . Don't be cross. All right?

LEONIDIK. He isn't cross. But he's in a hellishly awkward position.

LIKA [*smiles faintly*]. Don't let's go on about that.

LEONIDIK. All right, we can talk about something else. You're right. Dead right. By the way, I have an idea . . . First we'll have dinner in a not too shabby restaurant.

LIKA. A splendid suggestion. By the way, don't you think you're drinking rather more than you should?

LEONIDIK [*serious*]. You see, if you assume that I'm drinking to drown my sorrows, I'm probably not drinking enough.

LIKA. You keep on . . .

LEONIDIK [*pause*]. Am I a bore?

LIKA. Getting that way. And you really must face the fact that your health isn't up to much. You're going to our clinic for a check-up next week. I've arranged it.

LEONIDIK. Do you mean that I've had it?

LIKA. The war is over, my dear, time to be sensible.

LEONIDIK. All right. But today we'll get tight.

LIKA. In aid of what?

LEONIDIK [*taking some money out of the pocket of his uniform*]. First instalment.

LIKA [*pleased*]. The poems?

LEONIDIK. A satirical piece. "Dormidares does repairs."

LIKA [*a shade disappointed*]. I thought it was for your serious work.

LEONIDIK. Poetry is above the wage packet. Shall we get tight?

LIKA. Well, what will be will be.

LEONIDIK. We'll order some of that Lidya wine from Moldavia . . . Do you remember we drank a whole bottle on your birthday. Lidya, your name-sake. You liked it, you know.

LIKA. Very much. I drank a bottle and I sat and I wept. What a business.

LEONIDIK [*cautiously*]. Perhaps it will still come . . . his telegram.

LIKA. No, it's five days late. It isn't war-time, the post works all right. There won't be a telegram. The only thing is — why? Has he forgotten us . . . or is he dead? [*Her edginess breaking through.*] And what is your opinion, Comrade?

LEONIDIK [*quietly*]. There's no need to be cross with me. Is it my fault that I am back from the war alive . . . and he isn't?

LIKA [*slight pause*]. You don't believe he'll be back?

[LEONIDIK *does not answer.*]

But then . . . Why should you? You don't need him – that Marat Yevstigneyev, do you?

LEONIDIK [*clenches his fist*]. What are you . . . What are you trying to say?

LIKA. You know.

LEONIDIK [*shouting*]. Shut up!

LIKA [*sinks into armchair*]. Oh, it's so awful . . .

LEONIDIK [*slowly goes to the coat-rack, takes down his coat*]. I think I'll be going . . .

LIKA. No! Look, don't leave me . . . [*Quietly.*] I shall feel terrible if you go now.

LEONIDIK. Then I'll stay.

LIKA. Thanks. You're wonderful.

LEONIDIK. Wonderful, attentive, amazing.

LIKA. You think I still love him, don't you? I've nearly forgotten him. I only remember myself as I was. Brave, cheerful and happy! It's as though I belong to that little girl of 1942 . . . I obey her in everything.

LEONIDIK [*goes to her*]. Let's go and walk in the sun, shall we?

LIKA. Only don't think I'm unhappy . . . I'm studying for my favourite profession, I'll be a doctor . . . What can stop me now? Who can stop me? [*Cheerfully.*] Let's go out! [*She takes his coat, decides to help him put it on.*]

LEONIDIK [*sharply*]. I told you . . . Don't you dare help him! He must do everything himself.

LIKA. Sorry . . .

[*Two rings.*]

That's for us. Wait, I'll go and open the door. [*Goes and comes back at once.*] A boy has brought a note from downstairs . . . [*Opens the note.*] Marat!

LEONIDIK [*runs to her*]. What's happened to him?

LIKA. Read it . . . [*Gives him the note and leaning against the door absentmindedly stares at* LEONIDIK.]

LEONIDIK. "I have arrived. I'll come up. Tell the kid, if you've forgotten me or don't want to see me. And I'll vanish. That's all. Hero of the Soviet Union Marat Yevstigneyev."

LIKA [*without moving*]. He's alive . . .

LEONIDIK. You see.

LIKA [*feverishly*]. We must tell the boy. Where is he? [*Shouting.*] He's gone! [*Rushes out of the room.*]

LEONIDIK [*suddenly smiles*]. Marik . . . [*Takes out his comb for some reason and begins combing his hair.*]

LIKA [*back*]. You know, the light's gone in the corridor . . .

LEONIDIK. Stop worrying.

LIKA. I've opened the front door for him — that's all right, my dear, isn't it?

LEONIDIK. What's the matter with you?

LIKA. My head's going round a bit.

   [LIKA *starts pacing about the room.* LEONIDIK *watches her.*]

I'll go and meet him.

LEONIDIK. Throw your coat over your shoulders.

LIKA. Nonsense! [*Rushes towards the door.*]

   [MARAT *comes in through the open door. His greatcoat is unbuttoned. He wears the dress uniform of a Guards Captain. Oddly enough* MARAT *has hardly changed. He is still a boy, except that his skin is weathered and coarser. Seeing* LIKA *he stands without saying anything for a few moments, learning her as it were.*]

MARAT. Greetings!

LIKA. Are you alive?

MARAT. Of course. [*He moves towards her and suddenly notices* LEONIDIK.] You? [*Hugs and kisses him.*] We've been pretty lucky, haven't we?

LEONIDIK [*smiles*]. Yes. It could be a lot worse.

MARAT. What did you do?

LEONIDIK. Infantry. Then war correspondent. And you?

MARAT. Intelligence.

LIKA. Marat! You . . . you've forgotten me!

MARAT. Why, he's a soldier, silly. [*Kisses her.*] Well, that's that. Just let them try and beat us now. [*Throws off his coat.*]

LIKA. Who are you talking about?

MARAT. I don't know.

LEONIDIK [*looks at his decorations*]. Aha — a star!

MARAT. What did you think?

LIKA [*almost a whisper*]. But . . . why didn't you write?

MARAT. Lots of reasons. The important thing is I came back. The rest doesn't matter. [*To* LEONIDIK.] Isn't that so? [*Looks at them.*] Stop! . . . You haven't got married?

LEONIDIK. So far the problem has not been solved in a positive manner.

MARAT. Well done, chaps!

LIKA. Three days ago . . . I waited and waited for your telegram.

MARAT. The whole effect would have been completely ruined. Surely it wouldn't be as elegant as this?

LIKA [*with a touch of mockery*]. Look, Leonidik, do you think he stole that star?

MARAT [*indignant*]. What?

LIKA. Funny . . . And I thought you'd been killed.

MARAT. You don't know me. [*To* LEONIDIK.] True, isn't it? [*Slaps him on the arm and falls silent, realizing the arm is artificial.*] Sorry.

LEONIDIK [*apologizing, as it were*]. What can I do?

MARAT [*serious*]. I don't like it.

LEONIDIK [*smiles*]. Nor do I.

MARAT [*sharply*]. I like it even less than you do.

LEONIDIK. Why?

MARAT. I'll tell you some other time.

LEONIDIK [*to* LIKA]. I rather think I'll nip out and do some shopping. An excellent opportunity for a drink.

MARAT. What do you take me for? [*He produces a bottle of cognac from his greatcoat.*]

LEONIDIK. Marvellous.

MARAT. What did you think? [*Opens the bottle.*] Lika, you're more than beautiful . . . You're like the sun. I can't look at you without blinking.

LEONIDIK [*pours out the cognac, raises the glass*]. What shall we drink to?

MARAT [*thinks*]. We'll drink in silence.

2 May

Another sunny day. The windows are wide open. Distant music.
LIKA listens carefully to MARAT, restlessly pacing up and down.

MARAT. I flew by Douglas from Berlin. The weather was clear, not a cloud, and all that damned destruction was spread out in front of me. [*With a kind of inner fury.*] I'm going to the institute in the autumn. I am! Then we'll start building bridges. Bridges! A sacred business. The thing that joins. [*Thinks.*] I'll soon be twenty-two. I used to think it was half a life. Nonsense, of course. [*Goes to* LIKA.] What didn't we dream about way back in forty . . .

LIKA [*with a laugh*]. Yes . . . Like a film exposed to the light by accident.

MARAT. When I walked in a fortnight ago, I didn't know that things weren't all that simple. Berlin was taken a year ago, but it was only here in Leningrad I realized the war was finished. Irrevocably.

LIKA. Are you sorry?

MARAT. I'm rather frightened.

LIKA. Frightened?

MARAT. Well, lonely, perhaps . . . As if I'd lost my family again. [*Looks round.*] And there's no one.

LIKA. No one?

MARAT. I'm sorry. I have to get used to it.

LIKA. To what?

MARAT. Life. You. [*Laughs.*] I'm not always sure that I am alive . . . And that you are you.

LIKA [*quietly*]. Come and make sure.

MARAT [*concentrating on his own thoughts*]. These four years, sometimes they seem decades . . . Not easy to forget . . .

LIKA. Have you . . . loved anyone?

MARAT. There's been all sorts. We don't really have to talk about it. Let us rather look at truth in the face.

LIKA. All right, let's.

MARAT. What are you?

LIKA. Nothing much.

MARAT. Yes, it is funny . . . I have walked and walked about the world and it seems I don't know a damn thing about myself. [*Unexpectedly.*] Do you know anything about yourself?

LIKA [*flaring up*]. Everything!

MARAT [*sharply*]. Your "everything" is fiction!

[**LIKA** *does not answer.*]

What a beautiful medallion you have.

LIKA. Do you like it? You gave it to me.

MARAT. That's a lie . . . When?

LIKA [*in a kind of frenzy of gaiety*]. Last year on my birthday. An old woman had it for sale. It's true that I paid for it, but I was sure it was you . . . I shall always be sure.

MARAT [*slight pause*]. Thanks. [*Moves away to the window, turns.*] Did you make that up — about the medallion?

LIKA. Perhaps.

MARAT. Still, it's a beautiful thought.

[*The waltz to which they danced in '42, on her birthday, is heard in the street.*]

MARAT. Remember?

LIKA [*quietly*]. Yes . . .

[*They stand and listen in silence.*]

Then Leonidik walked in.

MARAT. And ate your parcel. [*Looks at the clock.*] Where is he, by the way? We said we'd meet at three.

LIKA. He'll turn up. He's punctual.

MARAT. He's changed a lot. I was the eldest in '42. Not now.

LIKA. Not then either.

MARAT. You know best. [*Pause.*] I often think of him.

LIKA. Me too.

MARAT. I want him to be all right.

LIKA. Very much.

MARAT. Are his poems worth anything?

LIKA [*thoughtfully*]. They're sort of involved.

MARAT. Is that bad?

LIKA. Perhaps. During the war I liked Turgenev, Tolstoy . . . I used to read and read like mad . . . But now I like children's books, especially if they're funny. [*Laughs.*] I think fourteen is the best time of one's life.

MARAT. Fourteen – it's fine!

LIKA. Khe-khe-khe! . . . [*Coughing sound.*] We're both like a couple of little old men.

MARAT [*unexpectedly*]. Yes, I'd like him to be happy.

LIKA. He had bad luck with his left arm.

MARAT. No, it was my bad luck. [*Looks at her.*] Has he told you he loves you?

LIKA. No . . . Not really.

MARAT. But it's obvious.

LIKA. You know, you haven't told me either.

MARAT. If you wait, I'll tell you. Perhaps.

LIKA. Perhaps?

MARAT. I don't like a crowd. [*Slight pause.*] Is it worth telling you?

LIKA. Tell me first, and then we'll see.

MARAT. Leonidik holds higher trumps than me.

LIKA. What?

MARAT. And then, Lika, I'm awfully proud. I'm so proud I'm disgusted with myself sometimes. They've given me a horrid little room at the hostel. I don't complain – I'm a hero after all!

LIKA. Marik, I've been wanting to say for a long time, this room belongs to you, of course, and . . .

MARAT [*interrupts*]. Shut up about that!

LIKA [*laughing at him*]. On that day they had an argument about the living accommodation.

MARAT. They had no argument. That's the trouble.

LEONIDIK [*almost running in*]. Konitiva! Konitiva! Good day in Japanese. [*Goes on bowing ceremoniously for a long time.*] Followed by the first of May distribution of presents. [*To* LIKA.] Snowdrops for you, and "yo-yo" for the Hero of the Soviet Union. Somewhat later, lots will be drawn for the main prize of the raffle.

MARAT. Respected war-correspondent, I think you're loaded.

LEONIDIK. A tiny drop was drunk, and what's more, with my dreary cousin. [*Puts on the table a bottle of wine he has brought.*] I thirst for more.

LIKA. I'm going to turn you out.

LEONIDIK. Marat won't let you. Marat loves me – he's the friend of the people.

[MARAT *fiercely blows a toy whistle.*]

Marat, tell her you love me . . . And finally where is the corkscrew?

MARAT. Give him the corkscrew.

LIKA. I wouldn't dream of it! He was examined at the clinic by the best specialists. He has thirty-three diseases and his heart just isn't worth a damn.

LEONIDIK [*winking*]. He's going to die soon.

LIKA. Fool.

LEONIDIK. Will you give us the corkscrew?

LIKA. No.

LEONIDIK. First of May – workers' international holiday!

LIKA. No.

LEONIDIK. Meeting of two comrades-in-arms!

LIKA. It's gone on for a fortnight.

LEONIDIK [*pathetic*]. I shan't do it again!

LIKA [*gives him the corkscrew*]. And mind it is the last time.

LEONIDIK. No question about it, my child. [*Goes to the window.*] But really today is somehow pre-war! Flags on the ships, music, dancing – as though there was no death and destruction, as though these five years have never been!

MARAT [*sharply*]. But they have. Lika, do you remember, we had an argument? I wanted everything to be just the same after the war. You were right. I realized it yesterday, at the parade. Bands were playing as before, troops were marching, parents were carrying their children. But it all meant something else. Suddenly I saw quite clearly that we are living in some chronologically new time. The past won't come back.

LIKA [*cautiously*]. Perhaps we have changed.

LEONIDIK. We? It would be interesting to find out, who are they, those "we"?

LIKA. We read children's books when we're grown up.

LEONIDIK. I was in the East, when the atom bomb was dropped on Hiroshima. I understood something that day. [*Slowly.*] Perhaps we are the survivors.

MARAT [*fiercely*]. No! The victors! That's just it, the victors! If we forget that, we've had it.

LEONIDIK. You're more drunk with victory than is right and proper, chum. Beware of sobering up. You know the greatest danger of victory?

MARAT. Expound.

LEONIDIK. Taking over the vices of the defeated.

MARAT. You're doing an awful lot of thinking.

LEONIDIK. Lika, please note – Marat doesn't want me to do any thinking. He's a despot. Russia is being overrun by the nomadic despot, at the gallop – hip, hip, hurrah!

LIKA. Stop arguing! It's boring.

LEONIDIK. Are you joining forces with the despot? Excellent. I love you for your clarity, Lika. But I love you – firm announcement on said subject to bystanders. Bystanders, do you receive me?

MARAT. It does rather look as if he shouldn't drink any more.

LEONIDIK. Oppression! And so, citizens, we have discussed what victory is. Let us now discuss the next question – what is love and what do you eat it with?

LIKA [*quietly*]. Leonidik, don't . . .

LEONIDIK. The speaker is Marat. Attention. The Hero of the Soviet Union on love. Over to you, sir!

MARAT [*goes to* LEONIDIK]. You gabble and gabble . . . My ears are wilting! [*Sharply.*] If you must know, a real man can do without love.

LEONIDIK. Excellent. How do you become a real man?

LIKA [*slight pause*]. I expect Marat gives lessons.

LEONIDIK [*to* MARAT]. Put me down from three to five on Saturdays. I should try, shouldn't I?

MARAT. I'm afraid you're beyond help.

LEONIDIK [*flaring up*]. I wouldn't joke about it if I were you.

LIKA [*anxious*]. Boys, stop it at once . . .

LEONIDIK. Well, of course, ladies adore Heroes of the Soviet Union.

MARAT. Exactly. And they can't bear slobs.

LEONIDIK [*going right up to* MARAT]. I didn't lose my right arm, you know.

[LEONIDIK *gives* MARAT *a hard sock on the jaw.* MARAT *falls slowly.*]

LIKA [*rushing to* MARAT]. You beast . . . What have you done to him?

LEONIDIK. It's nothing. Upper cut. Give Goliath some sal volatile.

LIKA [*rushing about the room*]. Where is it? I put it down somewhere . . .

LEONIDIK [*sits at table, ties on napkin*]. Haven't you got anything to eat? I'm terribly hungry.

LIKA. I must say . . . A fine pair . . . Started fighting . . .

LEONIDIK. He got what he asked for — that's all. Well, haven't you found the sal volatile?

MARAT [*on the floor*]. Damn . . . I don't need sal volatile. Just as well I fell with my head on the carpet.

LIKA. Have some water.

MARAT. I'm sorry, Leon — I talk too much.

LEONIDIK. All right, and don't you be angry with me . . . I didn't expect such luck.

MARAT [*rubs his chin*]. Yes . . . first rate.

LIKA. The fools! [*Looks at* MARAT.] He's got a bruise now . . . How can we go for a walk on the embankment?

MARAT. Why not? It's May Day — bruises are in order.

LEONIDIK. We must find a copper coin.

MARAT. It's what comes of underrating your opponent.

LEONIDIK. Put that in your pipe and smoke it until the next time.

MARAT. Look, Lika, he's threatening me again!

LIKA [*joking or not joking*]. That's nothing to a real man who can do without love!

LEONIDIK. And now for the raffle! . . . The best first-of-May present! To delight the children of the revolution! The luckiest wins! Therefore the winning straw is the longest. Attention . . . Pull!

[*All laugh.*]

26 May

Late evening, but it is still light outside. A wonderful patch of golden sky is visible through the open window. MARAT *and* LEONIDIK *are waiting for* LIKA.

LEONIDIK. What's the time?

MARAT. Quarter past ten. Our Lika's having a good time. [*Pause.*] Shall I turn on the light?

LEONIDIK. Why? Tonight there will be no real darkness.

MARAT. Talking in verse?

LEONIDIK. You're being silly. The white nights are a great miracle.

MARAT. Should we go home, do you think? It's getting late.

LEONIDIK. Go, if you want. [*Pointing to himself.*] He's staying.

MARAT. You – person!

LEONIDIK. He hasn't seen her for two days. He missed her very much. He isn't afraid of admitting it. Do you know why? He isn't a real man. He says what he thinks, does what he wants. He is all out in the open.

MARAT. How do you find it there – comfortable?

LEONIDIK. No draughts. [*Pause.*] Why are you staying? You were just going.

MARAT [*looks out of the window*]. It's true, it is a miracle. The sky is green and gold. [*Slight pause.*] Leonidik . . . Have you been to Saratov?

LEONIDIK. I've been through it.

MARAT. Liked it?

LEONIDIK. So-so.

MARAT. I may be going there. To study.

LEONIDIK [*turning towards him*]. You're daft . . . Why?

MARAT. A wartime friend asked me. [*Smiles.*] The Volga is wide there.

LEONIDIK. So what?

MARAT. It's beautiful. Besides I'm awfully fed up with you.

LEONIDIK. Nothing you did would surprise me.

MARAT. Quite. [*Very serious.*] What do you feel about me?

LEONIDIK. I cannot imagine life without you, my angel.

MARAT. Stop fooling. I love you.

LEONIDIK [*suddenly quite simply*]. I know.

MARAT. But it doesn't alter things. Got it?

LEONIDIK. Of course.

MARAT. One of us has got to go. Even if it's only for a time.

LEONIDIK. Perhaps.

MARAT. Leon . . . [*Very quietly.*] Why don't you go? It would be better.

LEONIDIK. Better for who?

MARAT. You. I'm sure of that.

LEONIDIK [*with a laugh*]. Shall I grow into a real man if I go?

MARAT. That's right. [*Passionately.*] We can't tell lies to each other. She doesn't love you.

LEONIDIK. That may be so, but we're going to ask her.

MARAT. Is that wise?

LEONIDIK. Don't you see, Citizen Marat, that he who has nothing is afraid to lose the little he has.

[LIKA *enters, turns on the light.*]

LIKA. What are you doing, sitting in the dark?

LEONIDIK. It's nice. With the white night outside the window.

LIKA. I was afraid you'd both gone home. How persistent you are.

MARAT. Leonidik is the persistent one.

LIKA. Of course, you wanted to run away, didn't you? Well then, go. Leonidik and I are going to have tea. I bought him some quince jam.

LEONIDIK. Marat, did you hear that?

MARAT [*with a dismissive wave of the arm*]. Women! [*Gaily.*] All right. I'm going to have some tea as well.

LIKA. First say you're sorry that you wanted to go.

MARAT. Bzzz! [*Rude noise.*] If you don't give me any tea – I'll shoot your Leonidik to hell!

LIKA [*roars with laughter*]. What fools! . . . [*Starts getting the tea ready.*] How extraordinary Leningrad is . . . The lilac's out in the Field of Mars, the scent is stunning. And the sunset over the Fortress is like the skin of a peach. Lovers are sitting on stone benches by the river. You'd think the whole town's gone mad. I was coming up the stairs just now, and there's a couple kissing on the first floor landing. [*To* MARAT.] Guess who? Your Lelya from Tbilisi.

MARAT. Shall I go and strangle her?

LEONIDIK. I didn't like girls when I was a little boy. I was simply jealous of them.

MARAT. Tell me, Leon, do you write little verses about love?

LEONIDIK. Sometimes.

MARAT [*to* LIKA]. Any good?

LIKA. Not bad.

MARAT. People adore it about love.

LEONIDIK. But, you see . . . Those poems aren't meant for publication.

MARAT. Who are they meant for?

LEONIDIK. Me

MARAT. Aha! So you know in advance – that's for other people, and this is for my own private satisfaction? You're going in for some kind of double-entry book-keeping . . .

LEONIDIK. A real poet, my child, must experiment. Take risks! It's silly to involve the readers who aren't prepared.

MARAT. Not everyone who reads for pleasure is a coward, you know. They want to take risks with the poet! Remember – all poetry journeys into the unknown . . . You want to journey there alone. Privately!

LIKA. Stop shouting. Go and sit in your place, the kettle's boiled. Marat, you're attacking Leonidik about nothing at all. Why does a person like his profession? Because it makes him take risks, try things, make mistakes, work his own way out. The most risky profession of all is medicine. That's why I love it. Now my mother was an ordinary G.P. When she was young she dreamt of being a great scientist. It didn't come off . . . [*Cheerful*.] But children are born into this world to succeed where their parents failed. I promise there will be no diseases left at the end of the twentieth century. I give you my word.

MARAT. Better give us some salami, you conceited creature.

LIKA. I'm starting on a thesis as soon as I get my degree. Sometimes I wake up and think, heavens, now who, who could stop me being a great scientist? Who is the enemy?

LEONIDIK. How about yourself?

LIKA. What?

LEONIDIK. Perhaps you are the only enemy you have.

LIKA. No, just a moment . . .

LEONIDIK. You're half-way to defeating your enemy when you find him.

MARAT. You didn't have to find Fascism. There's no worse enemy.

LEONIDIK. Who knows? The secret enemy is always more dangerous.

MARAT. I'm fed up with both of you. [*To* LEONIDIK.] You're quite impossible now that you've stopped drinking. You believe Lika, when she's trying to scare you.

LIKA. Marat, you aren't being helpful. Leonidik is weak and nervy by nature. Why do you tease him instead of backing me up?

LEONIDIK. Marik, don't tease me, I'm almost at death's door.

LIKA. You don't know the state you're in, you fool.

MARAT. Disgraceful . . . And because of him I can't even have a drink.

LIKA [*unexpectedly*]. We're all being very funny, but I feel sad, I don't know why.

MARAT [*firmly*]. Shall I tell you?

LEONIDIK. Wait . . . Don't.

MARAT. You wanted this.

LEONIDIK. She knows why we sometimes feel sad . . . The three of us when we're together.

LIKA [*after a long silence*]. Don't let's go on and on about it.

LEONIDIK. Sooner or later we'll have to. [*Nodding at* MARAT.] He's thinking of going to Saratov.

LIKA. You?

MARAT. I'll go and do it. You'll both cry a little without me. [*Pause.*] Funny. It's gone dark after all.

LEONIDIK. He told me to go away. Said you didn't love me.

LIKA. Our Marat knows it all.

LEONIDIK. Who's that playing the guitar?

LIKA. The neighbour on the balcony. He's musical.

MARAT. He's terrific.

LIKA. He sings too.

MARAT [*pointing at* LIKA]. Is he in love?

LIKA. Hopelessly. He'll be sixty soon.

LEONIDIK. A modern bridegroom. With legs and arms.

MARAT. Nicely put.

LIKA [*to* MARAT]. Where are you going?

MARAT. Saratov. Do you like it?

LIKA. I haven't been.

LEONIDIK. Not a bad little town. It has a medical school.

MARAT. It has everything.

LIKA [*looks at* MARAT]. Is that why you chose it?

MARAT. I have a friend there.

LIKA. Haven't you any friends here?

MARAT [*looks at* LEONIDIK]. I have. That's the trouble.

LEONIDIK [*smiles*]. Nicely put.

MARAT [*grim*]. All right. Someone has to go.

LIKA. You're the first, of course.

MARAT [*shrugging*]. Intelligence officer.

LEONIDIK. A real man.

LIKA. And you?

LEONIDIK. Not me. [*Shouting.*] No! I'll go only if you send me away.

PLATE 1. Judi Dench as Lika and Ian McShane as Marat in Act I,
Oxford Playhouse

PLATE 2. Judi Dench, Ian McShane and Ian McKellen as Leonidik, also in Act I

PLATE 3. Judi Dench in Act II

PLATE 4. Ian McKellen and Ian McShane in Act II

PLATE 5. Judi Dench, Ian McShane and Ian McKellen in Act III

PLATE 6. Judi Dench, Ian McShane and Ian McKellen in Act III

PLATE 7. The set in Act I, Lenin Komsomol Theatre, Moscow

PLATE 8. Olga Yakovleva as Lika and A. Zbruyev as Marat in Act II

PLATE 9. A. Mayorov as Leonidik in Act I, Central Theatre of the Soviet Army

PLATE 10. A. Pokrovskaya as Lika and G. Krynkin as Marat in Act II

MARAT. That's what he told me. You see.

LIKA [*very sharply*]. Shut up, you!

LEONIDIK [*helps himself to more jam*]. Curious . . . I've never seen quinces growing.

MARAT. They grow.

LEONIDIK. No, I told you a lie. I'll stay with you even if you send me away.

LIKA [*challenging*]. Why is that?

LEONIDIK. There will be nothing, if you aren't there.

LIKA [*to* **MARAT**]. What do you say?

MARAT [*almost cheerful*]. No point in drivelling.

LEONIDIK. Don't the neighbours object to us being here so late?

MARAT. We have nice neighbours. [*With a laugh.*] Oh, my living accommodation, my living accommodation . . .

LIKA. Yes, it's a funny expression.

MARAT. I was deeply in love with a young woman at Drogobich. As I left she said, "Marik, don't be silly, come back. I have such marvellous living accommodation."

LEONIDIK. Bravo!

LIKA. Leonidik, in what town were you deeply in love?

LEONIDIK. Leningrad.

LIKA [*to* **MARAT**]. You can't catch him up.

MARAT. I realize that. You haven't fallen out of love with Turgenev.

LIKA. What's the point of you laughing at me?

MARAT. No laughter, only tears. [*Gets up from the table.*] Right, we've had enough. Someone has to go. Me or him.

LEONIDIK [*numb*]. It will be as you say.

LIKA. Oh! So that's it! You know, I could choose the neighbour. With the guitar.

LEONIDIK [*listening to the neighbour playing*]. Yes, he is trying hard.

MARAT [*unexpectedly abrupt*]. I'm fed up with all the jokes.

LIKA. Don't let's say anthing for a moment. [*Slight pause.*] Marat, do you love me?

MARAT. Lik.., I could tell you, but I . . . [*He laughs.*]

LIKA. Did you say that because you're sure of me?

MARAT. I say what I say. You know, Lika, I'm a hero. Even the papers said so.

LEONIDIK. He loves you. He told me.

LIKA. Oh! So you're behaving like a real man!

LEONIDIK. It's catching . . .

LIKA. Now, tell me about yourself, not him.

LEONIDIK [*very seriously*]. I shall be lost without you. You're my sister and my mother. The whole wide world.

MARAT. What's the use?

LIKA [*goes to* LEONIDIK *and runs her hand through his hair*]. More tea?

LEONIDIK [*trying to smile*]. I could use a bottle of cognac.

MARAT [*pale*]. Tomorrow I'll bring some cognac for both of you.

LIKA. It's dawn . . . What a short night.

CURTAIN

ACT THREE

10 December 1959

The same room, but thirteen years later. A number of things have been replaced more than once. But has this not very expensive furniture found its final resting place? Probably not. The chairs, tables, divan and bookshelves are still searching.

There was a heavy fall of snow earlier in the evening. You can still see it coming down slowly against the street-lighting beyond the window. The clock strikes eleven. The corridor door opens and LIKA *and* LEONIDIK *come in.* LIKA *helps* LEONIDIK *to take his fur-lined coat off, drops down on her knees and takes his boots off, then goes behind the curtain and changes into her dressing-gown. At the same time,* LEONIDIK *changes his jacket and puts on his slippers.*

LIKA *looks in the mirror, winks at herself, and plugs in the electric kettle. The silence lasts for quite a long time.*

LEONIDIK *goes to the sideboard, brings the cheese out and tastes it.* LIKA *sees this, creeps up and slaps his hand.* LEONIDIK *puts out his tongue at her and moves over to his desk.* LIKA *starts laying the table for supper.* LEONIDIK *reads the newspaper.*

LEONIDIK. "Lenelectricwares have enlarged their stocks of metal crockery. How nice to replace your domestic utensils before the holidays." [*Pleased.*] "For sale, a domestic chimney 700 millimetres in diameter, seventeen metres in length . . ."

LIKA. At last.

LEONIDIK. "The Gastronome is organizing large sales of their products before the holidays . . ." "Meet the new year, 1960, in the Intourist Restaurants . . ."

LIKA. The bread is quite stale.

LEONIDIK. "Broadcasting, the 11th December. 4.45 – Open Your Hearts to Friends. Song Recital. 5.30 – If you're a Komsomol. 6.20 – Rheumatism in its early stages. 7.15 – Readings by the Poet, A. Sofronov. 7.40 – Village Fiddler . . ."

LIKA [*goes to him and kisses him on top of his head*]. That's enough.

LEONIDIK. Certainly. But at 8.15 "Oh, how good to live in our Soviet land."

[*The kettle boils.* LIKA *unplugs it and puts it on the table.*]

57

LIKA. Come and have some tea.

LEONIDIK. Certainly. [*Sits at the table.*]

LIKA. Shall I make you a sandwich?

LEONIDIK. Certainly.

LIKA. Cheese?

LEONIDIK. Sausage. [*Pause.*] It was a stupid play.

LIKA. No, why . . . Perfectly ordinary. [*Looks at the clock.*] It finished early . . . Eleven o'clock.

LEONIDIK. Your favourite people's artist was pulling faces today. Trying hard.

LIKA. He wasn't at his best.

LEONIDIK. No, why . . . He rumbled away in his bass as well as he could. [*Between sips of tea.*] If I had my way, I'd close all the theatres.

LIKA. Why?

LEONIDIK. You see . . . There's nothing wrong with the idea that all that is good is good and all that is bad is bad. But it begins to pall with repetition.

LIKA. You're a free-thinker. [*Brings a box of chocolates from the sideboard.*]

LEONIDIK. Ah! What's this over-indulgence in honour of?

LIKA. Have you forgotten? I'm getting a rise of 200 roubles from the first of January?

LEONIDIK. You might have provided something stronger for the occasion.

LIKA [*serious*]. Don't even think about it.

LEONIDIK. Still, we grow, we get promotion.

LIKA. No.

LEONIDIK. I shan't say a word.

LIKA. Lately, you've done awfully well, you know.

LEONIDIK. I serve the labouring masses.

LIKA [*smiles*]. Don't be a fool.

LEONIDIK. No fooling, no drinking allowed. Eating chocolate is though. [*Eats a chocolate.*] What are you going to be now?

LIKA. Attached supervisor.

LEONIDIK. Magnificent! I knew what I was doing when I married you. What are you attached to?

LIKA. Practice. I teach and I practise.

LEONIDIK. And what is better for a supervisor — to be attached or unattached?

LIKA. Unattached, I expect.

LEONIDIK. Meaning, it all lies ahead of us! Hip, hip, hurrah! By the way, I talked to the management. They promised us a flat soon. We're moving in spring. Aren't you pleased?

LIKA. I am. [*Quietly.*] Except that I'm used to this room.

LEONIDIK. Alack! Alack! We'll have to move just the same. [*Suddenly, very sharply.*] Damn this load of rubbish! They moved in and got dug in, the bums! [*Startled by his own tone of voice.*] Anyway, I couldn't care less.

LIKA. Will you have some more tea?

LEONIDIK. *Finito.* [*Rises from the table, kisses her hand.*] My biggest *merci.*

LIKA. Are you going to work?

LEONIDIK. Yes, I have to hand the proofs in tomorrow.

LIKA. You could do it during the day.

LEONIDIK. I'm fine at night. Oh, night-light, you are my friend, my brother, we shall go out together!

LIKA [*mildly*]. Darling, do be quiet. [*Pause.*]

LEONIDIK. For your information, there's no more ink.

LIKA. I'll buy some tomorrow.

LEONIDIK. And the good paper's finished.

LIKA. I'll buy some. [*Starts clearing the table.*]

LEONIDIK [*leafing through the proofs*]. Petrov is a scoundrel. So are Ivanov and Sidorov, I expect. An edition of five thousand copies! [*Suddenly really angry.*] Swine. [*Smiles.*] He promised ten thousand. Slim volume ... After all, it doesn't come out every year. [*Sharply.*] The other day your pet lay-about had an edition of a hundred thousand.

LIKA. Why mine?

LEONIDIK. You're always reading him.

LIKA. You liked him too, you know.

LEONIDIK. Yes ... He started well. And then? [*Fiercely.*] Why this cheap success? The vast editions? An inflated figure of a man! [*Silent and embarrassed.*]

LIKA. Don't, my dear. [*Slower.*] Well, if you like, I'll go and see Petrov and talk to him about the edition. Sometimes I have got away with it, you know ... Of course, five thousand isn't enough.

LEONIDIK [*coming alive*]. You're right, damn it ... Why ever not? Be my guardian angel once more, carry on with the good work, explaining to the Petrovs and the Sidorovs ... Oh my wife, purest of women.

LIKA. That's enough, that's enough. [*Strokes his hair.*] Off you go to your desk.

LEONIDIK. Sweet dreams, my attached supervisor ... My guardian angel. [*Holding the proofs, he half dances round the table several times.*] "Follow the blue-bird, follow the blue-bird as it flies through the sky ..." [*Finally he sits down in his armchair. He sits down heavily, as though tired by a long journey.*] There's no more ink.

LIKA. You've already said so.

LEONIDIK [*in French*]. *Pardon.*

[LIKA *turns off the light. There's only the light from the lamp on* LEONIDIK's *table.*]

LIKA. I'll switch on the tape machine ... very quietly.

LEONIDIK. Go ahead. Music helps with the proofs.

[*Slow waltz to which* MARAT *and* LIKA *once danced.*]

[*Smiles.*] Your favourite tune again?

LIKA [*quietly*]. Don't you like it?

LEONIDIK. Why not? It isn't a bad little tune.

11 December

After 3 p.m., but the December days are short in Leningrad, and it is growing dark outside.

Back home from her shift, LIKA *is busy with her housework. She clears the table and goes behind the curtain with a loaded tray.*

The clock strikes. Quiet knock at the door. It is repeated. The door opens slowly. It is MARAT. *He looks about him, takes a few steps to the window, looks out and presses his forehead to the window pane.*

LIKA *comes out from behind the curtain, places the washed up china on the table, turns and sees* MARAT. *They gaze at each other a long time.*

LIKA [*quietly*]. What have you ... What have you ... [*With a strange wave of the arm at* **MARAT.**] Why? You've gone mad.

MARAT [*swallowing air*]. No.

LIKA. It's pointless.

MARAT. It isn't.

LIKA. So many years! Surely you understand?

MARAT. So many years what?

LIKA. So many years after.

MARAT. Well, so what? [*With a shout.*] Wait! Stand still. Go on, don't move. Stand still. Stand still. Go on standing there.

LIKA. Marat, take your hat off. [*Slight pause.*] You're so ...

MARAT. What?

LIKA. Exactly like yourself. [*Pause.*] Have I grown old too?

MARAT. No. You're lovely in any case. [*Quietly.*] Once upon a time there lived an old man with his old woman.

LIKA. Be quiet. [*Whispering.*] Don't you see, I'm crying.

MARAT. I didn't know it was going to be like this.

LIKA. If you could feel the horror of it ... No! Don't come any nearer ...

MARAT. I shan't.

LIKA. Stand by the window.

MARAT. That's where I am.

[*Silence.*]

LIKA. Where do you live?

MARAT. Far away.

LIKA. That's as it should be. [*Smiles for some reason.*] Are you building bridges?

MARAT. Yes. [*Pause.*] When I come to Leningrad, I come here.

LIKA. Why?

MARAT. To look at the windows and go away.

LIKA. Nothing will come of it in any case. That's all now.

MARAT. I know.

LIKA. Go away. When is your train? Hurry up and go!

MARAT. I can't.

LIKA. Why not?

MARAT. I'm in a very bad way. And since I have come . . . That's all. [*Almost rude.*] Not to see you . . . I came to see you both. [*Quietly.*] You're all I have.

LIKA [*cautiously*]. And you're not going to start . . .

MARAT. No. Everything is decided. You've been married thirteen years. And I've been married quite a time.

LIKA. You're married?

MARAT. What did you think? We've all got our tickets.

LIKA. So you see . . .

MARAT. Yes, as we decided, so be it.

LIKA. Leonidik always blames you for going away – and everything . . . You haven't written once in all the thirteen years . . . Then he started saying you'd simply forgotten us.

MARAT. Did you think so too?

LIKA. No. It would be better if I had. [*Affectionately.*] What made you get married?

MARAT. No . . . [*With a laugh.*] All right. You see, I've got out of the habit of telling lies.

LIKA [*pause*]. You said you were in a bad way?

MARAT. I'll talk about it later. When Leonidik comes.

LIKA. Talk about it.

MARAT. No.

LIKA. Tell me!

MARAT [*pause*]. Well, how are things?

LIKA. All right.

MARAT. And work?

LIKA. I'm telling you – all right. Good polyclinic. Good area.

MARAT. Are you a practising G.P?

LIKA [*apologizing, as it were*]. That's right.

MARAT. But you wanted to . . .

LIKA [*sharply*]. It didn't come off. [*Calmly.*] But everything is all right. I've even been upgraded. Attached supervisor of the unit.

MARAT. Attached?

LIKA. It makes Leonidik laugh too.

MARAT. How is he?

LIKA. Everything going splendidly. His third book of poems is coming out. He isn't attacked by the press or at meetings. We're getting a flat . . . Moving in spring.

MARAT. What about this room?

LIKA. I don't know. We'll let it.

MARAT. Don't you mind?

[**LIKA** *does not answer.*]

[*Quietly.*] So Leonidik has everything under control.

LIKA. He has a seminar too . . . He teaches a bit.

MARAT [*cautiously*]. There's a lot of talk about poets just now. Even youngsters buy books of poetry . . . But there aren't any arguments about him.

LIKA. He doesn't try to be fashionable.

MARAT. I bought his little book, you know. It was a small edition, but they're lying about in the shops. [*Silence.*] Others have editions of a hundred thousand, and you can't get a single copy.

LIKA. It's just a cheap success.

MARAT. When books collect dust on the shelves — what kind of success is that?

LIKA [*flaring*]. Have you read his poems?

MARAT. I had occasion to.

LIKA [*trying to control her anxiety*]. Well?

MARAT. There weren't any mistakes. He writes without breaking the rules.

LIKA [*quietly*]. He doesn't publish his best work.

MARAT. I see.

LIKA. Wha:?

MARAT [*viciously*]. Everything.

LIKA [*pause*]. Marik . . . Don't tell him you've read him . . . Don't tell him any-thing.

MARAT. But, you know, that's . . . [*Quietly*.] It will be a lie.

LIKA. Let it!

MARAT [*walks across the room turns to* LIKA, *speaking passionately*]. How do you live here? [*Drops into a chair speaking quietly*.] I don't understand.

[*Door opens:* LEONIDIK *enters and sees* MARAT.]

LEONIDIK [*unable to look away from him*]. Marat Yevstigneykin!

The Same Evening

They sat down to supper an hour ago, but they're still at it.

LEONIDIK. . . . There's nothing to argue about. A person can never see him-self — what he is, who he is, if he has achieved it or hasn't . . . [*Pours him-self some wine.*] Only death clears it all up, and so here's to death!

LIKA [*takes his glass from* LEONIDIK, *drinks and smiles*]. You mustn't have any more.

LEONIDIK. This woman persecutes me . . . She's been persecuting me for thir-teen years! [*Laughs.*] Guardian angel, you understand? All the same, it's funny, you appeared an hour ago and it feels as if you haven't been away! Why are you silent?

MARAT [*quietly*]. I spent my childhood in this room.

LEONIDIK. So?

MARAT [*smiles helplessly*]. I don't know. [*Looks at them.*] How strange . . .

LEONIDIK. Strange? What exactly?

MARAT [*concentrating*]. There's a day I can't forget — first of May, the parade in '34 . . . I was nine. Father walked beside me in a new uniform. He held me tightly by the hand, and Kirov was standing and smiling on the rostrum. [*Passionately.*] If only everything could have remained as it was.

LEONIDIK. You're a naïve young man of the middle thirties . . . But we have seen the forties.

LIKA. And alack, we saw more than we understood, my poor Marik.

MARAT [*flares*]. Why do you call me poor?

LIKA. Because you believe in the impossible.

MARAT [*puzzled*]. Perhaps those who thought like me never came back from the war . . . [*Covers his face with his hands.*]

LEONIDIK [*cautiously*]. Hey! What's the matter?

MARAT [*lifts his head, looks at them carefully*]. How do we live? I think about it all the time. I'm thirty-five, so are you . . . and she's thirty-three . . . What have we done?

LIKA [*slight pause*]. You've had a lot to drink.

MARAT [*sharply*]. As much as I need! I'm not an alcoholic, so I don't have to watch it.

LIKA. How many of your bridges have you built?

MARAT. Six.

LIKA. Do you think that's too few or too many?

MARAT. It's enough.

LIKA. You see! And they publish his poems. While I look after people's health. All that we dreamed about has happened. [*Gaily.*] Well? Isn't that right?

MARAT [*looks at her*]. I always believed you. Not now!

LIKA [*slight pause*]. What do you want from us?

MARAT. I wanted you to help me. [*With a laugh.*] But I didn't know you were worse off than me.

LEONIDIK. We lost everything in the siege. But we found each other. [*Sharply.*] You had no right to leave us!

MARAT. Don't you think that my reasons for leaving matter?

LEONIDIK. I expect they do to an ordinary man. But you're Marat.

MARAT. I love flattery. All the same, let's talk frankly.

LIKA [*gaily*]. Do let's. Have you a nice flat? How many rooms?

MARAT [*to* LEONIDIK]. You see, she's afraid.

LIKA. What am I afraid of?

MARAT. The truth.

LEONIDIK. It can be tiring in large doses. Maximalism nearly destroyed mankind.

MARAT [*hotly*]. Now, let's think. When is a man finished? When he suddenly realizes his whole life is decided and he will never be more than what he is already. I don't mean jobs, I mean something bigger . . . [*Goes to* LEONIDIK *and puts his hand on his shoulder.*] Are you tired of living?

LEONIDIK [*pause*]. Why not — I'll speak up and tell the truth. I don't mind.

MARAT. Stop playing the fool.

LEONIDIK [*unexpectedly*]. I am tired.

MARAT. Why?

LEONIDIK. Eh, dear boy, a man gets most tired when he stands still.

MARAT [*to* LIKA]. What have you done to him? Answer me.

LIKA [*blazing*]. Dear friend, kindly explain your right to that tone of voice.

MARAT. Thirteen years ago I left you together in this room. The room where I spent my childhood. [*Choking with excitement.*] That's why I can ask you in any tone of voice I please — understand that? Are you happy?

[*Long silence.*]

LEONIDIK. We get by. We visit the clinic regularly, we are upgraded. [*Goes to* LIKA.] The dreams of childhood . . . Who got in their way? Leonidik. The result is rather poor. I write badly, don't I?

MARAT. Why? You write correctly.

LEONIDIK. You're polite, sir.

LIKA. Marat!

MARAT. Lika said you don't publish your best poems.

LEONIDIK. I have been guilty of that.

MARAT. Do you write them now?

LEONIDIK. I've lost the knack. [*With a laugh.*] He's a silly fool. He published the simple rhymes, the rest he kept to himself, refining word sequences to make it more amusing. But, you see, poetry requires a reaction.

MARAT. How long have you known this?

LEONIDIK. He has known it a long time but he wouldn't admit it to himself.

LIKA. Shut up! Don't you see, Marat is longing to convince us that your life is wasted. [*Acidly.*] It doesn't seem very polite in front of me. Besides, for a judge, he's rather an interested party, isn't he?

MARAT. That was below the belt, my child.

LEONIDIK. So Marat is a wicked breaker-upper, while we are happy and it's all running on wheels.

[*Long silence.*]

LIKA. Marat, it's late . . . Go away.

[MARAT *goes to the coat-rack, puts on his fur jacket, and stands silent in the middle of the room.*]

MARAT. Perhaps it really wasn't worth my coming here . . . [*Wraps his scarf round his neck.*] It's a long way to your village. [*Puts on his deer-skin cap.*] Makes you remember all sorts of things. Which I did. And how, the things I remembered . . . and how. [*Goes to the door, turns.*] Bridges! [*With a kind of fury.*] The best type of installation in the world! Six bridges – six pages of life. Do I consider any of them as the height of achievement? The summit? [*Pause.*] I had a friend. A design engineer. We built three bridges together. A confident chap. But he wasn't satisfied either. Then he was given this bridge to design . . . An installation without precedent! It was hard going. There were people who raised objections – and how! But you know he succeeded in getting me appointed works manager. [*Is silent and looks at them as if he had just seen them.*] Right . . . Why am I telling you? It's late, Lika, isn't it? [*Goes to the door and suddenly takes off his cap and turns to them.*] It could have been my life's work. It could! . . . But it isn't. [*Sharply.*] I abandoned my friend. I went and abandoned him. Unthinkable, isn't it? I abandoned him . . . [*Hurriedly.*] I convinced myself and others I wasn't ready, wouldn't manage, couldn't . . . [*Thinks a moment.*] Perhaps it really was that? [*Viciously.*] Whether it was or it wasn't, I managed quite neatly to get myself transferred to another job . . . A letter arrived there: "Hullo Marik, hullo you extinct volcano." Exactly. He wrote those words to me. [*Talking feverishly, hurriedly.*] He's in a bad way, my old friend. The quiet-lifers dubbed it a doubtful project . . . [*With a laugh.*] No, the point isn't that he despises me, perhaps even hates me . . . I can't come to terms with myself! [*Slowly.*] I expect I'll never come to terms with myself.

LEONIDIK. A sad story. [*Sadly.*] Has it ever occurred to you that it's barely credible?

MARAT [*desperate*]. Why?

LEONIDIK. Don't you see, it isn't logical.

MARAT [*fiercely*]. You assume life is logical! Write a poem about it. The evening rag slobbering with glee will print it! [*Sharply.*] Has all that happened to you been logical?

LIKA [*affectionately*]. My darling, we aren't children any more, and really let's leave Cloud-cuckoo-land to the younger generation. Our time there is up; it's time we came down to earth.

MARAT [*flaring*]. Don't want to!

LIKA. We aren't super-men, my dear.

MARAT [*passionately*]. Who told you that? . . . People should be terribly grateful to providence for allowing them to live! Well, think how many people died so that we should remain alive! Remember '42, the winter blockade, all the suffering? Hundreds of thousands died, so . that we should be extraordinary, triumphant, happy. Look at us – you, Leonidik, me? . . . Try and remember what you were, your promise. And where is it? Where is the promise? [*Quietly*.] Well . . . Why are you silent?

LIKA [*suddenly very simply*]. I'm afraid.

MARAT [*goes to her, affectionately strokes her hair*]. At last. [*Smiles*.] Oh, Lika, Lika . . . Sometimes it does you good to be afraid. There are plenty of cowards among optimists, child. [*Thinks*.] No, this is what I want to believe now – that on the eve of death it isn't too late to start one's life from the beginning.

[LIKA *wants to object, but can't find the words, and all she can do is smile, frightened and lost*.]

[*Cheerfully*.] And now I shall try and be logical. You never can tell, Leonidik. The thing is . . . I could tell you, Lika . . . And I shall tell you. The lot. [*Goes up to her very close*.] I lost you and I lost everything. Even the birds don't sing in the morning . . . They're silent, I don't know why. The stars in the sky have gone; the sky is empty now. Do you understand? Not a single star! There's silence, darkness. [*Pause*.] Well, there you are . . . You were longing for logic, you silly fools . . . [*Turns to* LIKA.] How is it all going to work out now? I don't know.

LIKA [*after a pause, she gets up and says very firmly*]. As before, only better. [*Goes to* LEONIDIK.] He will be happy. I swear it to you.

MARAT. Goodbye! [*Runs out of the room*.]

LEONIDIK. Bring him back, Lika, bring him back!

LIKA [*suddenly almost runs to the door, then stops with tears pouring down her face*]. I can't . . . I can't . . .

31 December

The festive table is laid for two, but LIKA *and* LEONIDIK *are sitting on the divan and playing cards.*

LEONIDIK. That's it! Your hour has come!

LIKA. I'm not afraid of you.

LEONIDIK. How about this!

LIKA. And how about that!

LEONIDIK. He has lost. It's beyond me. Fooled again.

LIKA. Once again! For the third time.

LEONIDIK. Triple fool of the Soviet Union! Marvellous!

LIKA. You're simply inattentive.

LEONIDIK. Not attentive or wonderful or amazing.

LIKA. But you have an incredibly beautiful tie.

LEONIDIK. I have that. [*Looks at the clock.*]

LIKA. What's the time?

LEONIDIK. Forty minutes to the New Year. *Finito*. [*Goes to the window.*] Crowds and crowds of citizens hurrying to meet the New Year at table . . . Funny.

LIKA [*smiles*]. You immediately think of your childhood.

LEONIDIK. The streets will be empty at midnight . . . [*Declaims.*] "And only meet a lonely passer-by . . ." [*With a theatrical gesture he throws a rug over himself, takes a stick, and, doubled up, hobbles across the room.*] As in a fairy tale. [*He laughs and is suddenly quiet.*]

LIKA [*pause*]. What are you thinking?

LEONIDIK [*unexpectedly*]. Marat!

LIKA. Yes. He's alone now. Five thousand miles away. [*With a laugh.*] Three weeks gone and that's that.

LEONIDIK. He's a darling.

LIKA. Don't.

LEONIDIK. Oh, dear — let's have another game. [*Cheerful.*] Perhaps I'll get my revenge.

LIKA. Today you're sort of . . .

LEONIDIK. They're approaching, damn them.

LIKA. Who?

LEONIDIK [*pulling a face*] . The sixties.

LIKA. You utter fool. [*Kisses him on the back of the head.*]

LEONIDIK [*quietly*] . Don't.

LIKA [*uncertainly*] . You're being rather nice today.

LEONIDIK. Now that's true.

LIKA. You've been playing the fool all evening. [*Cautiously.*] You'll be bored . . .
seeing the New Year in with me.

LEONIDIK [*singing*] . He will not be bored . . . [*Jumps up from the divan, goes
to the table.*] I really have made a colossal salad. Why aren't I a cook! My life
is wasted.

LIKA. Why do you keep looking at the clock?

[*Bell.*]

LEONIDIK. Well, that's all now. Open the door!

[LIKA *looks at him with a lost expression.*]

LEONIDIK. That's all. *Finito*.

[*Knock at the door.*]

Come in, Marik.

[*The door opens.* MARAT *stands there, in his fur jacket, covered in snow.*]

LIKA [*in fear and hope*] . You?

MARAT. As you see.

LEONIDIK. I was so afraid . . . [*Slaps him on the back.*] But you never fail.

MARAT. I react.

LEONIDIK. Marat, you're the friend of the people.

MARAT [*taking off his jacket*] . How did you find my address?

LEONIDIK [*significantly tapping his forehead with his finger*] . Understand? But
I was afraid the plane would be late. Now I can relax.

LIKA. What have you been up to? Tell me.

LEONIDIK. Lika, I got you something. A surprise in a way. It's with the neighbours. But the hour has come . . . I'll bring it. [*He goes.*]

LIKA [*goes to* MARAT *and says slowly, dragging out the words*] . I thought I
would never see you again.

MARAT. Me too. [*Clumsily strokes her hand.*]

LIKA. Your hand is so cold.

MARAT. It was difficult getting here from the airport. The New Year. All the taxis taken. [*Presses her hand to his cheek.*]

LIKA [*quietly*]. Are you sure you ought to have come?

MARAT. Not quite, child. [*Takes out a telegram.*] Yesterday I got this wire.

LIKA [*reading*]. "Catch plane immediately. Lika needs you. Mind, not later than the thirty-first. Leonidik." [*Looks at* **MARAT.**] I didn't know anything.

MARAT [*flaring up*]. Stupid jokes! Do you think it was easy to drop everything and fly over? [*Goes to the table and stuffs something into his mouth.*]

LIKA [*helplessly*]. Why do you use your fingers?

MARAT. I'm hungry!

LIKA [*smiles slightly*]. Don't make so much noise. [*Pause.*] Poor thing, you're tired . . .

MARAT. I expect so. [*Looks at her.*] I had a strange dream today . . . I was standing on an enormous bridge. It wasn't finished, you know . . . And I had to complete the job. A howling wind all round . . . I looked about me and saw both banks. My childhood on one bank, the May Day parades, the battleship "Marat" and father with his friends; and on the other post-war peace, the new life . . . But I'm standing on the unfinished bridge, the waves getting bigger and stronger and I can't, I can't join the opposite banks . . .

LIKA [*quietly*]. What will be will be . . . [*Astounded.*] What will be will be!

MARAT. What's that about?

LIKA [*slight pause*]. You left and I thought everything was all right between Leonidik and me . . . I gave you my word, you know, and now . . . three weeks later . . .

[**LEONIDIK** *returns, carrying a package.*]

LEONIDIK [*a finger to his lips*]. Sh-sh-sh . . . [*Goes to the table, takes the bottle.*] Now I'm going to pour myself out some wine . . . No, Lika, don't start! I'm going to drink it. [*Raises his glass.*] My health! [*Drinks.*] Not bad. Quite pleasant. [*Unwraps the package which contains flowers.*] The flowers are for you. Lucky I managed to get some. I'm very pleased about that.

LIKA. Thank you, but . . .

LEONIDIK. What can I say . . . We've been together for thirteen years and I love you as I loved you the first day. But I love you in my own way. No less but no more. Though I expect that isn't the point. I just haven't justified your hopes. You put so much into me. You even forgot yourself. But it was all for nothing.

LIKA. Must I believe that?

LEONIDIK. I must be alone. Today. If not today, you know, I'll never do it. Lika, don't let me be weak.

LIKA. No! . . . [*Desperately.*] Marat, why don't you speak . . . Tell him . . .

MARAT. I'm not going to!

LEONIDIK. My train leaves at 00.50. It's a nice nice business trip. [*Pause.*] I'm just an egoist and I've realized I have to be alone. [*To* LIKA.] To leave your care, your protection . . . [*To* MARAT.] You have nothing to fear. You're stronger. [*Slight smile.*] Anyhow, you can't live without each other, I know. [*To* MARAT.] Tell me, and no lies mind, I am right, aren't I?

[*MARAT doesn't answer.*]

Don't be a coward — well?

MARAT. Yes.

LEONIDIK [*affectionately*]. And why are you so silent . . . Lika?

LIKA. Goodbye.

LEONIDIK. Well done! You both understand. I knew you would. [*To* MARAT.] Remember what you said, that on the eve of death it isn't too late to start one's life from the beginning? That's overdoing it, of course. But it made an impression on me. I don't know why.

[*The clock strikes.*]

MARAT. Twelve . . .

LEONIDIK [*smiles*]. Twelve. The New Year . . .

[*In silence they go to the table and* LIKA *pours out some wine.*]

[*Raises his glass and says quietly.*] Don't let's ever betray our winter of forty-two . . . Right?

MARAT [*raises his glass and says*]. Or ever come down to earth. [*To* LIKA.] You promise?

LIKA [*raising her glass and speaking very fast, almost in a whisper*]. I promise you both.

[*Pause.*]

LEONIDIK. Well, now . . . Time to be off. He packed his suitcase earlier. The man has foresight. He'll come back, he'll ask you to his house-warming . . . We'll be seeing each other, shan't we?

MARAT. You mean that you aren't as great a coward as I am?

LEONIDIK. In a sense. [*To* **LIKA.**] Perhaps because I love you less than Marat does. [*Kisses her hand.*] Who knows. [*Goes towards the door, stops by the table.*] But don't forget, there will be a bit of me here today in this room. Yes, don't hurry . . . Let me get farther away from you. [*Takes a fork, tries the salad.*] Not bad. [*Pours out some wine, drinks.*] I think it was his last glass of wine. [*Smiles.*] I have given you up — I'll give that up too . . . Just think of that! [*Looks at them.*] Till we meet! [*He goes.*]

[**LIKA** *looks at the laid table, smiles rather strangely. With trembling hands* **MARAT** *strikes a match, lights a cigarette, drops into a chair.* **LIKA** *goes to him and puts her hand on his shoulder.*]

MARAT [*his voice unsteady*]. You know . . . On the first of May in '45 we got into the courtyard of a toy factory. It was in Breslau. There we were bombarded by mortars. We were seven. Only I survived.

LIKA [*quietly*]. My God . . . Why are you telling me this?

MARAT. It's a funny thought, you know, I might have died . . . [*Holds her hand tightly.*] And this moment — this very moment — it wouldn't have been.

LIKA. Marat . . .

MARAT. What?

LIKA [*quietly*]. He's alone, out there in the street.

MARAT. No — just don't pity him, do you hear? Today everything has started for him from the beginning. [*Passionately.*] You must believe in him again, Lika. [*Slight pause.*] Is living together going to be all that easy for us?

[*He falls silent, a little afraid, which* **LIKA** *understands.*]

LIKA. No, no everything's going to be all right . . . [*Not loud.*] The sixties . . . I believe in them. They will bring happiness.

MARAT. They can't fail to. Such hopes!

LIKA. Only, don't be afraid, don't be afraid to be happy . . . Don't be afraid, my poor Marat!

FINAL CURTAIN

The Promise

In his letter of 9 November 1965 Aleksei Arbuzov wrote about *My Poor Marat* in the production by Efros: "The theatre worked with great enthusiasm and the production as a result is probably no less successful than *It Happened In Irkutsk*. In any case all the tickets for the performances advertised have been sold. The actors are young and were unknown but after the première they are famous and that's the joy of it . . . I am convinced that of all my plays [it] is the most suitable for abroad. I can just see Judi Dench in it . . ." He had seen her the year before in *The Twelfth Hour*. He sent his regards to "dear Hauser" and went on: "Oxford is unforgettable. If you don't send for me for the première of *Marat*, I shall come to London in the summer of 1966 for the football world final". Of course, we sent for him.

Re-reading his letter now I recognize the pointers to his personality as a dramatist.

(1) Since the audience reaction showed the play was a success, Arbuzov had little more to say about it. His belief that it would succeed abroad showed the practical appraisal and quick action of an all-rounder, i.e. the man equally interested in football.

(2) His comparison of the success of *Marat* – a cast of three – with the success of *It Happened In Irkutsk* – a cast of nineteen plus the chorus – gives an idea of his range as a dramatist. That is not counting the difference in subject matter and treatment. There is one thing the plays have in common – both are about private people against an historic background; one had international while the other had national significance.

(3) His suggestion of Judi Dench for Lika, his pleasure at the success of the young and unknown actors in Moscow implies a very broad and lively awareness of and commitment to the theatre. He has a reputation for writing wonderful parts for actors and especially for actresses. In Moscow and Leningrad, where the theatre is more stable than in London, Olga Yakovleva and Alisa Freindlikh, who were the outstanding Likas, appear in his plays over the years.

Critical reaction to *My Poor Marat* in Moscow was summed up by *The Literary Gazette* critic. He found the play more ambivalent on the stage than on the printed page. One production had acclaimed the author's youthful idealism; another had wept for the trauma of a generation; a third had stressed the importance of being alive, man's right to happiness and "that on the eve of death it isn't too late to start one's life from the beginning". Incidentally, that is a recurring theme in Arbuzov's plays.

As a title *My Poor Marat* had the wrong associations here because of the RSC Marat/Sade production. Arbuzov was in favour of *My Poor Hero*. *The Promise* was dreamed up by Frank Hauser and gave a clue of the original U.K. interpretation. It focused on what Marat says to Lika in the last act when he reminds her of the blockade: "Hundreds of thousands died, so that we should be extraordinary, triumphant, happy. Look at us – you, Leonidik, me? Try and remember what you were, your promise. And where is it? Where is the promise?"

The press was unanimous in its praise. The play and Ian McKellen received a couple of awards. It has been produced world-wide in the theatre; also filmed, televised and broadcast on radio; it is still being done from time to time.

It is easy to miss the point of Act One. "What is so special about the time Lika, Leonidik and Marat spend together during the siege? It's miserable – they are always cold and hungry," I was told by a young American actress after I had seen a lugubrious preview. Of the three acts, Act One is the funniest and liveliest. The Arbuzov paradox is that physical deprivation gives an edge to inner experience. Act One is not a naturalistic portrayal of adolescent semi-starvation, though I remember at Oxford Playhouse we all agreed that semi-starvation could impede overt adolescent sex.

The point or points of Act One are in the dialogue and the stage directions. In the midst of destruction, three adolescents find each other. They have no one else. "No more silence", says Lika. They share their experiences – during an air raid the dream of kissing and eating toasted tea-cake with raisins, as well as Leonidik's account of the death of his father, his mother and the "man". They also feast – and what a celebration it is – the stew from the food parcel eaten very slowly, every biscuit crumb savoured. They share and fuss and brag and bully and dream of a future and they fall in love. At the same time they emerge from their den into acres of destruction; in Leningrad spring is on the way which is very special (see the note at the end of *The Twelfth Hour*); they have survived and they go their different ways till Act Two. Arbuzov's spoken stage direction was: "In Act One they are just like puppies – lots of fuss and bother".

CRUEL GAMES

Dramatic scenes in two parts (eleven scenes)
Poems by Igor Shklyarevsky

Cruel Games was first performed in London by students of the Guildhall School of Music and Drama, January 1980, with the following cast:

Kai Leonidov	Nicholas Reader
Nikita Likhachov	Reece Dinsdale
Terenty	James Andrew Morgan
Nelly	Sarah Berger
Mishka Zemtsov	Giacomo De Filippo
Masha Zemtsova	Jackie Downey
Konstantinov	Shane Collins
Loveiko	Rolf Saxon
Oleg Pavlovich	Joseph Long
Nelly's mother	Sharon Willmott
Lyubasya	Emma Rogers
Girl like an angel ⎫ Girl not like an angel at all ⎭	Stella Goodier
Soprano recorder	Somsak Ketukaenchan
Violin	Karen Markus
Clarinet	Joy Farrell
Guitar and music composed and directed by	Lori McKelvey
Choreography by	Graham Turner
Directed by	Gillian Cadell
Designed by	Richard Curtis Berry

Zhestokiye Igry (*Cruel Games*) was first performed in the Soviet Union, May 1978, at the Griboyedov Theatre of Russian Drama, Tbilisi. It was directed by A. Tovstonogov.

The play was first performed in Leningrad on 3 September 1978 at the Gorky Theatre with the following cast:

Kai	V. Yushkov
Nikita	G. Bogachev
Terenty	A. Tolubeyev
Nelly	E. Popova, LGITMIK student
Mishka	Y. Demich
Masha	N. Tenyakova
Konstantinov	G. Gai
Loveiko	G. Vasilyev
Oleg Pavlovich	M. Volkov
Nelly's mother	Z. Sharko
Girl like an angel ⎫ Girl not like an angel at all ⎭	N. Danilova
Head of production	G. Tovstonogov
Directed by	Y. Aksenov
Designed by	A. Orlov

And as he grew . . . he walked evenly between us . . .
a hand out to each of us for what we could offer by way
of support, affection, teaching, even love . . .

Edward Albee — *Who's Afraid of Virginia Woolf?*

CHARACTERS

KAI LEONIDOV, twenty-years-old
NIKITA LIKHACHOV, twenty   } friends from school
TERENTY, twenty
NELLY, recently arrived in Moscow, nineteen
MISHKA ZEMTSOV, doctor, thirty
MASHA ZEMTSOVA, geologist, thirty-nine
KONSTANTINOV, Terenty's father, fifty
LOVEIKO, Zemtsov's neighbour, thirty-eight
OLEG PAVLOVICH, Kai's stepfather, forty-three
NELLY'S MOTHER, forty-four
LYUBASYA, Nikita's younger sister, eighteen
GIRL LIKE AN ANGEL
GIRL NOT LIKE AN ANGEL AT ALL } the author suggests that the same actress plays both parts

The action takes place in the late seventies in Moscow and at the oil fields in Tyumen region.

[*This time the author recommends a naturalistic setting.*]

80

ACT ONE

Scene One

It is the end of September in the seventies. A house in Tverskoy Boulevard, built at the beginning of the century. A somewhat neglected, spacious three-room flat on the first floor.

In an armchair in the room that used to be the nursery, KAI is sitting in his usual posture. He is twenty, carelessly dressed, with a short hair-cut. He was good-looking as a child. It is growing dark outside but from the window one can still see the yellowing leaves of the boulevard. It is raining hard.

NELLY is standing in the doorway gazing into the twilight room. There is a simple look about her; the girl does not belong to Moscow as yet. There is a cheap little suitcase on the floor beside her.

NELLY [*looking carefully at* KAI]. Hullo. Your front door wasn't locked . . .

KAI. So what?

NELLY [*with disapproval*]. Well, you're alone in the flat.

KAI. So what?

NELLY. Burglars could walk in.

KAI. They don't.

NELLY. You might turn the light on. It's dark outside. What's the point of talking in the dark?

KAI [*turns on the table lamp. Looks at* NELLY.] Where do you spring from like that?

NELLY. Like what?

KAI. Wet, love.

NELLY. Why do you call me love? It won't do.

KAI. Who do you want?

NELLY. Leonidov.

KAI. Strange. I never thought anyone would want me.

81

NELLY [*looks round*]. Your flat's in a mess.

KAI. No doubt, my darling.

NELLY. Dust all over.

KAI. That is so, my sweet.

NELLY [*indignant*]. Can you talk sense?

KAI. I'm lazy, my friend.

NELLY [*looks at the easel*]. Are you an artist?

KAI. I'm not quite sure.

NELLY [*sees the aquarium*]. But you like fish?

KAI [*with a wry smile*]. More than anything in the world. [*Pause.*] Go on.

NELLY. Do you remember Iveta Gorshkova?

KAI. I'm not crazy about her.

NELLY. She sent me.

KAI. What for?

NELLY. Take me in. [*Quietly.*] Shelter me.

KAI [*pause*]. Are you — not quite right in the head?

NELLY. Where can I stay? Look, Leonidov, I've spent two nights at the railway station.

KAI. Tears won't help. No tears, if you please.

NELLY. I'm not going to cry. I've had all that. [*Slight pause.*] You have a three-room flat and you're alone here.

KAI. That's rational and correct. Now will you get out of here.

NELLY. Don't be rude. I'm talking to you like one human being to another. I'm in a bad way, you know. I haven't got a Moscow residence permit. I've nowhere to go. You realize that? For a couple of months I stayed with Iveta — we met at the Storm Club. At that time I was very low. She saw that at once. "You're funny," she said "come and stay with me." But, you know, her flat is bedlam, to put it mildly. Never the same crowd. Music plays. Doors bang. Some people stay the night. Laughter and tears. Still, it was a roof over my head. Suddenly she got a wire — her parents were coming back. She burst into tears and then gave me your address. "Off you go", said she, "there's something about him."

KAI. Why are you in Moscow?

NELLY. I had to come.

KAI. More details, please.

NELLY. You want to know everything.

KAI. I see. A simple story. What entrance exam have you failed?

NELLY [*slight pause*]. Medicine.

KAI. You failed badly?

NELLY. So badly, I was quite surprised.

KAI. Have you come a long way?

NELLY. There's a town called Rybinsk.

KAI. Go home.

NELLY. I haven't got a home, Leonidov.

KAI. And parents?

NELLY. I hate them. I'm sorry for my mother on the whole. And my father. I hate them all the same.

KAI [*looks closely at her*]. What's your name?

NELLY. Nelly.

KAI. That's a dog's name, if I'm not mistaken.

NELLY. Actually I'm Lena. They called me Nelly at school.

KAI. Are you soaked, Elaine?

NELLY. Yes, actually, I'm frozen stiff. It's the end of September but so cold.

KAI. There's a little bottle beside you. Pay attention. Also glasses. Pour it out. That's quite a vodka.

NELLY. I see. Not a little bottle.

KAI. In that case, let's have a good swig Elaine. Or you'll catch a cold.

[*They drink.*]

That's quite normal. How old are you?

NELLY. I was nineteen on Thursday.

KAI. You look older. You're lying to me, aren't you?

NELLY. I often tell lies. You must remember that, Leonidov.

KAI. Want some more?

NELLY. But don't fill it up – or I'll go to sleep. Have you got a bite of something to go with it?

KAI. Eat some sweets. They're in that box.

NELLY. This is rather childish.

KAI. In Chicago they only drink vodka with chocolate.

[*They drink.*]

Have you got some money?

NELLY [*concerned*]. Do you need a lot? I haven't got much.

KAI. Take this. Ten roubles. [*Holds out the money to her.*] And that's the end. Bye, old girl.

NELLY. What? Are you sending me away? You miserable fool! You're very lucky I came.

KAI. Really?

NELLY. I did all the housework at Iveta's – I made the tea; I did the shopping and the cleaning, even the laundry! I'll do the same for you. Your parents are abroad, you're alone here. You don't have to pay me. I'll find a job, get a residence permit and then take myself off. [*Tries to smile.*] You'll remember me.

KAI. You're overdoing it, Elaine.

NELLY. But why? It's quite true. [*Unsure of herself.*] Are you afraid of me, perhaps? Don't be . . . [*She smiles but sounds pathetic.*] I'm a lot of fun.

KAI. I see, you're game for anything.

NELLY [*very quietly*]. What?

KAI [*slight pause*]. Why don't you like your parents?

NELLY. They crossed everything out for me. [*In a shout.*] The lot? Do you see? All right. We'll shut up.

KAI. You can stay.

[*For a long time they sit without saying anything.*]

NELLY. How old are you?

KAI. A score.

NELLY. You're older than me. What are you called?

KAI. Kai.

NELLY. That's not human either.

KAI. Yulik. Mother called me that as a child.

NELLY. Did she? Kai's better. I shall call you Skiffy.

KAI. Why Skiffy?

NELLY. Doesn't matter. You studying?

KAI. They wanted me to be a lawyer. The second year I quit. I'm taking a correspondence course.

NELLY. You're complicated. Iveta told me.

KAI. She's absurd. I like to be quiet, please note. If you're going to fool around, do it quietly.

NELLY. I'll try. But don't let's be beastly to each other, all right? [*Pause.*] Where am I going to sleep? Here?

KAI. What do you mean, here?

NELLY. Well . . . With you . . .

KAI. Anything else!

NELLY [*shrugs*]. You're so strange. [*In some surprise.*] Thank you.

KAI [*opens the door of the next room*]. There's a small sofa in the corner. You get settled there, got that?

NELLY [*looks round*]. It's neglected.

KAI. There is space enough. [*Pause.*] People used to have fun here. There was a Christmas tree. Father Christmas came. Everyone danced and there was a lovely woman in a white dress . . . Stop! The kitchen! [*Almost vicious.*] Your work is there.

> [*Fade out. Fade up again in a few moments.* NELLY *is asleep in the arm-chair.* KONSTANTINOV, *an elderly, villainous-looking man is sitting motionless in another corner. He has his coat on and his cap as well.* TERENTY *appears, an easy going, bright and willing lad. He has come in his blue overalls straight from work. He sees* KONSTANTINOV.]

TERENTY. You here?

KONSTANTINOV. A long time. I thought you weren't coming. The rain.

TERENTY. The rain nothing! We've been electing the warden of the hostel.

KONSTANTINOV. Have you elected him?

TERENTY. Had to. Where's Kai?

KONSTANTINOV. Out. I came about an hour ago. He wasn't here.

TERENTY [*seeing the sleeping* NELLY]. Fancy that! [*Goes to her.*] What is that?

KONSTANTINOV. No idea. She was asleep when I came.

TERENTY [*holds the bottle to the light*]. They've been drinking. Empty. I expect Nikita brought her.

KONSTANTINOV. Busy body.

TERENTY [*looking at* NELLY *closely*]. A new one . . .

[*Pause.* KONSTANTINOV *looks a long time at* TERENTY.]

KONSTANTINOV. What news?

TERENTY. Nothing new.

KONSTANTINOV. Tell me something.

TERENTY. We met the day before yesterday.

KONSTANTINOV. Still . . . Time passes.

TERENTY. The hunchback nearly fell off the scaffolding this morning.

KONSTANTINOV. There you see . . . One must be more careful. [*Pause.*] Let me look at you – your hair seems to be going dark.

TERENTY. I don't think so.

KONSTANTINOV [*carefully*]. Of course, it's pointless . . . You said not to . . . But I got some more cinema tickets. Next door at the Replay, they've got Shukshin . . .

TERENTY. Dad, we are not going to the cinema together. [*Returns the tickets to him.*] There is no point . . .

KONSTANTINOV [*with a quaver in his voice*]. What are you doing?

TERENTY. Kai will be back . . . He'll have something to say . . .

KONSTANTINOV [*goes to the door, returns*]. I brought you a scarf. Take it. [*Gives him the parcel.*] It's going to be cold.

TERENTY. I can buy that.

KONSTANTINOV [*quietly*]. Take it . . . son.

TERENTY [*pause*]. All right. Off you go.

KONSTANTINOV. Don't be angry . . . I'll look in. [*He goes.*]

[*From his shopping bag* TERENTY *produces a packet of sugar, eggs, a sugar loaf and two bottles of Buratino wine.* NELLY *wakes up. She watches* TERENTY's *activities with surprise.*]

NELLY. And who are you here?

TERENTY. Terenty. Here and everywhere. Wherever I go, I'm always Terenty.

NELLY. Fancy that.

TERENTY. Did Nikita bring you?

NELLY. What Nikita?

TERENTY. Don't you know Nikita?

NELLY. Your Nikita is all I need!

TERENTY. What are you doing here?

NELLY. Living.

TERENTY. Been here long, have you?

NELLY. A couple of hours.

TERENTY. That explains why you weren't here when I looked in yesterday. What are you to Kai? A relative?

NELLY. If you must know — fate sent me to him.

TERENTY. To drink vodka?

NELLY. If you like.

TERENTY. And you made yourself comfortable in the armchair . . . fast asleep, you know.

NELLY. I haven't slept two nights. I sat in the railway station. Got that, mushroom.

TERENTY. Now why mushroom?

NELLY. You're like one.

TERENTY. I don't think so.

NELLY [*pause*]. Why have you brought the food?

TERENTY. We're going to have tea.

NELLY. Forget it — about bringing the food. Not your responsibility any more.

TERENTY. I'm a friend of his.

NELLY. You don't look it.

TERENTY. Why not?

NELLY. You're much simpler than him.

TERENTY. What a lot you know. We're a fraternity — Kai, then me and Nikita. Haven't you met Nikita?

NELLY. Why do you keep on about Nikita! All from the same stable, are you?

TERENTY. No, why? I live in a hostel. I'm building Moscow. Nikita has countless relatives. We all live our own way. But the main thing is here — at Kai's.

NELLY. What's here?

TERENTY. We just come here, that's all. I'm afraid you're going to be in our way.

NELLY [*slight pause*]. Listen, mushroom, don't give him that idea. I've nowhere to go. Nowhere at all. I've left my parents. I'm a stray.

TERENTY. I bet you made trouble for them.

NELLY [*quietly*]. They made trouble for me.

TERENTY [*with a wry smile*]. Well . . . parents can. [*Pause.*] What's your name?

NELLY. Nelly.

[NIKITA *enters. He has long hair. He is very good looking, affable and fun. He is simply dressed but with an eye to fashion. Taking no notice of the others, he takes his time to remove his shoes and without saying anything he lies down on the divan and stretches himself.*]

NIKITA. Hullo folks.

TERENTY [*with respect, to* NELLY]. Nikita.

NIKITA [*staring at the ceiling*]. It seems we have a woman?

TERENTY. Not seems, it is so.

NIKITA. An intelligent woman helps us to shorten a rainy evening. That is, if they're good looking. Oh! I'm being vulgar. Senility setting in. It's a bad sign.

NELLY. What are you — a psycho?

NIKITA [*turning to* NELLY]. Who's she?

TERENTY. Kai brought her.

NIKITA. Love at first sight. The lot. [*He slaps* NELLY *just below the middle of her back.*]

NELLY [*losing her temper*] . Listen you!

[KAI *enters. They all go quiet.*]

KAI. I think I've got my feet wet.

NIKITA. Where have you been?

KAI. Looking at the rain. [*With some interest.*] It really is curious. Rain is lead. [*Goes to the easel.*] Now if I were to paint that – a naked man and the drops puncture his skin, sharp drops of lead.

NIKITA. The sausage is on the table. Tea, Terenty!

NELLY. Come on, mushroom. [*She goes with* TERENTY.]

NIKITA. What is this new venture of yours?

KAI. She's out of luck. Alone in Moscow. She can sleep here.

NIKITA. She looks a bit of a mess.

KAI. She'll clean up. [*With a wry smile.*] She'll sweep the floor. She'll get the tea.

NIKITA. The trained secretary?

KAI. I think she's had a rough time. She was very anxious to please. Imagine, all of a sudden she asked – was she going to sleep with me?

NIKITA. She thinks she owes it to you. Your noble action. [*Looks in the direction of* NELLY's *exit.*] Yes, she looks nice. [*Smiles.*] Shall I drop a hint?

KAI. What?

NIKITA [*playful*] . I'm her host here as well . . . up to a point.

KAI. One should be more discriminating, old thing.

NIKITA. Think so? [*Turns.*] One old grumpy complained to me: "Life" he said "is very short". [*He goes.*]

[KAI *goes to the window, watches the rain, then returns to his easel. He picks up a brush and paints a great fat red question mark across the picture.*]

KAI. No . . . Always no and no.

[TERENTY *enters.*]

TERENTY [*with a glance at the picture*] . But why? . . . You spent a long time drawing it.

KAI [*furious*] . Painting! Painting, not drawing! How many times do I have to tell you . . . Idiot!

TERENTY [*short pause*]. Why are you like that?

KAI. Sorry.

TERENTY [*smiles suddenly*]. Nikita has started making up to the girl . . . He never gets fed up with it. [*Unexpectedly.*] I went to an amateur concert yesterday. I was interested. For instance, you perform and people listen to you. They don't even interrupt. Yes . . . it's interesting . . . [*Pause.*] Tell me, Kai, how would you explain the word: self-awareness?

KAI. Self-awareness – I expect it's an escape from self. To see yourself, know yourself, you've got to step aside, not to notice yourself, to go away . . . Then suddenly you turn and you see yourself . . . without thinking.

TERENTY. Clever. [*Another pause.*] Now, what's the best thing in the world?

KAI. Childhood.

TERENTY. What do you think about most?

KAI. Kindness.

BLACKOUT

Scene Two

Middle of November towards evening. KAI's *room again. In his armchair* KAI *is sketching something in a large sketching pad. A* GIRL LIKE AN ANGEL *is sitting at his feet on a low stool. She is knitting.*

GIRL [*after a long pause*]. You mean, you love no one?

KAI. No one.

GIRL. But your mother?

KAI. Her husband loves her. That's enough for her.

GIRL. And no one else?

KAI. What for?

GIRL [*slight pause*]. I shall light a cigarette.

KAI. Only open the fan-light.

GIRL. All right. [*Smiles.*] I'll wait.

[KONSTANTINOV *enters and dithers by the door.*]

KONSTANTINOV. Good evening . . . Has Terenty been?

KAI. He'll be along.

KONSTANTINOV. It's snowing . . . Shall I be in the way?

KAI [*indifferent*]. Sit down.

KONSTANTINOV. Thank you.

GIRL. Is your front door always open?

KAI. Always.

GIRL. Why?

KAI. I'm waiting. Someone might come in.

GIRL [*knitting all the time*]. What do you feel about the atom bomb?

KAI. Nothing, I suppose.

GIRL. Aren't you at all sorry for people?

KAI. I'm not sorry for myself.

GIRL. I'm sorry for myself.

KAI. You're a silly girl.

[NELLY *enters with a bag.*]

NELLY. Good evening all! I'm frozen. I have holes in my mittens, that's why. Uncle Seryezha, greetings!

KONSTANTINOV [*brightens up*]. Hullo. What news at work?

NELLY. I'm wall-papering. [*Cheerfully.*] A benefactor has come forward – he promised me a residence permit. I'm like a bird in transit without any rights. My boss is scared stiff.

KONSTANTINOV. A residence permit would be all right. They'll find you a hostel. Like Terenty.

NELLY. I'll have everything – in time. [*Unpacks the food.*] Kai, Kai – I got some sausages. Shall I cook them?

KAI. I'd like coffee . . .

NELLY. You'll also have your coffee, Skiffy. [*Looks at the* GIRL, *then at* KONSTANTINOV.] You know, you may be in their way?

KONSTANTINOV. They let me come in.

NELLY. Then stay where you are. Where have they put my broom? [*Goes into the kitchen.*]

KONSTANTINOV. She's bright and cheerful . . . Now if we could get Terenty engaged to her . . .

[KAI *has finished his sketch; he examines it.*]

GIRL. Show me.

KAI. It's rubbish. [*Tears the sketch.*]

GIRL. What was wrong?

KAI. I wanted to draw your thoughts.

GIRL. Do you know my thoughts?

KAI. I know everything. [*Thinks.*] I can't do anything.

[NIKITA *enters.*]

NIKITA. How goes it? . . . Are we happy?

KAI. So-so. You are tough — you've stayed away for three days.

NIKITA. Fuss and bother. At work and in my private life. I came first in everything. Have the ladies phoned me?

KAI. Non-stop. Your ladies never tire.

NIKITA. Cover up for me till next Sunday. Say "He's out of town."

KONSTANTINOV [*half-rising*]. Perhaps he isn't coming?

KAI. Wait a bit longer.

[KONSTANTINOV *sits down in embarrassment.*]

[*To* NIKITA.] I have news. I went and saw the vice-chancellor this morning. My correspondence course has gone by the board. Over. I'm free!

NIKITA. I don't approve. Or understand. I enjoy studying. Especially coming first.

KAI. I'm not like you. I'm incapable of being first.

NIKITA [*thinking it over*]. What will the parents say?

KAI. They'll calm down in the end.

[NELLY *returns and sees* NIKITA.]

NELLY. So you've turned up?

NIKITA. Where else would I go, Yelena Petrovna?

NELLY. Have you got the prize?

NIKITA. There has never been a Maths Olympics which I haven't won. [*Looks her up and down.*] Oh! You've got new shoes.

NELLY. You noticed?

NIKITA. You can't hide anything from me.

[*The* GIRL *folds her knitting and gets up.*]

KAI. Are you coming tomorrow?

GIRL. Must I?

KAI. Are you bored with me?

GIRL. Perhaps with you. Perhaps I'm just bored. I'll have to think.

KAI. Go ahead and think. It's an idea.

[GIRL *goes.*]

NELLY. Jingles, listen – I know you like Aero chocolate. I got some for you. It used to be one rouble ten. I bought some for one rouble fifty. It's either better or there's more of it. Help yourself.

NIKITA [*takes the chocolate*]. That's nice of you.

[TERENTY *enters.*]

TERENTY. Hullo! I've got five bottles of Buratino wine. They're giving it away on Kalininsky Prospect. [*Sees* KONSTANTINOV.] You here?

KONSTANTINOV [*dithers*]. Well? What news?

TERENTY [*angry*]. We see each other almost every other day. What news can there be? I'd rather you came to the hostel.

KONSTANTINOV. But you spend your evenings here.

TERENTY [*slight pause*]. They want to up-grade me.

KONSTANTINOV. There, you see ... [*Cautious.*] I bought a portrait of the writer Shukshin. I got it framed too. Hang it up where you like.

TERENTY. You should have thought of that before. [*Goes into the kitchen with the wine.*]

NELLY [*to* NIKITA *with a smile*]. When you chew your ears move, very nearly.

NIKITA. That's impossible.

NELLY. I wish you'd take me to the swimming pool when you're breaking a record.

NIKITA. I'm afraid you'd pass out with the excitement.

[KONSTANTINOV *sees that no one is looking at him and goes away quietly.*]

NELLY. Uncle Seryezha's gone . . . He waited and waited . . . I don't approve of Terenty. After all it's his father.

[GIRL *reappears. Without a word she sits down on the stool at* KAI's *feet and brings out her knitting.*]

People come and they go . . . The front door's open, of course.

GIRL. What are you sketching now?

KAI. What the puppy thinks.

GIRL. Do you like animals?

KAI. I liked them as a child.

GIRL. Then you stopped liking them?

KAI. I did something horrible. I killed a cat.

GIRL [*horrified*]. Why?

KAI. It reminded me of someone.

GIRL. I'm going to have a cigarette all the same.

KAI. I didn't mean to kill it. I just hit it. But the cat died.

GIRL. Were you sorry for it?

KAI. I was sorry for myself.

NELLY [*seeing her doll on the floor*]. The monsters! My doll is on the floor and they never noticed.

NIKITA. The doll suits you. You're sensational.

NELLY [*affectionately*]. She's my little friend . . . We've been together for fifteen years. [*Pause.*] Now, Jingles, tell me – you and Terenty come here nearly every evening. What for?

NIKITA. Who knows? [*Shouts.*] Kai, Nell's asked me why we come here?

KAI. Nobody knows . . . A piece of nonsense.

NIKITA. That's the point. Now, take me, for instance . . . I come here and that's certainly quite amazing. I have an exemplary family – lots of people! Brothers, sisters, nephews, parents. Even my great-grandfather is alive. He was a terrorist, by the way, he killed a Governor of a region. Briefly, masses of a great variety of people – all alive, all well, all with a future.

NELLY. Then why don't you make for home?

NIKITA. No reason why I should. I wouldn't find anyone at home except for great-grandfather. And we all eat at different times.

NELLY. Why?

NIKITA. Because there isn't one single idle person amongst the lot of us. We're all terribly busy. We're damnably progressive. That's why. We don't see each other for weeks. My younger sister woke up one day and said to me: "Listen, young man, what's your name?"

NELLY [*laughs*]. You're making it up.

NIKITA. I'm giving you the general outline. Sometimes we meet in the summer. On Sundays. That's when we find out that we're all doing terribly well.

GIRL [*gets up*]. No . . .

KAI. No what?

GIRL. I don't think I'll come again. Never.

KAI. Don't.

[GIRL *quickly kisses* KAI's *hand and runs out*.]

Pity there's no champagne.

NELLY. Don't fret, Skiffy . . . I'll also be leaving you soon. They're giving me a hostel.

KAI. Will that be a great improvement?

NELLY. I should be working for my exams.

NIKITA. Haven't you changed your mind about disembowelling corpses?

NELLY. I'm not going to change my mind. To be a doctor – that's my real ambition.

TERENTY [*comes out of the kitchen*]. What a business – I've eaten some-body's sausages.

NELLY [*horrified*]. Not all?

TERENTY. I'm a sensitive person – I left three.

NELLY. That's all right then. Give them to Kai.

KAI. I've been waiting for coffee for half an hour.

TERENTY. Take a seat. I've brought your coffee.

[KAI *and* TERENTY *get down to their supper.* NIKITA *leafing through a magazine reads out in French.*]

What's that?

NIKITA. Everyone's advised to go to Madagascar.

TERENTY. It will be done.

NELLY [*goes to* NIKITA]. Nikita . . . What I want to say to you . . . is . . .

NIKITA [*tearing himself from the magazine*]. What exactly?

NELLY. Don't go home tonight . . . Stay with me . . .

NIKITA [*smiles, runs his finger down her nose*]. I can't.

NELLY. Why not?

NIKITA. I have a training session at the swimming-pool tomorrow morning. I must be stretched like a string on a violin.

NELLY [*slight pause*]. Do you feel all right about me, Jingles?

NIKITA. Wonderful.

NELLY. And you aren't a bit afraid of me?

NIKITA. Definitely not.

NELLY [*smiles*]. Supposing I went and had a daughter by you?

NIKITA [*cheerfully*]. I think we can do without.

[*As a joke* NELLY *begins dandling her doll.* NIKITA *watches her, then shakes his finger at her.*]

Look out, Nell!

TERENTY [*rises*]. Quiet all! [*Recites solemnly.*]

> "Be gone, thou brooding, doubting spirit!"
> The Messenger of Heav'n replied.
> "Enough of thy defiant triumph.
> The hour of judgement now is come
> And God's decision blessed stands!"
>
> The fallen demon curs'd himself,
> He curs'd those insane dreams of his,
> And once again, that spirit proud,
> Adrift in space and time eternal,
> Was all alone — no hope, no love.

[*He stops and looks at them all.*]

KAI [*shattered*]. What is that?

TERENTY. I'm reciting that at our amateur evening. It's beginning to get me. A strong pull.

NIKITA. Have you decided to be an actor?

TERENTY. No, why — I like my work. This would be a hobby.

[*The phone rings.*]

KAI [*lifting the receiver*]. Well . . . he is not here. He hasn't been for three days. Who is the cooing dove? . . . All right, I'll tell him. [*Hangs up.*] I'm fed up with your women.

NIKITA. Tell them to go to . . . Just a moment, who was it?

KAI. Olenyeva.

NIKITA. Lelya? Pity you hung up. She's special. If she rings again, tell her — Saturday as agreed.

TERENTY. Can I recite Turgenev's: "How lovely, how fresh the roses used to be."

NIKITA. Hang on, will you . . . [*Leafs through his notebook.*] I haven't even got her phone number.

NELLY [*unexpectedly*]. Are you kind, Nikita?

KAI. He is not cruel.

NIKITA. Not cruel doesn't mean he's kind.

KAI. Quite right. Terenty is kind. Nick is not cruel. I am cruel. That's how we rate.

TERENTY [*suddenly heated and somehow out of context*]. No, that is not the main thing! It's something else . . . You know, Nell, we've been together from childhood . . . When we're together we don't have to talk — not about any subject! We are not fools — we don't play cards! It's great — not having to talk to each other. Not everyone knows how . . .

[NELLY *sits in the corner and weeps quietly.*]

KAI. Leave the room.

BLACKOUT

Scene Three

Late evening at the end of January. KAI's *room has finally been tidied up. It is even cosy; today at any rate. Subdued lighting.* MISHKA, KAI *and* TERENTY *are sitting at the table. There is an open bottle of cognac.* TERENTY *is drinking tea.*

MISHKA [*sings quietly, accompanying himself on the guitar*].

> Behind the sauna, woodshed and
> the dunes, the fisherman awake
> all night, sat scraping his bayan;
> the woman stared at the moon.
> On Saturday the moon was full.
> The fisherman went on and on,
> all night he scrap'd the same low notes,
> all night he scrap'd the same slow tune,
> while she sat staring at the moon,
> a cold and white and distant moon.
> She did not weep nor hum a tune.
> The woman simply sat and stared.
> The fisherman would end his song
> and start again the same old tune.
> He'd end his tune and start again.
> The woman simply sat and stared.

[*Puts down his guitar and pours out the cognac.*]

[*To* TERENTY.] You've had enough tea, young man. Get down to business.

TERENTY. I told you, I don't drink.

MISHKA. This is cognac?

TERENTY. I won't drink — I'd rather die.

MISHKA [*to* KAI]. Where did you find this miracle?

TERENTY. I'm his friend from childhood.

MISHKA. Takes a lot of finding . . . [*Raises his glass to* KAI.] The parents!

KAI. That's depressing.

MISHKA. Don't you get on?

KAI. I've lost the knack. It's the second year we're apart. True, your aunt, my mother, to put it simply, spoils me, always writing letters to me. She keeps up appearances on the whole.

MISHKA. You still dislike your stepfather?

KAI. Why should I. He's a handsome young man. Of course, I'm sorry for them – it's their second year in Iceland among the geysers. It can't be much fun.

MISHKA. Do you ever see your father?

KAI. Where could we meet? At the railway station? He has a new family in Leningrad. I heard, he has a son. [*With a wry smile.*] My baby brother. [*Holds out his glass.*] A splash.

MISHKA [*slight pause*]. Don't be so dramatic . . . It's hardly worth it. My parents are great fun: the letters they write – you'd die laughing. [*Raises his glass.*] Do as you like but I'll drink to them!

[*The door opens and* NIKITA *comes in from the cold.*]

NIKITA [*looks around*]. You have guests?

KAI. Meet my cousin. He got stuck in Moscow and he's staying the night here. He's eleven years older than me. But there are centuries between us.

MISHKA [*holds out his hand*]. Mishka Zemtsov. Medico. I play the guitar.

KAI. Don't run yourself down. He's a great character, an enthusiast of the sixties. Have you heard of them? He sits on the oil in West Siberia and cures the bears in its marshy forests.

NIKITA. A fashionable place. I've lost an uncle out there. He supplies things. With some success.

KAI [*to* MISHKA]. You have a great mathematician before you. He always gets five out of five.

NIKITA. What can I do, it's a must. As a child I was trained to go to the top.

MISHKA. Really?

NIKITA. My family has no use for misfits.

MISHKA. I see. You know all about success. Do you know about failure?

NIKITA. What, what?

MISHKA. All right, time will tell. [*Pours out the cognac.*] Now, to my daughter! The one and only!

TERENTY. You got one already?

MISHKA. Child of the marshy forests. She'll be born in five weeks.

TERENTY [*touching* MISHKA'*s glass with his teacup*]. You're obviously a man of sense – go forth and multiply.

MISHKA. Conditions are difficult. If I lived in Moscow, I'd have fourteen of them. [*Again picks up the guitar and sings.*]

> I ate a litttle – thought a lot,
> You thought a little – ate a lot.
> With what result? The following:
> You know you're clever – I'm a fool.
> You burst out laughing – I start crying.
> You save it up – I squander it.
> Your memory is good – mine bad.
> You know what's what, which I do not.
> But if you have forgiven me,
> I never will forgive, not you.
> I ate a little – thought a lot,
> You thought a little – ate a lot.
> With what result? The following:
> You know you're clever – I'm a fool.

[NELLY *comes in from outside. She listens to* MISHKA *singing.*]

NELLY. Good evening all.

TERENTY. Why so late?

NELLY. I was celebrating. I've got a hostel.

TERENTY. So . . . Our happy times are over. I'll have to do the shopping again.

NELLY. I had beer and cheese with the chaps. So that's it, chaps. [*Goes to the next door room.*]

MISHKA. Who's she?

TERENTY. Our trained secretary.

KAI. I took her in temporarily. She helps with the housework.

MISHKA. Nice girl.

KAI. Nikita thinks so too.

NIKITA [*sharply*]. Rubbish.

[*Short pause.*]

TERENTY. How are the wild beasts out there – many and varied?

MISHKA. Not too many. There are bears and countless snakes.

KAI. Have you got a bearskin?

MISHKA. It's a disaster. I shot my old friend, the bear, in the spring. I skinned him but it moults. It's in the spring the bear moults. We can't get rid of his hair now for six months.

[NELLY *comes out of her room and listens intently to* MISHKA.]

On the whole our life is interesting. There's marshy forest all round – it doesn't look like a Health Centre. And if you set out with a search party into the wild, life is of very special order. You crawl across the marsh as through a minefield. One careless movement and it's – Mishka goodbye! One kilometre can take you five hours, no less. Or fording a river in a blizzard, if you hesitate – you freeze to the ice. Yes . . . I've seen a thing or two. At first I simply couldn't go to sleep out there, especially outside the tent, if one had to sleep by the campfire. Rustling all round, rustling. I felt stripped, as it were – without cover, if you like. Then I got used to it and never slept better. You hang up your shirt on some stakes over your head and you have a house! You sleep and dream as nowhere else. You wake up with the first sunlight, open your eyes – life!

NELLY. What's your name?

MISHKA. Mishka Zemtsov.

NELLY. I'm Nelly.

MISHKA. A big hullo to you!

NELLY. I'll be a doctor too.

NIKITA. Don't be in such a hurry to show off. You haven't been accepted.

MISHKA. You failed?

NELLY. So what? I'll get what I want.

MISHKA. Go and work in a hospital as a nurse in the meantime. You need experience.

NELLY. I've done that. In Kineshma I nursed the sick for six months. It didn't help with exams.

MISHKA. If I had a nurse like that, I'd pay her weight in gold. [*Picks up the bottle of cognac.*] Let's drink to this. There's a drop left.

NELLY. The beer I had has gone to my head.

MISHKA. All right . . . I'll drink it up. [*Walks over to the wall where* KAI *has put up his drawings.*] Yours?

KAI. Imagine. I play at it.

MISHKA. What is it?

KAI. That's part of the rules of the game. [*Holds out his portfolio.*] Look at these.

[MISHKA *examines the drawings.* NIKITA *goes to* NELLY.]

NELLY [*with a wry smile*]. Well, my darling, my joy, my sunshine? What are you looking at?

NIKITA [*unsure of himself*]. I hope you aren't leaving today?

NELLY. Your hopes are justified – not today. [*Laughs quietly.*]

NIKITA. Why the laughter?

NELLY. I'm thinking – I'll go and I'll not give you my address. You'll start looking for me everywhere. You'll consult the missing persons bureau. You will wring your hands in despair. Isn't that so, my poor little boy.

NIKITA. All right . . . [*Almost affectionate.*] Stop it, Nell.

NELLY. And really it is all over between us. It's goodbye, Jingles, my little orphan.

NIKITA. You know something . . . You listen to me . . . [*Takes her by the elbow.*]

NELLY [*snatches her arm away*]. Let go of me! [*Brings her face right up to him.*] Perhaps I dislike you more than anyone else in the world? Move away from me. Move away for ever.

NIKITA. Why so moody? I don't get it.

NELLY. What if I'm pregnant by you? Six months? [*Wry smile.*] That frightened you . . . Oh, my precious little top-marksman!

NIKITA. Talking to you today is . . . [*With a dismissve gesture he joins* TEREN-TY.]

TERENTY. Have some tea. And don't argue with women – they're always right.

MISHKA [*handing the portfolio back to* KAI]. These are sharper. [*Thinks.*] Perhaps it's good. I'm no judge, of course . . . [*Slight outburst.*] Only why do you always have rain, rain, rain? Is sunlight out of fashion?

KAI. I put down what I see. Why should I pretend.

MISHKA. Perhaps you have a mean way of seeing things. Seeing is also an art.

KAI. Well, there's a way out. I'll buy a camera and get some good weather snaps for you.

MISHKA. I don't mean that, Yulik. Look, it's all dead . . . No light, no day-light . . . [*Heated.*] You're rebelling, you left college. But whose money are you living on? Your mummy sends it to you. I don't see the logic of it, my friend.

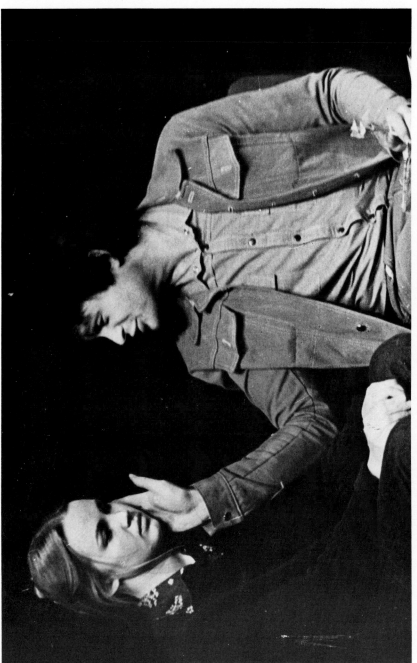

PLATE 11. E. Popova as Nelly and G. Bogachev as Nikita, Gorky Theatre, Leningrad

PLATE 12. E. Popova and N. Tenyakova as Masha

PLATE 13. M. Rogov as Kai and A. Baikov as Terenty, Lenin Komsomol Theatre, Moscow

PLATE 14. G. Smirnov as Konstantinov

NIKITA. Mishka, aren't you being very superior?

MISHKA [*pause. He smiles unexpectedly.*] You're right — I'm shouting him down. That's ugly. [*Thinks.*] Honestly, though, your lives are dim here. Rather sour, on the whole.

NIKITA. I can't see, that applies to me. I have a good time. Quite.

MISHKA [*furious*]. Do you know what a good time is, you little fool? [*Makes a rude gesture.*] That's what you know!

NELLY. But why make a noise? You should be sorry for them.

BLACKOUT

Scene Four

The beginning of March in West Siberia. The settlement of an oil-prospecting expedition.

ZEMTSOV's room in a two-storey log-cabin. There is no order here, no sign of a woman's touch — things are at odds with each other.

It is evening with wind and snow outside; inside the stove crackles, it's warm. LESSYA, two-months-old, is asleep in a home-made cradle in a corner.

MASHA ZEMTSOVA is sitting at the table, drinking tea, and MISHKA is writing something in a notebook. MASHA will soon be forty but she looks older. She is robust and beautiful with mocking, restless eyes.

MISHKA. Once upon a time there lived Mashka and Mishka. There lived Mashka and Mishka once upon a time.

MASHA. Don't you get bored? You've been saying that all day.

MISHKA. The combination of words flashed through my mind at dawn. As soon as I woke up. Once upon a time there lived Mashka and Mishka . . . Don't you like it?

MASHA. It's amusing.

MISHKA [*glancing at the sleeping baby*]. Look at her. She fell asleep at once.

MASHA. It's the air of the marsh. We went past the turn late afternoon. They're drilling a new hole there.

MISHKA. Careful you don't drop her out of the sledge.

MASHA. Anikin is in charge of the drilling. He got what he wanted.

MISHKA. Damn your Anikin ... Look after your daughter or I'll give you such a bashing! [*Goes to her from behind, embraces her hard, kisses her.*]

MASHA. You fool! You spilled tea over me.

MISHKA. Never mind. [*Turns on the tape-recorder.*] Let's dance, Mashakins.

MASHA. Let's, why not, madman.

[*They rock and roll.*]

[*Stops.*] Let me get my breath.

MISHKA. What? Old age creeping up? [*Kisses her.*] There lived Mashka and Mishka once upon a time ... [*Kisses her for a long time.*]

MASHA [*freeing herself*]. Hey, careful! At the age of thirty-nine I produced a daughter for you. Now you want to start a son ... Perhaps we should wait, Mishakins?

MISHKA. No, you are not romantic, Mashakins. True passion is beyond you.

MASHA [*sharply*]. Stop it.

MISHKA [*cautious*]. What is it?

MASHA [*sinks onto a stool, speaking quietly*]. I'm bored. Oh, so bored.

MISHKA. Hullo! Bored already. You only had her ten weeks ago. Are we so dull?

MASHA. You know me, don't you? I can't stay at home.

MISHKA. That's why all your husbands scarpered.

MASHA. Only two.

MISHKA. Isn't that enough? Relax, Masha — take a look at this lovely baby you've produced.

MASHA. She doesn't feed at my breast.

MISHKA. Oh, you make me angry.

MASHA. You shouldn't have married a grown-up woman. Forty in a few days. I'm nine years wiser than you.

MISHKA. Yes ... That's quite a subject.

MASHA. Full of sadness. I hop around like a fool in a cage.

MISHKA. There you go again. Now it's a cage.

MASHA. Isn't it? You're a doctor. You can be called out any time of day and night and for as long as you're needed? But I've got to sit with her, there's no way out.

MISHKA. Be patient . . . We'll soon take her to the crèche.

MASHA [*flaring up*]. At the end of the summer we had just reached a new seam. But no, my expedition was called back, my area was said to be doubtful. The oil is there! I must prove it. I must put my case. It's up to me. But here I sit with you both, dilly-dallying.

MISHKA [*almost with admiration*]. You're a wild beast!

MASHA. I'm a geologist. Everything else comes second! My place is out there. I started something and it's up to me to finish it.

MISHKA. Yes . . . The child was bad luck.

MASHA. I warned you. You should have listened to me, my dear boy.

MISHKA. It's a disaster. I love you. [*Smiles.*] That's the disaster.

MASHA. My very own darling . . . Bear with it. I'll be an old woman soon.

[MASHA *turns on the tape-recorder. They rock and roll like mad. There is a knock on the door.*]

MISHKA. Come in.

[LOVEIKO *enters. He is thin, lanky, pale, with wild hair and mad eyes. He is thirty-eight-years-old.*]

LOVEIKO. Why are you dancing, dear neighbours? The house is shaking. I have neuralgia! Listen, Mishka, give me something for my head — I'm dying.

MISHKA. You're always dying, Loveiko, but I don't see the grand finale.

LOVEIKO. All right, I'll die shortly. In the meantime give me a pill to swallow.

MISHKA. Here, greedy guts. You'll soon finish my entire stock.

LOVEIKO. Couldn't you give me something for my heart . . . It keeps stopping.

MISHKA. Some people just go on living. They should have died last year but they're still running around.

MASHA. Now, don't listen to him. Have some tea.

LOVEIKO. No. Mishka is a super doctor. I haven't had a word of comfort from him. So I go on living to spite him. [*Goes to the table.*] What have you got with the tea?

MISHKA. Have a pastry.

LOVEIKO. Good enough for a bachelor.

MISHKA. You should get married. Women adore the sick. Gives them something to do, carrying chamber-pots. Get married, Loveiko. You'll have someone to walk behind your coffin.

MASHA [*angry*]. My God, I'm going out.

LOVEIKO. All right, we'll stop joking . . . [*Sipping his tea.*] Listen, Masha, I've been to see Rebrov. He is not providing the wherewithal for a survey. He said your area was not promising. All his geological élite agree on that point. "Loveiko, don't fool yourself," said he, "and tell Zemtsova to look after her child."

MASHA [*very troubled*]. Now don't worry, Loveiko, don't worry. I'll go and see Rebrov and take Lessya with me. I'll shake him.

LOVEIKO. Spring is just round the corner. If we don't get our survey allowance now, the summer will burn itself out.

MASHA. I've just told you – I'm going to shatter Rebrov.

MISHKA. You're gangsters! The set I've got into.

[LOVEIKO *begins to cough.*]

Surely you aren't taking this sick man into the marshy forests with you?

LOVEIKO. I'm a platform driller – a high-class master craftsman. God intends me to die in the open.

MASHA. He doesn't need pills, he needs the wide open spaces. Loveiko, believe me, once we get there you will rise like a phoenix from the ashes.

LOVEIKO. It's possible, quite possible. As you say, like a phoenix. Only get the estimate before May.

MISHKA. Yes, I've had my summer. Your area is fifty kilometres across the marsh. You won't be looking me up on your off days.

MASHA. Let me prove my point. After that I'll go to Sochi with you, if you like.

MISHKA. Will you? You'll find a new testing ground, Zemtsova. And it won't be any nearer. [*To* LOVEIKO.] Listen, you ailing thing, have yesterday's papers arrived?

LOVEIKO. They have.

MISHKA. I'd like to have a look at them. [*He goes out.*]

LOVEIKO [*looking at* MASHA *who is standing by the cradle*]. Well? Have they clipped your wings, birdie?

MASHA. We shall see.

[LOVEIKO *follows* MISHKA *out.* MASHA *bends over the cradle.*]

[*Partly affectionate, partly distressed.*] Well, beautiful? Are you punishing me?

[*The door opens quietly.* NELLY *enters cautiously with a bundle and small suitcase.*]

NELLY [*sees* MASHA *and nods*]. It's me. Good evening. The cold here. I'm frozen. Can I go to the stove?

MASHA [*astounded*]. Please do.

NELLY. Does Mishka Zemtsov live here? I've come to see him.

MASHA. Why, are you . . . ill?

NELLY. Why should I be?

MASHA. Where have you come from?

NELLY. Moscow. [*Slight pause.*] The heart of our country.

MASHA. Has Mishka . . . I mean, did he ask you to come?

NELLY. Not ask, exactly . . . He sort of hinted.

MASHA. What are you going to do here?

NELLY. Me? Live. [*Pause.*] Who are you in relation to him?

MASHA. His wife.

NELLY. He has a wife? I didn't know that. All right. Fine.

MASHA. Thank you for allowing it.

NELLY. No, why not.

MASHA. Are you good friends?

NELLY. I suppose so, on the whole. The point is I liked him a lot. He's a human being. [*Sees the cradle.*] Is the child also his? He never told me about that either. The point is — I'm very fond of small children.

MASHA [*very slightly mocking*]. Really? It's all turning out very well for you.

NELLY. Do you think so? Possibly. [*Firmly.*] Is your tea hot? If not, please make some more. the hotter, the better.

[MISHKA *returns, sees* NELLY *and looks at her closely.*]

Good evening! Well, I've come.

MISHKA [*puzzled*] . A big hullo to you! [*Looks her over uncertainly.*]

MASHA. You're the host, Mishakins, she's your visitor.

MISHKA. That so? How nice . . . [*Thinks.*] Wait, where have I seen you before? Go on, take your hat off . . . Mother of God, my best friend, Tamara!

NELLY. I'm Nelly.

MISHKA. That is not important. [*With interest.*] Why are you here?

NELLY. You told me yourself – I'm worth my weight in gold.

MISHKA [*happy*] . Now I recognize you, hedgehog! [*He starts unmuffling her.*] Masha, look, she was working for my cousin as a stewardess . . . I really took to her!

MASHA. Obviously. Since you asked her to come.

MISHKA. You've come at the right moment, Nelly. The very moment. My nurse has been kidnapped by a helicopter pilot. There's no one to look after my patients. How did you know? Anyway, well done! And shall we enjoy your company for long?

NELLY. We'll see, shall we. Next autumn I must have a go at my medical entrance again. Will you help me?

MISHKA. You can rely on that. [*He sits her down by the stove.*] Well, what messages from my cousin?

NELLY. They don't know I came to you. I left without saying goodbye. That's all. So long! They probably think I left them to go to the hostel. [*A moment's pause.*] Interesting to know what they think. [*Wry smile.*] They don't think anything, right? Why should they think, on the whole? What is there to remember? [*Leisurely.*] Yes, what a laugh, here I am with you . . . Life goes racing by Mishka . . . It races by and doesn't wait. [*Looks at* MASHA.] And this is your wife? How old is she?

MASHA. I'll be forty very soon, little girl.

NELLY. Not young. [*The warmth makes her sleepy.*] All right, we'll sort things out. Give me some tea quickly – I'm quite frozen. [*She closes her eyes.*]

MASHA. She's a god-send to you.

BLACKOUT

Scene Five

Moscow. KAI's *flat again. The middle of May. The day is overcast.*

KAI, NIKITA *and the* GIRL WHO IS NOT AT ALL LIKE AN ANGEL *are talking over a bottle of wine. The tape-recorder plays quiet music.*

GIRL. Rain and more rain . . . They call it spring. And nothing happens. When the weather's good, there's always something.

KAI. You vanished for a long time.

NIKITA. There were complications at the institute.

KAI. What were they?

NIKITA. The same. I keep getting five out of five.

KAI. Isn't that boring?

NIKITA. It's a habit. [*Slight pause.*] Funny, I'd like to go away somewhere.

KAI [*surprised*]. That's something new.

NIKITA. You're right, I've got out of control. Somehow I don't feel too good, Kai-Yuly.

KAI. The girls have worn you out.

NIKITA. I've quietened down.

KAI. You're joking. [*To the* GIRL.] He's an interesting man, isn't he?

GIRL [*shrugs*]. We'll see.

NIKITA. She's very amusing!

KAI. I'm helpless with laughter, as you see.

GIRL. It's no way to live. I'm already twenty-one but I haven't been to Daghestan. They say, the monasteries there! Everyone goes there. Only fools go to Sochi now.

NIKITA [*goes to easel*]. Done anything new?

KAI. Take a look. [*Shows him a drawing.*]

NIKITA. Nelly . . .

KAI. From memory.

NIKITA. Whatever for?

KAI. I felt sad that evening. Like it?

NIKITA. Very much.

KAI. Thought so. My one and only success. The rest is rubbish. All rubbish.

NIKITA. Will you give it to me?

KAI. No. [*Slight pause.*] Remember Mishka?

NIKITA. Your cousin?

KAI. Beard. Guitar. Decorative. Crawls over marshes, knows about life. [*Thought-ful.*] Perhaps he shook me. Somehow nothing is the same since. [*To* GIRL.] Why are you chain-smoking? Like a monkey.

GIRL [*thoughtful*]. It's odd all the same. All the years I have lived — but I've never been to the zoo.

NIKITA. Does Terenty still come?

KAI. Regularly, though not for long. He's a keen amateur, you know. He leaps about or sings or dances. Anyway, he's making progress.

GIRL. We are not going to Zagorsk or Kolomenskoye. We should go and look at the churches. Lyubochka Intelman walked to Optina desert. Bare-foot.

NIKITA. Where did you dig her up?

KAI. She turned up on her own.

GIRL. Silly fool — I bring luck. Ask Stasik.

NIKITA [*rather hesitant*]. Kai, it's quite funny . . . Imagine, I dreamt of Nelly a few nights ago. [*Embarrassed.*] No reason why I should . . . The dream was sort of inconclusive. It made an impression.

KAI [*pause*]. Well?

NIKITA. I felt sort of disturbed . . . Of course, it's nonsense, but I decided to look for her. I didn't find her at the hostel. Remember how hard she tried to get a residence permit. Then suddenly she chucked it all up and left Moscow.

KAI. Why are you so worried?

NIKITA. Well, she really is a peculiar creature . . . She teased me often — I'll have a daughter by you . . . Or she'd announce all of a sudden — I may be six months gone . . . Little jokes like that.

KAI. Well, we'll have some fun. Fatherhood will suit you . . . Jingles!

NIKITA. The timing is right. Why else would she leave Moscow? . . . And my dream fits in.

KAI. Yes, you've had it.

NIKITA. Why, no, it's nothing . . .

[*Pause.*]

GIRL. Actually everyone's going to Lev Tatarsky's summer cottage . . . They have all kinds of mystical experiments there. The last holiday they discussed Dostoyevsky.

NIKITA [*gets up*]. I'm going.

KAI. Have you found her address?

NIKITA. She hasn't left it. [*Significantly.*] That's another factor. She's a strange girl. You don't know what to expect. [*Long pause and sudden smile.*] A little flame. Honestly, I keep thinking of her.

KAI. She was amusing.

NIKITA. She was a dear. You can laugh if you like, but with her I had it so . . . The trouble is, Kai-Yuly, I can't find the right word.

KAI [*pause*]. Come tomorrow late afternoon. Terenty will be here. We'll discuss it.

NIKITA. I'll look in. [*Looking at the* GIRL.] Get rid of this one.

KAI. I'm sorry for her. Her husband left her last week.

NIKITA [*goes to the* GIRL, *pats her on the cheek*]. All the best. [*He goes.*]

GIRL. What a fool.

KAI. But why?

GIRL [*pleading*]. Let's go for a boat trip on Moscow River.

KAI. It's going to rain again.

GIRL [*suddenly quite simply*]. Do I depress you?

KAI. Everyone leaves me cold.

GIRL. You don't know me. [*Wants to embrace him.*]

KAI [*moving away*]. What is there to know. [*Points at* NELLY's *portrait.*] Now she was kind.

GIRL [*looking at the portrait*]. Were you together for long?

KAI. She made good coffee.

GIRL. Is that all?

KAI. That's enough to remember.

GIRL [*thinks*]. Shall I go?

KAI. Where will you go? Sit down.

[OLEG PAVLOVICH *appears in the door. He is forty-three but looks younger; besides, he is well-shaved, fresh and good-natured.*]

OLEG P. You weren't expecting me? [*Cheerfully.*] It's me.

KAI. Good day, Oleg Pavlovich.

OLEG P. Your door is open as usual.

KAI. That's pure coincidence, Oleg Pavlovich.

OLEG P. Really? You're joking. Don't let me frighten you — I'm only in Moscow for a couple of days. I came for a few minutes — I must dig round in my study. I'm spending the night with my parents. The old people miss me.

KAI. What's to be done, Oleg Pavlovich?

OLEG P. How are you doing on your own? [*Glances at the* GIRL.] Everything O.K.? You don't look too good. Not studying too hard, are you?

KAI. I labour day and night. [*With a nod at the* GIRL.] We're just preparing for a session.

OLEG P. Well . . . Best of luck.

KAI [*suddenly shouts*]. Damn!

OLEG P [*jumps, then smiles*]. A ringing cry. You even frightened me. Everything in order at the institute?

KAI. As usual.

OLEG P. Your mother worries about how you manage without us. She often has dreams about you. [*Places a parcel on the table.*] Here's a lot of presents from her. Enjoy yourself.

KAI. I'm most grateful, Oleg Pavlovich.

OLEG P. She begged me to spend the evening with you but I can't make it . . . Though we could go and watch the football together . . .

KAI. I'm very grateful, Oleg Pavlovich. But I don't go there any more.

OLEG P. Why not?

KAI [*going right up to his stepfather and speaking very earnestly*]. I don't understand any more why they keep taking the ball from each other.

OLEG P [*embarrassed*]. You're joking. [*He goes into the room next door.*]

KAI. Well, how is he? Impressive?

GIRL. His jacket is very well tailored. Who is he?

KAI. A young man of forty-three. He is married to an old friend of mine. Love at first sight – imagine that? And all around is engulfed in flames. In the morning she prepares raw steaks for him and he swallows the bloody meat without chewing it.

GIRL. You're a schizo.

KAI. Probably. Though his jacket is a tailor's model. And tie, an incredible grey, colour of hell! And that barely noticeable spotted shirt! Apparently only fifteen years ago, he used to create merry hell at Yevtushenko's evenings. Oh, what has become of you, you proud generation of the polytechnics! How fiercely your boots are polished now!

OLEG P [*returns*]. It has all worked out, I found what I was looking for. Well, I'm glad everything is all right. Mind you don't forget your mother . . . [*Happily.*] Oh, yes! I'm hopelessly senile . . . Her letter! I nearly took it back to Iceland with me.

KAI [*quickly opening it*]. Typewritten . . . [*Raising his voice.*] It's typewritten!

OLEG P [*at a loss*]. Well?

KAI [*slight pause*]. Everything is fine, Oleg Pavlovich. Happy journey.

OLEP P. Keep well, dear boy. [*Kisses him.*] Work well. [*Waves cheerfully to the* **GIRL.**] Arrivaderci. [*He goes.*]

KAI [*stands motionless*]. Give me your handkerchief.

GIRL. What for? [*Gives him her handkerchief.*]

[**KAI** *wipes his lips with it and without looking tosses it out of the window.*]

Have you gone completely crackers?

KAI [*closely examines the pages of the letter*]. No mistakes! Very smooth . . . I used to love the letters she wrote by hand. I used to guess what she was thinking by the look of the words. I used to guess what she wanted, you know?

GIRL. I don't know anything . . .

KAI [*holds out the letter to her*]. Read it.

GIRL. I'm not going to. It's written to you.

KAI [*in a rage*]. Read it! You hear?

GIRL [*reads*]. "Yulik, my dear, I can't tell you how I miss you. We haven't seen each other for a year and a half and it turns out that we only get our leave next summer. But then we'll have two whole months. Oleg's been lucky. He was suddenly called to Moscow. He's so glad, he'll be seeing you. Imagine, he's longing to go and watch football with you . . . I hope you have a wonderful evening, only stop Oleg from smoking — it's bad for him . . ."

[KAI *goes to the tape-recorder and turns it right up. The Rolling Stones blast away. KAI listens without moving, tapping out the rhythm barely noticeably with his foot. The GIRL keeps waiting for something, then goes to the tape-recorder and turns it off. There is silence. But KAI keeps tapping out the rhythm with his foot.*]

GIRL. That's enough. I'm going.

KAI. She was like a cat . . . That same cat . . . But perhaps she was a little like you? [*Seizes her arm.*]

GIRL. What is this — have you gone mad, scum?

KAI [*strikes her face*]. Don't go!

GIRL. You've got something coming to you . . . [*Goes quickly.*]

[KAI *switches the tape-recorder on again. In contrast to the blast of the music and out of rhythm, slowly like a blind man, he circles round the room.*]

BLACKOUT

Scene Six

The oil-prospecting settlement in the second half of July. ZEMTSOV's room. Today disorder reigns more than usual.
    It is morning but the heat has started. MASHA is packing things in a sack. LOVEIKO is watching her.

LOVEIKO. Shall I help?

MASHA. Stop interefering. [*Slight pause.*] Are you packed?

LOVEIKO. I'm ready to go. [*Looks out of the window.*] Pity . . . We shan't say goodbye to Mishka.

MASHA. A doctor here has no time of his own. I've spent three years waiting.

LOVEIKO. He's also waited for you three months on end.

MASHA. Three months is nothing. To wait every evening — that's hard.

LOVEIKO. All right, cheer up. Our life is beginning. Under canvas! Your little cage is wide open . . .

MASHA. All the same I am a mother. I don't know what kind of mother.

LOVEIKO. I don't see anything special to worry about. The child is pampered at the crèche. Nelly is a help. You're a geologist first and last.

MASHA. It all looks easy from outside.

LOVEIKO. Then why don't you stay?

MASHA. You're wasting your breath, Loveiko. My main interest is out there! Our area has been described as doubtful. Right! If there is no oil there, it is up to me to prove that! I'll come back and say — I was wrong. I'll sign the statement.

LOVEIKO [*looking at her in admiration*]. Say what you like, it's fun to be with you.

MASHA. You're glad you're coming?

LOVEIKO. I'll say. I'll gaze fondly at you from early morning. To the small hours of the night.

MASHA [*grim*]. Will you stop looking at me like that. It won't get you any-where. Understand?

LOVEIKO. With my ailments, Zemtsova, I'm not counting on anything. If you embraced me, I'd drop dead from coughing.

MASHA. I shouldn't count on that if I were you. When a geologist is on the job, his ailments avoid him like the plague. I'm afraid, you're going to be trans-formed out there.

LOVEIKO. I like the smile of your promise, Masha.

MASHA. The only trouble is my smile holds few promises. [*Pause.*] Right, the subject is closed.

LOVEIKO. Untimely. [*Wry smile.*] I'm absurd.

[NELLY *enters carrying* LESSYA, *muffled up.*]

NELLY [*glancing round*]. So Mishka isn't back yet?

MASHA. Why have you dragged Lessya here.

NELLY. To say goodbye.

MASHA. I said goodbye to her yesterday at the crèche.

NELLY. That was yesterday. You're leaving today. For several months, perhaps. Say goodbye to her once more.

MASHA. I suppose you walked out of the hospital when you were on duty.

NELLY. I've got a stand-in. And Lessya's been fed. [*Puts her in her old cradle.*] You've grown, my lovely. She's almost too big for the cradle.

LOVEIKO. The helicopter will be here in half an hour. I'll fetch you. [*He goes.*]

NELLY [*looking in his direction*]. He's taking a suitcase packed with medicine. He spent a whole hour at the chemist yesterday.

MASHA [*staring at* NELLY]. What interests me . . .

NELLY. Well?

MASHA. Do you like me, Nelly?

NELLY [*slight pause*]. You put the question very bluntly.

MASHA. You don't like me. What a pity, little girl. All the same, keep an eye on Mishka, don't leave him on his own . . . He's bright and cheerful of course, but he can't stand living alone.

NELLY. I'll work it all out for myself. I'm no fool, honestly. Perhaps you noticed that?

[MISHKA *comes into the room. He is dressed as before and has a rucksack.*]

MISHKA. Greetings to the labouring masses! Glad to see you! Masha, look at all the ducks I shot. We'll cook them for your journey . . . [*Glances around.*] Why is Lessya here?

NELLY. She came to say goodbye to her mother.

MISHKA. Why today? You're going tomorrow . . .

MASHA. It's been altered. We're going today. In half an hour.

MISHKA [*pause*]. I see. [*Takes a duck and examines it closely.*] Pity, there was no point in killing them. [*Suddenly angry he throws the rucksack down on the floor.*] How ugly!

MASHA. Don't break your instruments.

MISHKA. What a muddle . . .

NELLY [*embarrassed*]. I'm going to the shop . . . [*She runs out.*]

MISHKA. We shan't say goodbye. Our night together has gone up in flames.

MASHA. All right. Let's forget it.

MISHKA. I've forgotten almost everything. When I met you and went mad about you. You were so special then. Now all I remember is how we say goodbye to each other.

MASHA [*strokes his hair*]. This isn't the time for self-pity. You're a man of iron.

MISHKA. There is that. [*Drops down on the bed*.] Only I'm very tired after five days. I had a difficult operation — I only just managed to bring the crook back to life.

MASHA. Why crook?

MISHKA. He always wins at cards. The manager said to me as I left: "Well, doctor, thank you, but we never expected you'd let him live. Now he will ruin the lot of us."

MASHA. Darling fool . . .

MISHKA. Why have you stopped loving me?

MASHA. I'm not used to these games.

MISHKA. Don't run yourself down, I remember a few things.

MASHA. Possibly. But I don't like empty talk.

MISHKA. Will you come over for a couple of days?

MASHA. I doubt it. It would take me three days to get here from across the marsh.

MISHKA. That means Loveiko is my only hope. As soon as he begins to die, I'll be right over.

MASHA. Not likely. There in the open, he'll stretch his wings.

MISHKA [*pause*]. You know, you have a careless attitude to life?

MASHA. Mishka, we'll be careful in our coffins.

MISHKA. You'll make one joke too many. And you don't understand, I'm not talking of death. You're careless about people. You play around. And you don't look at people, you don't notice them. But life wants to be noticed, accounted for, in a manner of speaking.

MASHA. A grave dissertation, exactly like an old professor. Isn't it a bit early at thirty, my little boy?

MISHKA. You have a grown-up son in the army. Have you written to him this month?

MASHA. He'll be back in a year. We'll have long talks. [*Slight pause*.] Don't you think this conversation is boring?

MISHKA. It is . . . You're going away — just the time to enjoy ourselves. [*Goes to the tape-recorder*.] Shall we have a last dance?

MASHA. I'm not going to.

MISHKA [*picks up his guitar*]. Will you listen to this love-song? In farewell.
[*Sings.*]

> When we're in love, the forests walk
> into our sleepers on the train.
> The poplars, stations, bridges, fields
> all come and go; and silence flows
> uniting us when we're in love.
> We are together still and yet
> apart. We're also silent now.
> You ask me things. I don't reply.
> The poplars, stations, bridges, fields
> and all the world comes roaring out
> and meeting you. And all the world
> in silence now recedes from me.

[*Without a pause.*] I got so hungry when I was near home. It's passed somehow. Right, I'll stuff myself after you go. Nell will come up with something.

MASHA. There's no point in fetching Lessya home from the crèche. Not so
much trouble for you either. Dance in the evening. The tape-recorder is working. Have all the fun you can together.

MISHKA. Thanks for your parting advice. You have outlined our course of
action. But I shall kiss you all the same. [*Embraces her and kisses her for a
long time.*] Once upon a time there lived Mishka and Mashka . . .

NELLY [*enters carrying some bread*]. That's it, Comrade Zemtsova, the helicopter's waiting.

MISHKA [*pats* MASHA *on the shoulder*]. All right, have a good time.

MASHA. Same to you.

MISHKA. We'll try. As far as possible.

LOVEIKO [*enters with his things*]. Hail and farewell, doc! You know what —
Masha and I aren't the only ones to go. You're also for the road.

NELLY. Now what?

LOVEIKO. They've just phoned from the office. They're sending a car for you.
In Baikul a cook's been trapped under a tree. They said you must go at once.

NELLY [*fiercely*]. To hell with the lot of you! He hasn't had anything to eat
or drink!

LOVEIKO. Shut up, don't be rude.

NELLY. There's a limit to everything. I shan't let him go.

MASHA. You're wasting your breath making a noise, little girl. Take a look at his face – he's very pleased. During our whole life together, I had perhaps eight dinners with him. You must get used to it, my dear.

NELLY. I've had enough of your jokes – you know.

MASHA [*turning to* MISHKA]. Pleased? Your eyes shining?

MISHKA. Remember me like that. Farewell, my joy. And you're looking pleased – you've escaped!

MASHA. I admit it.

MISHKA. Well, off you fly to meet your fate, old lady!

LOVEIKO. Stop making speeches!

MISHKA. That sick man is trying to hurry you up . . . Quite right. Take large stocks of medicine, Loveiko. Don't forget to take sweets. Zemtsova adores "kiss-kiss". There's a serious person for you – a riddle of a woman. Only don't drop her on the way. She's all I have.

MASHA. Enjoy yourself, speechmaker. [*To* LOVEIKO.] We're off.

[LOVEIKO *and* MASHA *leave. A long pause.*]

MISHKA. You swore and you were coarse. I can't stand that in women. You must bear that in mind.

NELLY [*obediently*]. I shan't do it again.

MISHKA [*looks at the bread*]. Let me break off the crust. [*Bites it off.*] It's hot . . . lovely. [*Takes his rucksack.*] I expect it's raining in Moscow and people don't know what to do. All right, I'm off. I have a right to work, that's why. We'll keep our pecker up, slyboots! [*He goes.*]

NELLY [*goes to the sleeping child*]. Well, your parents have run off this way and that way – they've forgotten Lessya's birthday. You'll be six months tomorrow. Enjoy yourself, silly – here comes your youth.

CURTAIN

ACT TWO

Scene One

The middle of August. ZEMTSOV's *room; its been cleaned and tidied up.* MISHKA *and* NELLY *are finishing their tea. The rain is swishing down outside. There are crashes of thunder nearby.*

MISHKA. Don't get depressed, all right . . . have some more tea.

NELLY. I couldn't. This is my third mug. I must go home.

MISHKA. In this downpour?

NELLY. What's the time?

MISHKA [*looks at his watch*]. Ten minutes past nine.

NELLY. I've stayed too long . . . it's night.

[*Crash of thunder nearby.*]

MISHKA. The fury! . . . The whole world trembles.

NELLY. It's been pouring over an hour.

MISHKA. When do you go on duty?

NELLY. Early morning. At eight.

MISHKA. You'd better stay. Or you'll drown on the way.

NELLY. What will the neighbours say?

MISHKA. Shucks the neighbours!

NELLY. Masha will hear.

MISHKA. She couldn't care less. That's what she feels about me.

NELLY. In that case I'll enjoy it. Haven't you got anything stronger to drink?

MISHKA [*slight pause*]. You're a bad lot.

NELLY. No worse than anyone else.

MISHKA. It's August, Nell . . . your entrance exams are nearly over.

NELLY. I've postponed it for another year. I told you.

MISHKA. You haven't explained why.

120

NELLY. I'm getting my strength up. And I'm watching you with interest. Now let's say you're eating porridge. I watch you in amazement — how beautifully he eats his porridge! Or I watch you operating — it's a picture. I can't take my eyes off you. Educational is the word.

MISHKA. Let's dance . . . [*Goes to the tape-recorder.*]

NELLY. Why, no! It's late. We couldn't dance together. You have a different style — after all there's twelve years difference. If you like I'll dance alone for you quietly? I've got this number for connoisseurs — it's called "The goose a-walking went". I used to do it in the fourth form at school. There's no accompaniment. I shall hum it. [*She dances her rather surprising dance.*] Well, along those lines. It gets more interesting later, but I've forgotten it. A lot of people gave me admiring glances afterwards. [*Thinks.*] My father wasn't pleased — he tore my dance-frock and gave me a hiding. Mother locked me up for a week without shoes. They were earnest people. They gave me a hard up-bringing. They loved me, that's why — that's what they said. They crossed out my youth. I wanted to be happy . . . You know, Mishka, from childhood I wanted to be madly happy — always good weather, music playing everywhere, festivals and parades, kind people all round, happy and glad of each other. But they crossed it all out. They watched me non-stop. [*Wry smile.*] But not enough. When I was in my last form at school, they went away for a week and left me alone. Then I plunged into the abyss, as it were. I allowed myself everything . . . without a backward glance, to spite them.

MISHKA [*quietly*]. What happened next?

NELLY. Nothing good, on the whole. I had to pay for it in the summer. They took me away soon after the school finals. [*Thoughtful.*] I think I should have had a daughter. I didn't — my parents crossed that out. Then I ran away from home. [*Flares up.*] I couldn't stand being shut up . . .

MISHKA. And your boyfriend?

NELLY. He's around. I packed my things and rushed over to him. It was October. It was cold. "Let's run away together", I said. But he replied, quite cheerfully on the whole: "Get away from me" . . . When I remember his words, I want to die, Mishka . . . [*Repeats them.*] "Get away from me" . . . I've met that quite often since — one does so want to believe it's for real, with affection and friendship. But I go on living and living and living and I don't find that.

MISHKA. It's all there! You must believe me . . . It's such torture at times, Nell, such ecstasy . . . Believe me, you will have it all, all of a sudden, the lot. You'll close your eyes tight and gasp with love, I give you my word.

NELLY. It isn't likely, Mishka.

MISHKA. I tell you — you will! It'll come! You'll see! It comes to all of us but we must recognize it, grab it. That's mine! And then we're happy for ever. Whatever happens later, till our dying day we'll remember with a smile — it happened to me!

[*Somewhere quite close there is a flash of lightning and a clap of thunder. Frightened, NELLY flings herself at MISHKA, presses herself to him and hugs him.*]

What's the matter, silly . . .

NELLY [*breathless, in a whisper*]. Marry me, Mishka, marry me, my dear. Save me, please.

MISHKA [*quietly*]. I mustn't.

NELLY [*weakly*]. Why not?

MISHKA [*apologizing, as it were*]. I love Masha.

NELLY [*moves away from him to the table, thinks*]. Would you like some more tea?

MISHKA. I've had enough. [*Touches the teapot.*] And it's cold.

NELLY. Pity I left the shortbread at home — I never brought it . . . It was a present to me for work done.

MISHKA. Nell!

NELLY [*turns towards him*]. Well?

MISHKA. Why do you want me?

NELLY [*slight pause*]. You're the best of the lot — so reliable. If only I could get a bit of rest . . . I'm so tired of the emptiness; I can't trust anyone any more.

MISHKA. You don't love a man because he's the best of the lot.

NELLY. Why then?

MISHKA. That's a great mystery. Insane love cannot be explained. It's a law unto itself.

NELLY. Is that true?

MISHKA. Certainly! Now, give me your hand — I'll tell you your fortune. [*Takes her hand.*] Well, I can see it at once — you don't love me, Nell. It's obvious, you love someone else. You wanted me so as to thrust him out of your heart, to free yourself of his power.

NELLY [*weakly*]. Where did you get that?

MISHKA. It's all in the palm of your hand! He humiliated you and you couldn't bear it. You forgave everyone but him. But you can't forget him.

NELLY. That's a lie! I don't love him. I simply hate him. I despise him, that's why. He's a bastard, that's what. He won me over deceitfully, he pretended I was indebted to them.

MISHKA. And his name is Nikita.

NELLY. That's the one. [*Pause.*] He was dangerous — he had an affectionate laugh. Sometimes he was so kind, such fun, and he used such marvellous words. I never heard anything like it. But he said them casually. Without thinking. Because I didn't matter to him — it didn't matter if I was there or not. [*Pause.*] I couldn't stand his neglect. I ran away as far as I could. [*Suddenly flares up.*] Only don't think I suffered him in silence. Oh, no! He got it from me too.

MISHKA [*smiles*]. In what way did he get it?

NELLY. I made him angry. In revenge. I got him rattled. I told him lies, that I was pregnant. [*Puzzled.*] I wanted to frighten him, I suppose? No, that's not right! You read a love story and it's all so tidy. It's not the same in life — just muddle. Really a disaster.

MISHKA [*thoughtful*]. There is that. But don't make up your mind too soon. As long as you're alive, everything is possible.

NELLY. Are you trying to comfort me?

MISHKA. Aha . . . Myself at the same time.

[MISHKA *picks up his guitar and sings very quietly. Barely audible,* NELLY *repeats after him.*]

"The sky's drawn down and stands in silence low above the river.
I do not know why we have parted — why we meet again.
I do not know, I do not know . . . Nor does the autumn wind
Know why it lifts the fallen leaves so high, high off the ground
Or why at night it places them in drifts on fields and slopes
And tosses them again at the bare branches of the birch.
The sky's drawn down and stands in silence low above the river.
I do not know why we have parted — why we meet again."

NELLY [*listening*]. The rain's dying down . . . [*Looks around.*] It's nice here . . . at home.

MISHKA [*goes on playing*]. Great! But the trouble is, you know, Masha has left us . . . For sure. [*Slight pause.*] She's taken up with Loveiko out there. I don't know why.

NELLY [*quietly*]. How did you find out?

MISHKA. There are kind people everywhere.

NELLY. Don't believe them.

MISHKA. But I do. [*Pause.*] All right. She knows best. But no one can take away what we've had. Oh, fiddle – nobody.

NELLY [*whispers quietly*]. How good, how splendid that in this world you are with me . . . Mishka, dear, I'm so grateful for that . . . No, I don't know how to put it.

[MISHKA *goes on playing the guitar and finally gets the tune of "the goose a-walking went".* NELLY *looks at him and sobs – either crying, or laughing.*]

BLACKOUT

Scene Two

End of September in Moscow. It is evening. In KAI's *room the table is laid. There are the remains of supper.* KAI *is sitting in the armchair,* TERENTY *is still eating something,* NIKITA *is restlessly pacing about. Their conversation has a savage quality.*

TERENTY. Hey, Nikita, relax.

NIKITA. Good we didn't go to a restaurant! . . . Quite super to celebrate one's twentieth birthday in a restaurant . . . It's vulgar! [*To* KAI.] You organized everything beautifully, old man . . . Herring, potato and vodka . . . Austere. Worthy of men. As for the total absence of girls! It's a new note. Yet another proof that the age of infancy is behind us. We're people. We're not the same now. We're other people.

KAI. We may be other people, but what kind of people? Nobody knows. All is shrouded in darkness.

NIKITA. Quite right. We'll have a last drink. That will be that. [*Looks at* TERENTY.] He's been swallowing orange juice all evening. His friend is twenty. But did he take one little sip in my honour . . .

TERENTY. I won't – I'd rather die.

NIKITA. There's something about him, isn't there, Kai? In his own way he's splendid. [*Sincere.*] He's better than me!

KAI. Stop gabbling. It's stuffy . . . Who closed the window?

NIKITA. Kai-Yuly, what's the matter?

KAI. A strange September . . .

NIKITA. I've drunk a lot. I've crossed a frontier. Everything must change. There's something very funny.

KAI. What's funny?

NIKITA. I'm over-exposed?

TERENTY. What, what?

NIKITA. Over-exposed to the wide world. It's the same wherever I go. No one's glad of me. They laugh but they're not glad – do you understand?

TERENTY. All right, don't bellow! We're celebrating a birthday. [*Looks at the table.*] There's a lot of washing-up . . .

KAI. You sorry Nelly isn't here?

TERENTY. Not the point. I'll manage. [*Points to* NIKITA.] He's the one to be sorry!

NIKITA [*in a sudden fury*]. Why? That's a lie . . . Why should I be sorry?

KAI. Hey! Come to think of it . . . [*He brings out a cardboard box, opens the lid and brings out* NELLY's *old, ragged doll.*] One of my last finds.

TERENTY. Now what's that?

KAI. A forsaken child.

NIKITA. Nell's . . .

KAI. A forgotten infant. I found it yesterday under her sofa.

TERENTY [*examines the doll*]. It's worn . . . She had it as a child, I expect. [*Gives it to* NIKITA.] Go on, nurse it, why not . . .

NIKITA [*stumbles away from him*]. Go to hell!

TERENTY. Your conscience not easy?

NIKITA. No, you tell me, am I to blame? Am I to blame – yes?

TERENTY. Stop showing off . . . [*Grunts.*] You are over-exposed.

NIKITA. Is that so? [*He throws himself on* TERENTY.]

[*The door opens.* KONSTANTINOV *enters.*]

KONSTANTINOV. Enjoying yourselves?

TERENTY. But I told you not to come on the seventeenth.

KONSTANTINOV. I couldn't help it. I'm sorry. [*Goes to* NIKITA.] I apologize for breaking it up. Here, please take the dog, a memento, I made it out of wood. People think it's a great likeness to the living model.

NIKITA. It's a good dog. Thanks.

KONSTANTINOV [*to* TERENTY]. Do you like it?

TERENTY. Well, the dog is like a dog.

> [*There's a quiet knock on the door.* NELLY'*s* MOTHER *stands in the doorway. Her face is tired and grey. She is plainly dressed. She carries an old handbag and a shopping bag.*]

MOTHER. Excuse me . . . I did knock. There was no answer. I want Comrade Leonidov.

KAI [*gets up*]. Me.

MOTHER. So I found you . . . Thank you. [*Slight pause.*] My husband is ill . . . That's not the point, of course. I'm trying to find my daughter . . . a little girl, Yelena Petrovna. Actually she's called Nelly. Do you know her?

TERENTY. That's right. We do.

MOTHER. I've been to Kineshma and now it's my third day in Moscow. I've been going from one address to the next. [*Smiles, quietly.*] She's been moving so often – I can't think. Today they gave me your address, thank God . . . [*Long pause.*] Where is she?

KAI. She's gone away.

MOTHER. From you as well? [*Pause.*] You'll give me her new address, won't you?

KAI. No.

MOTHER [*upset*]. But why not?

TERENTY. She hasn't left her address. He tried to find her.

MOTHER [*to* NIKITA]. Can you tell me anything?

> [NIKITA *makes a strange gesture and says nothing.*]

Has she been gone a long time?

NIKITA. Six months.

MOTHER. My God! Perhaps she isn't around any more? Not anywhere? [*Looks at* NIKITA.] Young man, why don't you say something?

NIKITA [*with a sudden shout*]. I don't know!

MOTHER [*notices the doll lying on the table*]. That's hers . . . She had it as a child. Why hasn't she taken it with her? She must have been in a hurry. [*Looks round the room.*] Where did she sleep?

KAI. Next door. On the sofa.

MOTHER [*timidly*]. But why was she living here? It's confusing . . . What for?

KAI [*pause*]. No reason.

MOTHER. I see. Can I see where she slept?

TERENTY. This way. [*Opens the door.*]

> [*Without any hurry,* **MOTHER** *goes next door.*]

KAI. It's like a dream. [*To* **NIKITA**.] What do you say? Are we dreaming about ourselves? It's an idea!

NIKITA [*quietly to* **TERENTY**]. Well? What's she doing?

TERENTY [*stands in the doorway*]. She is sitting on the sofa. She's thinking.

> [**NIKITA***'s younger sister,* **LYUBASYA**, *runs into the room. A red-head, she is inconsistent, quick to react and very agitated. She is carelessly dressed, in the fashion.*]

LYUBASYA. There, I knew it – you're here! You've let yourself go completely. Mother's in the country, madly unhappy, and you're squatting here, drunk of course! A fine brother . . . The table's laid for him – well he is twenty – we got lampreys and eel, Aunt Sonya has arrived from Sochi. She hasn't seen you for three years, she wants to take a look at you – but you're here for some reason.

NIKITA. Scram, Lyubasya.

LYUBASYA. Why, have you gone mad? We've got five tins of crab. You're twenty after all. Mother's lost in wonder – she only comes up from the country once a month to see us – and there's Aunt Sonya specially arrived from Sochi.

NIKITA [*slowly*]. Apart from Aunt Sonya, the crabs and the eel, is there anyone at home?

LYUBASYA. No, not yet, but they may arrive. They're sure to. Father phoned from work, he'll be late but it seems there's every chance he'll make it. Gary and Julia have Mexicans staying with them in the country but they may be coming. Rufina is coming by plane from Leningrad, it's possible she'll get here in time . . .

NIKITA. It's possible! It seems may be! Kai, do you hear . . . What if you and I maybe seem to be? And really we're not here, like father who's at work. Aunt Sonya and the lampreys are real!

LYUBASYA. You're a nutcase! The woman's brought you an enormous melon!

NIKITA. Shut up!

[NELLY's MOTHER *comes in from the next-door room.*]

MOTHER. It's all right, it's a good sofa . . . What sort of coat was she wearing when she left? Did it have a fur collar?

TERENTY. Something like that.

MOTHER [*to* NIKITA]. No, definitely. Was it fur?

NIKITA. Definitely. It was fur.

LYUBASYA [*furious*]. Why, are you making fun of me? They're waiting for you at home, they've laid a super table for you. But you are saying I don't know what to I don't know whom!

MOTHER. No why, why scold him, little girl? He's a good lad, it shows at once. He was the only one who looked for her. [*Long pause.*] It means we've lost her trail . . . I must go home. [*Opens her bag.*] I brought a few things for her . . . Apples from the garden. Why carry them back. Help yourselves. [*She tips the contents on the table.*]

KAI. Thanks.

MOTHER [*to* LYUBASYA]. Don't be upset, little girl. Taste it. [*She holds out an apple to her.*]

LYUBASYA. It's funny, why are you shoving this fruit at me? As though we haven't got any. [*To* NIKITA.] Come home immediately. After all, in one hour I must catch the plane to Tbilisi. [*She runs out.*]

MOTHER. She was offended. I don't know why. She's restless. [*Pause.*] This is my address, in case you hear anything. [*Gives* NIKITA *a bit of paper.*] Thank you. [*Goes to the front door and opens it. In the doorway.*] I think my husband's dying. He was very determined I should find Lena. "I want to forgive her for everything and I'll ask her to forgive me," he said "if only I could see her for the last time." He cursed her when she left home, said not to look for her. He was a harsh man. Religious. Perhaps he wanted it for the best. But it has turned out – I'm afraid to think. What has life in store for her? . . . I'm sorry . . . [*She goes.*]

KONSTANTINOV [*after a long pause*]. She was bright and cheerful, bright and cheerful, but look what she's done.

TERENTY [*fiercely*]. We don't yet know who's more to blame.

NIKITA [*unexpectedly*]. You think I'm to blame too?

TERENTY. Why thrust yourself forward? No one asked you. Go home. Aunt Sonya's waiting for you.

NIKITA. Don't pretend! I can see that you blame me!

TERENTY. What if I do! Who was she running away from in Moscow — thought of that? She was bright like a swallow. She took care of us all. She was fun. Kai never touched her. But you? Always trembling, afraid she'd give you a child. Right now she may be having a rough time with him, God knows where. When did you decide to make enquiries about her? He had a dream about her, don't you know. You're kind . . . Very kind, if it's no trouble.

KAI. We're all just the same. Leave him alone. We're all shit.

KONSTANTINOV. Why go on like this, boys . . . It's a birthday.

TERENTY [*losing his temper*]. You have no say in this . . . Observer! You've made yourself at home here as if in the theatre . . .

NIKITA. No one is glad. No one! I do amazingly well in my studies and swimming down my lane and in private. I am universally admired! [*Quietly.*] But no one's glad of me.

TERENTY. Get along with you!

NIKITA [*shouts*]. I'm helpless! I have lived expecting a miracle. I hoped someone would come, appear, arise . . . and we'd share things. No one appeared. Pointless! And my beloved family! Ha-ha! They were infatuated with me, when they could spare the time. From infancy I was destined to play a leading part! They never had the shadow of a doubt that I would, they were so preoccupied with themselves.

KAI [*desperate*]. You're lying, you've forgotten it all! We were such happy children. Don't you remember Christmas here? Always presents under the Christmas tree and father performing his magic tricks. Mother sang. They loved each other. And it was all destroyed in one day! After she left, father looked at me and said: "You're like your mother, look in the mirror — an exact replica of her!" And he flung me away into a corner. It was all over then — I stopped loving everyone. I never felt sorry for anyone. I stopped loving everyone.

TERENTY. I remember — I remember what you were like before. You laughed easily. You were kind, even stupid . . . And what fun we had — remember?

NIKITA [*afire and ecstatic*]. We came and stayed with you in the country, Kai. You said: "Nothing in the world is better than strawberries", and other such nonsense.

KAI [*hurrying*]. And that Sunday when Terenty began to drown. We went bathing in the rain and suddenly there was nobody — remember? We got to the shore but Terenty shouted in the water: "I'm drowning. Help!" We roared with laughter, we thought he was pretending but it was real. You dashed into the water first and when you got him out, we thought he was dead — no signs of life at all . . . I flung myself on him and started pumping him. When he opened his eyes and we saw he was still alive, you remember how you hugged me, Nikita? We were roaring with laughter, quite ecstatic . . . All that happened, it did!

TERENTY. Me too . . . I expect I was more glad than anyone else. [*Heatedly.*] It was me, me, that you saved. I remained alive in the world — that's good . . . I remember, I remember . . .

KAI. What a day that was . . . Remember?

NIKITA [*feverishly*]. I remember — he was lying on the grass, his eyes closed. We thought that's the end, the lot . . . But then, Kai, it was you . . .

TERENTY [*ecstatic*]. And then it was him . . . Yes?

KAI. And then I — I flung myself on you!

[KAI *knocks* TERENTY *off his feet, hugs him,* NIKITA *leaps on top of them and like children they thrash about on the floor.* KONSTANTINOV *watches them in silence.*]

NIKITA. That's when I knew — there was three of us!

KAI. And I knew that. There's three of us — we are afraid of nothing.

TERENTY. You even gave me your water-pistol. You were kind, Kai.

KAI. Kind?

[*And all of a sudden they fall silent.*]

TERENTY. What now? What's happened? Why have we grown like this?

KAI. Like what?

NIKITA. You know. [*Goes to the table.*] We must have a drink!

KONSTANTINOV [*takes the bottle from him*]. Perhaps you've had enough, boys?

NIKITA [*in icy tones*]. You're welcome to sit here — no one's throwing you out. So just go on sitting. [*Sharply all of a sudden.*] Terenty, why does he come here?

KAI. Nikita, don't touch him.

NIKITA. No, but why? You told him not to.

TERENTY [*pause*]. I haven't the authority. I haven't the right.

KONSTANTINOV. You are not cruel. Thanks. [*Goes to the door, stops.*] Won't you listen to me this time? The house is empty. [*Hopeful.*] Let's go, shall we?

TERENTY. This is pointless. Go alone. [*Out of control.*] Out you go!

KAI. Oh, Terry . . . [*With a wry smile.*] Where's the kindness?

KONSTANTINOV. No don't you go blaming him. I'm not worth it. He was never talkative. He never talked about his father. Maybe he should.

TERENTY. It's too late.

KONSTANTINOV. I'll tell you. I drank. From the age of five, I threw him out of the house at night. He waited afraid in the barn for the dawn and only then crept back into bed. It was the same in winter. My wife didn't survive. She died. Either of grief or my fists. That's how they are. Have a look. I'm not a locksmith for nothing. That's when he left home as well. I woke up one morning, looked around – I was alone. [*He glances at* TERENTY *who turns away.*] All the best. [*He goes.*]

BLACKOUT

Scene Three

In the last ten days of October. ZEMTSOV's *room as neat as the last time; everything is in its place with a kind of defiance.* MASHA *is sitting at the table; she hasn't removed her outdoor clothes, not even her hat with ear-flaps. Only her jacket is unbuttoned. She sits motionless staring in front of her.*

LOVEIKO *is sitting expectantly on the other stool, also in his travelling clothes. It is a late autumnal morning, dark and hopeless.*

LOVEIKO [*breaking the silence*]. Nell isn't coming.

MASHA. They've gone to fetch her.

LOVEIKO [*insistent*]. I'd like to get the office news if we have the time. We must put in a claim for a second stop-cock.

MASHA. Think when you talk. It's all the same to me now.

LOVEIKO. You should control yourself. Grief is grief but the work goes on. Just now people are waiting for us to produce results.

MASHA. Should I dance for you, perhaps?

LOVEIKO. You're humiliating me, Zemtsova.

MASHA. You may be temporarily cured, but don't expect good luck all round. Don't count on that. Everything's changed.

LOVEIKO. I shan't say what I feel, I'm a quiet man. Especially as you're the mistress, in every sense. But however great your grief, I shan't let you forget the job.

[NELLY *enters, looks at* MASHA, *controls her tears and goes to her.*]

MASHA. You've lost weight. [*Embraces her.*]

NELLY [*quietly*]. Who'd have expected it. [*Pause.*] Are you here for good?

MASHA. I'm going back tomorrow.

LOVEIKO. We're about to strike oil.

NELLY. Congratulations. I'll take half a litre.

MASHA. Don't you dare!

NELLY. What's he doing here?

MASHA. Go away, Loveiko.

LOVEIKO [*gets up from his stool and goes to* NELLY]. Why are you glaring at me? Wicked girl! Are you afraid I'm glad?

NELLY [*furious*]. Get out of the house!

LOVEIKO [*to* MASHA *on his way out*]. I'll wait for you out in the open. [*He goes.*]

MASHA [*pause*]. Tell me what happened.

NELLY. The 18th October, Wednesday. It happened . . . The geophysicist at Shadrinsky had gangrene. We had an S.O.S. The station is a hundred kilometres away surrounded by marsh. They flew out, not realizing the weather was breaking up. A time and place had been fixed for his arrival. They got there but the force of the wind had increased. The helicopter pilot shouted: "We're going back!" But Mishka said: "Drop the ladder!" The helicopter hovered, their petrol was limited, enough for a fifty seconds' descent. There were people waiting below . . . He began to go down the ladder when they were thrown sideways by the wind. [*Slight pause.*] He fell into the marsh. That's all. There were people within a hundred metres — everyone saw it.

MASHA [*after a long pause*]. Have you got a cigarette?

NELLY. I don't smoke.

MASHA. I stopped. What's the point? Why stop?

NELLY. Mishka left a stub. [*Gives* MASHA *the box.*] I kept it.

MASHA. Give me. [*Examines the stub. Strikes a match.*] I'll finish it. [*Pause.*] He died as he lived. [*Wry smile.*] That was just the way he was.

NELLY [*watches as* MASHA *smokes*]. The smoke's drifting away.

MASHA. What?

NELLY. Nothing.

MASHA. They say you sleep here. Do you?

NELLY. Aha. And I fetch Lessya from the crèche for the night.

MASHA. But why?

NELLY. I don't know . . . It must stay warm with life here, without interruption.

MASHA [*quietly, desperately*]. Oh, you, my God . . . [*Pause.*]

NELLY. Tell me please, how did you find Mishka? How did you meet?

MASHA. In the marsh, during an expedition. We noticed each other. The night was cold. We slept under the same quilt and in our sleep we both kept pulling it over.

NELLY. That's fun.

MASHA [*thinks*]. I suppose so.

NELLY [*unexpectedly*]. He was my salvation. [*Smiles.*] I had stopped believing in people. When I got to know him — I believed again. Gladly.

MASHA [*puts out the cigarette end*]. I've finished it. That's all.

NELLY. Did you know he was the best?

MASHA. I guessed that. Occasionally, more's the pity.

NELLY. He knew everything . . . about Loveiko.

MASHA. I wasn't hiding anything.

NELLY [*thoughtfully*]. I'd kill you, if I could.

MASHA. You'd be right.

NELLY. He was desperate the last few months. At Pechuga there was a roaring jet and he walked into the flames. He stopped being afraid.

MASHA. So it's my fault. [*And all of a sudden her despair breaks out.*] I'm a slut! An animal.

NELLY [*shouts, almost viciously*]. Oh no . . . Don't flatter yourself! You assume it was because of you. But for a long time now you meant nothing to him. He fell in love with someone else — madly in love if you must know!

MASHA. Who was that? Well, tell me, child.

NELLY [*drunk with her own lie*]. Me! He cared nothing for anyone else. We really were infinitely happy together! So keep quiet. That's all.

MASHA [*slight pause*]. Eh, little one . . . [*Goes right up to her.*] Well, look at me. [*Takes hold of* NELLY's *head.*] Why are you telling me lies?

NELLY [*weakly*]. It's all true.

MASHA. I'd be happy to believe you.

NELLY [*utterly feebly*]. It's true, it's true.

MASHA. Are you sorry for me, is that it? [*Kisses her unexpectedly.*] In that case thanks for the lie. [*Wry smile.*] The trouble is I don't believe you.

NELLY. No, it isn't you I'm sorry for. You've got it wrong again. [*Suddenly smiles, trusting.*] I wanted a fairy tale. Surely it would be a great happiness if a man like Mishka fell in love with you? Then why not with me? Why should you be so happy? Why should other people know happiness, while I only know disaster and deceit. I'm kind. I take trouble. The man who married me would be very lucky. I'm convinced of that. I invented my love for Mishka to be rid of another love. I met a man who was not faithful to me. Oh, it is not easy for me to forget him, for him it's nothing, no trouble. I don't suppose he remembers there was someone called Nelly. He hasn't thought of her for ages. [*Pause.*] But your Mishka has left you happy for ever – super just remembering the kind of man who loved you.

MASHA. You finished well, like a knife in my heart. All right, carry out my death sentence, you kind little girl.

NELLY. I shall never understand you – not now and I didn't before.

MASHA. What is there to understand. I'm an old woman. In ten years I'll be fifty. He'd have been a boy. No . . . Why find excuses for myself. I don't know how to love – there, imagine, what a drama.

NELLY. You mean, your parents haven't taught you?

MASHA. I had no parents. The war carried them off. I come from an orphanage. I'm free. The life and soul of the party. Singing, dancing, thank God! My real pleasure is in my job, my work. I haven't the gift of warmth, Nelly. So I missed out on happiness.

NELLY. He'll always stay alive for you.

MASHA. Don't try and comfort me, child. You don't know how. Besides why comfort me. There's no enjoyment for me ever.

NELLY. With your character?

MASHA. The games are over. I've fooled around, it's enough. [*Pause.*] Heavens, my God, how casual we are about living . . . When Mishka said goodbye he said we're "so careless". The trouble we create without a backward glance.

[*She sees* MISHKA*'s tape-recorder, goes to it, turns it on. The familiar dance tune is heard.* MASHA *listens in silence without moving. Then she turns it off.*]

Did you dance with him?

NELLY. Sometimes.

MASHA. Take it as a memento.

NELLY. I mustn't. He recorded a song here . . . Perhaps to you?

MASHA [*slight pause*]. Switch it over.

NELLY. Why not? Listen . . .

[*She turns the switch.* MISHKA*'s guitar is heard; his voice sings:*]

We're two white clouds adrift in azure skies.
In blinding heat we meet at last.
We only parted for a time on earth,
We never parted for eternity.

Above the living who don't think of us,
Above the cold blue Dnieper river,
Above the graveyard where we lie apart,
Today we drifting go together.

We're two white clouds adrift — one rosy pink
In greeting of the day below;
It casts its shadow on the second cloud
That dare not drift and part again.

The smoke will come our way! And you will grieve
As you remember your young days.
I'll send a heavy downpour on your grave
But you won't spare a drop for mine.

In fiery skies you'll turn to vapour first.
I'll follow clanging in pursuit.
But will you wait for me in clover, wheat,
But will you wait in wormwood, clay?

We're two white clouds adrift in azure skies.
In blinding heat we meet at last.
May be we never parted down on earth,
Not ever, not even for a time.

[*The song comes to an end.* NELLY *turns the tape-recorder off and holds it out to* MASHA.]

NELLY. Take it.

MASHA. I haven't the right to it. Keep it.

NELLY. Thanks.

[LOVEIKO *enters. He stops by the door.*]

MASHA. You here? What bliss.

[LOVEIKO *goes to her.*]

Give me a cigarette, Loveiko. That's right. Now a light. [*Smokes.*] And now your part is over. I'm going back alone.

[LOVEIKO *looks at her in despair.*]

There's nothing to say. Off you go.

[LOVEIKO *goes in silence.*]

[*To* NELLY.] Did you like that?

NELLY. It's too late now.

MASHA [*wry smile*]. That's true.

NELLY. When will you be back?

MASHA. In a month, I think. We've struck oil.

NELLY. Well then . . . Good luck.

MASHA. I'm leaving Lessya with you. Do what you like. Sleep with her here, or leave her at the crèche.

NELLY. I'll be here. Looking after her makes me happy.

MASHA. Whatever your heart tells you.

BLACKOUT

Scene Four

Moscow. The beginning of December. KAI's *room, late evening.* TERENTY *and* NIKITA *come in from outside.* KAI *is standing by his armchair as though he has been waiting for them for a long time.*

The other side of the window snow is falling and the wind is blowing; there is also a sense of disturbance in KAI's *domain.*

KAI. Quiet!

TERENTY. Why quiet?

KAI. Don't slam the door.

TERENTY. Why phone people at night, telling them to come over? Can't you think of something better?

NIKITA. Have we come again to nurse your insomnia, dear boy?

TERENTY [*pause*]. What's happened here?

KAI. Nell's back.

TERENTY. Stop it!

NIKITA. What . . . When?

KAI. Two hours ago.

NIKITA. Well, go on.

TERENTY. Where has she come from?

KAI. She said from far.

NIKITA [*pointing to the door to the next room*]. Is she there?

KAI. Don't go in. You mustn't.

NIKITA. What am I to understand by that?

KAI. She hasn't come alone. She has a child with her.

TERENTY. What child?

KAI. Hers, I suppose. It caught a cold on the journey.

TERENTY. A boy?

KAI. A girl. Kind of funny. She coughs, looks around, won't go to sleep.

NIKITA. But who . . . who is this little girl?

KAI. Hers. I told you.

NIKITA [*furious*]. Why are you smiling?

KAI. Go to hell!

TERENTY. Now, wait . . . Kai, stop it. Tell us the details.

KAI. She turned up at ten-thirty. Outside a snowstorm. She was covered with snow. "Take me in — for old times' sake", she said. "My little girl fell ill on the journey . . ." Well, what else . . . She came in, drank some tea, asked how Terenty was.

NIKITA. That's not what I want to know!

KAI. I asked you not to shout. She's lulling the child to sleep.

NIKITA. Who was she living with? How did all this happen?

KAI. She said, she stayed with distant relatives in Solihard.

NIKITA. She's telling lies as usual. She makes things up.

TERENTY. But why? Why shouldn't she go to Solihard. I want to know why you got us out of bed?

KAI. What else could I do? [*Smiles incredulously.*] I lost my head. Word of honour. [*Gestures.*] I completely lost my head.

TERENTY. You're sort of . . . as you were as a child.

KAI. And what has it got to do with me? Let Nikita sort it out.

NIKITA. Why me? That's funny, you know . . .

KAI. You must know what to do, you fool . . .

NIKITA. You're smiling again?

TERENTY. Isn't he allowed to smile? The child is ill, well, take it home with you. You have a house full of people, there'll be someone to look after it . . .

NIKITA. Are you out of your mind? [*Looks at his watch.*] It's late. I'm going.

KAI. Now, isn't that super! Nikita, you're a sight for sore eyes.

> [NELLY *comes out with* LESSYA. *She looks at them all in silence and sits down.*]

TERENTY [*too late*]. Nelly!

NELLY. Greetings, mushroom . . .

KAI [*cautious*]. Well, how is she?

NELLY. She is asleep at last.

KAI. Put her down here. On the sofa.

NELLY. Let's try. [*Takes a long time settling* LESSYA, *surrounding her with cushions.*] She's not too demanding. It's only a cold.

KAI. We'll get a doctor in the morning.

NELLY. We'll wait. I'm trained now. [*To* TERENTY.] You're better-looking, Terry. Have you put on weight? How's the hobby?

TERENTY. I perform.

NELLY. You have a different haircut.

TERENTY. Semi-Sassoon.

NELLY. It suits you. [*Slight pause.*] Kai, don't worry. I'll go as soon as Lessya is better.

NIKITA. Where?

NELLY [*pretending she has just noticed him*]. Hey, look who's here by the door, his fur hat jammed over his face . . . Looks so intriguing. Not our Nikita? Isn't that nice to see you. Greetings, dear comrade.

NIKITA. What's funny? I don't get it . . .

NELLY. You've missed me, you're worn out with worry. Were you going? Well then, good night. [*Very sharply.*] All right, get out!

NIKITA [*timidly*]. Nellikins!

NELLY [*livid*]. What now?

[NIKITA *comes up close.*]

[*Her voice breaks.*] Don't touch me, Jingles.

NIKITA. You have a smudge on your face. Side of the nose. And on your cheek.

NELLY [*quietly*]. A smudge? Have I?

NIKITA. You have.

NELLY. A big smudge? [*Very quietly.*] Honest to God?

NIKITA. I'm telling you.

[*They stand there in silence.*]

NELLY [*taking a hold of herself*]. It's the journey . . . Don't worry! I'll go and make myself beautiful. [*She goes.*]

KAI [*wry smile*]. Yes . . . You're moulting all the same.

NIKITA. Oh, hell! I felt awfully sorry for her, standing there with soot on her face . . . [*Sharply.*] And you! Couldn't you tell her to go and have a wash?

KAI. I was concerned with other things. She came in. The child was crying. I completely lost my head.

TERENTY [*goes to* LESSYA *and looks at her*]. I was always sorry I didn't have a little sister.

[*Very cautiously* NIKITA *approaches the sleeping child.*]

KAI [*to* TERENTY]. Make room for our leading man. [*To* NIKITA.] Well, what do you feel, old man?

TERENTY. Is there something going on inside?

NIKITA [*slight pause*]. I'm working it out . . . She's a bit large for her age.

KAI. Your thoughts lack elegance, *mon ami*.

NIKITA. After all, why me?

KAI [*thoughtfully to* TERENTY]. Shall we beat him up?

NIKITA. You're enjoying yourself.

KAI. Oh, you poor thing.

TERENTY [*to* NIKITA]. No, you must understand . . . After all what's the difference? Well? Everyone loves children.

NIKITA. To listen to you . . .

NELLY [*comes in*]. She hasn't woken up?

TERENTY. She is asleep. [*Pause.*] How old is she?

NELLY. She'll be a year in due course.

NIKITA. Enjoying yourself?

NELLY. Why should I mind? [*Suspicious.*] You aren't doing sums, are you? You're wasting your time! She's a big girl, even though she was premature. Everyone thinks she's older. [*To* NIKITA.] Why do you keep fussing over her? You've come in from the freezing cold. She's ill.

NIKITA. I've warmed up.

NELLY. I don't care, move away.

TERENTY. What did you call her?

NELLY. Lessya.

NIKITA. What does that mean?

NELLY [*with daring*]. Who knows?

NIKITA [*suddenly furious*]. Stop playing the fool. Tell me — what did you call her?

NELLY. Why are you making the loudest noise? What right have you?

NIKITA [*controlling himself*]. Who else has the right? True, isn't it?

NELLY. Oh, my dear, what a laugh . . . What are you thinking, stupid? [*Fierce.*] Go on, move away! She is not your child.

NIKITA. That is not true! [*Quietly.*] Whose child is she?

NELLY. You've got it wrong. [*Calm.*] That was before you.

NIKITA [*looks at* LESSYA]. No. I don't believe you.

NELLY. I wish you would. Then you'd learn.

NIKITA [*quietly*]. Who's the father?

NELLY [*with challenge*]. I don't remember.

NIKITA [*shaken by her words*]. I apologize. [*He goes to the door.*]

NELLY [*suddenly rushes after him and stops him*]. But would you have wanted her, wanted her to be yours? Tell me, would you?

NIKITA. Get away from me! [*Rudely he pushes her aside. He goes.*]

[NELLY *drops down on a chair. She does not say anything. Tears run down her face.*]

KAI. Don't you dare! I've always forbidden it. Do you hear?

NELLY. Go away!

KAI. If you're going to be rude, I'll throw you out.

NELLY. Oh, never. [*She weeps more loudly.*]

TERENTY. Listen, Nell . . . Really, why not . . . I'm serious, let's get married.

NELLY [*through her tears*]. Oh, how stupid you are . . . You're most awfully stupid. I never thought you were so stupid . . . You couldn't be more stupid . . . [*She hugs him.*] You are so stupid.

KAI. He isn't at all stupid . . . It may seem funny, but he's quite bright.

BLACKOUT

Scene Five

The last days of December. KAI's *room again.* LESSYA *is asleep in a new pram by the window. On the shelves by* KAI's *easel there are several figurines of the child in plaster, clay and wood.* KAI *keeps glancing at* LESSYA, *sketching something on his pad.*

The day is drawing to a close . It's gradually getting dark outside. The lamps are being lit on the boulevard. The snow is coming down slowly. NELLY *appears from the corridor with a fairly small but bushy Christmas tree.*

NELLY. Look, Kai, surprise for you . . . You're always remembering your Christmas tree, the fun you had here. I got one. Our neighbour, Kolya, rustled it up. And he made a cross, take a look.

KAI [*goes to the tree and touches it*]. It's bushy. Our Christmas tree usually stood here.

NELLY. Then put it there. In the boxes on top of the cupboard I saw you had the toys for it. Get them down, Skiffy, don't be lazy.

KAI [*brings a box down, opens it*]. The dust here . . .

NELLY. Clean it. Here's a duster.

KAI [*going through the toys*]. It's amusing . . . All the familiar faces.

NELLY. Our neighbour is very sweet and provided us with candles. Kolya is so nice. Perhaps he means to marry me?

KAI. You do go on . . .

NELLY. Don't be impatient – I'll be gone soon. Now Lessya's recovered, I can leave. Father has died and mother has asked me to go back home. Will you miss me?

KAI. I don't believe you're going to leave me. [*Smiles.*]

NELLY [*examines the figurines*]. You've done so many Lessya's. And they're all different. They're marvellous, honestly. [*Thinks.*] Perhaps you are talented?

KAI. We'll find out in due course.

[*Absurdly made up,* TERENTY *appears from the other room.*]

NELLY. Oh, Terry! [*Roars with laughter.*] You frightened me.

KAI. Half-wit!

TERENTY. The performance is on Saturday. I'm getting ready, trying to find the right make-up.

KAI. What are you doing in the bedroom?

TERENTY. I'm trying out moves in front of the mirror . . . I've been getting up from the chair in different ways, to give it more expression. [*Turns.*] A Christmas tree!

NELLY. We'll light the candles, when it's quite dark. I've cooked a special treat – all the things we like. And then we'll dance till we drop! [*Goes into the next-door room.*]

TERENTY [*sits down at the little table with his mirror and make-up*]. Now I shall be an old muzhik. That will make you gasp.

[*Slowly* KAI *decorates the Christmas tree.* NIKITA *appears and walks about the room.*]

NIKITA. Painting your mug again?

TERENTY. The ghost of Hamlet has arrived!

NIKITA. Decorating a Christmas tree? Idyllic! [*Goes to* LESSYA *and looks at her.*]

KAI. You can't keep away. And here you are.

NIKITA. Only you are allowed to indulge yourselves. [*Nods at* TERENTY.] And he's a fine one — proposed marriage to her, took her to the registry office, very nearly. [*Pause.*] Has Lessya quite recovered?

KAI. Have you decided to show concern?

TERENTY. She told you — it is not your child.

NIKITA [*flaring up*]. She's always telling lies. You can't believe what she says! [*Pointing to the sleeping* LESSYA.] As I look at her, right here, in my heart if you like, I get flashes of things ... Let's say, five years later she's at the Olympic swimming pool and I'm about to beat the world record.

TERENTY. So what?

NIKITA. And she'll be glad of me ... Got it?

KAI. Yes ... You're in your second childhood, poor thing.

[NELLY *comes in again.*]

NELLY. Greetings, dear friend! Have you come to gaze fondly at your one and only daughter? [*Wheels* LESSYA *out in her pram and returns.*] A little goes a long way.

NIKITA [*not quite knowing how to behave*]. What's so funny?

NELLY [*serious*]. You are so cruelly right — there's nothing funny. It's sad, Jingles ... [*Simply.*] You know, I'm so sorry for us both.

NIKITA. But why, why are you sorry? If needs be, I'm always ready ...

NELLY. I know — you're a great little pioneer ... Always ready. Only it's too late. It's too late, my dear.

NIKITA. What are you going on about? It's impossible to understand you.

NELLY. Thank God for that! [*Passes her hand over his face.*] All right, what will be will be but I don't expect to be happy.

[KONSTANTINOV *enters uncertainly.*]

KONSTANTINOV. Good evening. Enjoying yourselves? That's good. Seasonal greetings . . . I've got a present for Lessya here. It's a mechanical toy – a pedestrian that you wind up.

NELLY. Thanks, Uncle Seryezha . . . The pedestrian will come in useful.

KONSTANTINOV [*to* TERENTY]. I have an extra-loud alarm clock for you. They say, it simply throws you out of bed.

TERENTY [*turns to his father*]. That's what I need. [*He has glued on a grey beard and moustache and added to his make-up.*]

KONSTANTINOV. What a joke! You, Father Christmas? Actually you look like Nikanor, the watchman. [*To* KAI.] I also got some coloured candles, by chance.

NELLY. They'll also come in useful. I adored them as a child – pity they're scarce now. [*Turns on the tape-recorder.*] Here we go! [*Music.*] Put out the light, Kai . . . And light the candles!

[*The light is out; music plays; the boys light the candles.*]

The festive opening of the grand ball. The ladies' waltz. The ladies invite the gentlemen to dance! Come, Terry . . . Let's dance!

[TERENTY *and* NELLY *whirl around. The door opens. In the semi-darkness a woman appears at the door.* KAI *turns on the light.* MASHA *enters the room;* TERENTY *happens to be beside her.*]

MASHA. What's this?

TERENTY. A walking cripple.

MASHA. Will you move aside, please.

[MASHA *looks around the room in silence.* NELLY *emerges from behind* KAI *and approaches her in silence. She stops and looks down.*]

Have you nothing to say?

NELLY [*quietly*]. You left her . . . you simply deserted her. I thought you didn't want her.

MASHA. Think what you're saying! [*Pause.*] What did you expect?

NELLY [*helpless*]. I thought . . . perhaps you wouldn't find me.

MASHA. I have found you. I made the effort. [*Stares at her.*] You are heartless.

NELLY. I thought you were heartless.

MASHA. Where is she?

NELLY [*points to the door*]. In here. [*She goes into the next-door room.*]

[MASHA *follows her.*]

NIKITA. Who's that?

KAI. Don't know.

TERENTY [*he guesses*]. So that's what it is . . . [*He removes his beard, sits down.*]

[MASHA *and* NELLY *return.* MASHA *carries the sleeping* LESSYA, *wrapped in a blanket.*]

NELLY. Careful outside. She's been ill.

MASHA. I see. We go on playing and playing – we never have enough of it.

NELLY. Who do you mean?

MASHA. Me as well. [*Sees the tape-recorder, with wry smile.*] That thing's familiar.

NELLY [*intimately and almost affectionately*]. How are you?

MASHA. Not well. I proved my point about the site. But here [*Points to her breast.*] everything's gone silent. My dancing days are over. [*With a shake of her head.*] All right, keep going. And stop playing games or you'll kill yourself. [*Goes to the door.*]

NELLY [*rushes to her, shouts*]. Let me say goodbye!

MASHA. No. You'll wake her up. [*She goes quickly.*]

NELLY. That's how it is . . . The dancing is postponed.

TERENTY. Don't say anything.

KAI [*goes to his shelf, picks up one of the figurines, looks at it, glances round*]. Funny how empty the room is.

NELLY [*looks at them all*]. Forgive me!

NIKITA [*suddenly furious*]. Liar! What a liar you are!

NELLY [*with hope*]. Are you upset? Are you? Yes?

NIKITA. What are you? Lies! Nothing but lies.

NELLY. But she could have been . . . She could have been our daughter, Jingles . . .

NIKITA [*savagely*]. Out of my sight!

[*In silence,* NELLY *puts on her fur jacket, throws the kerchief over her head, then gets her suitcase and starts packing quickly. They all stare at her as in a trance.*]

KONSTANTINOV [*goes to her, not hurrying*]. Don't leave them, little girl.

[NELLY *says nothing.* KAI *slowly goes to her and removes her jacket.* NIKITA *goes to her and removes her kerchief.*]

KAI [*to* NIKITA]. Pass me the matches.

NIKITA. What for?

KAI. I'll light the candles on the Christmas tree.

TERENTY [*turns on the tape-recorder*]. Here's some more music for you . . . Pity it's sad.

KONSTANTINOV. I'm off. Keep well, son.

TERENTY. The kettle's boiled. Enjoy your tea. [*Puts on his jacket.*] Let's go, dad . . . It's late and we have a long way to go.

[KONSTANTINOV *says nothing but takes him by the arm and leads him off.*]

NELLY. How lovely . . .

KAI. You mean, Terry?

NELLY. Hm . . . [*Glances at the Christmas tree with all the candles now alight.*] What a beautiful Christmas tree . . . [*Pause.*] Have you forgiven me?

NIKITA. Will you be glad of me? [*Quietly.*] You are my only hope.

NELLY. I'll be whatever you like.

[KAI *puts on his coat, turns off the light. Only the candles on the Christmas tree light up the room.*]

NIKITA. Where are you going?

KAI. I'm going for a walk. I'll look up at this window from the boulevard. I'll see the Christmas tree, the candles burning as in my childhood. [*He goes.*]

NELLY [*slight pause*]. Not really?

NIKITA [*touches her hand*]. Quiet . . . Quiet . . . [*He speaks so quietly, he is barely audible.*]

FINAL CURTAIN

Cruel Games

In Moscow in the summer of 1980, I was involved in a violent argument about *Cruel Games*. The occasion was a dinner party with Arbuzov's two daughters, his two son-in-laws, one a dramatist, the other a film director, and their friends who were mostly aged between forty and fifty. The argument began on the naturalistic level. How convincing are the play's two environments to which Nelly latches on? She is an adolescent lost waif from yet a third environment.

There is Kai's room in Moscow. It is a refuge, like the room in Leningrad where the threesome of *The Promise*, three adolescent strangers, find each other and survive. Kai's room is not a refuge from the physical deprivation of war. For the three boys, old schoolfriends now twenty, it is their pad, an escape from emotional deprivation and confusion, from parents, ambition, pressures and privileges. Two of the boys, Kai and Nikita, are of Moscow's privileged class. Everyone at the dinner agreed that the Moscow environment was portrayed with great authenticity. They were amazed that Arbuzov at the age of seventy could portray contemporary twenty-year-olds with such subtlety. That had also been the reaction of the press.

The second environment is Mishka's and Mashka's home in the oil-fields' settlement of the Tyumen region. Emotionally, life is claustrophobic. The area is vast and dangerous. Mishka, the doctor, travels to his patients by helicopter; Mashka, the geologist, is not able to return home for the weekend when she goes prospecting for three months. A version of the second environment appears in Arbuzov's plays in many guises. In *The Promise* Marat returns to Lika from a distant place where he is building bridges. In *Lovely to Look At!* Vasya chooses to go to Ustegorsk where there are no concerts or games of volley-ball.

Arbuzov's second environments could be described as imagined worlds. Applying their measure of authenticity, the dinner company insisted that the second environment in *Cruel Games* was not authentic. They found the characters incredible. "Only because the Lenin Komsomol Theatre production opts out of the problem", I said. Mishka is made to look out of place and slightly ridiculous in Kai's room, which is interesting. But the scenes in Mishka's and Mashka's home barely exist in a half-set suggesting heavy industry and a fun-fair at the same time — flashing lights and a great metal wheel on which Mishka dies crucified. Compare how Nelly describes his death in the dialogue. In the production, finally the boys in Moscow and Nelly turn into clowns, putting on white make-up with red blobs on their cheeks and noses. The play ends in a pointless caper.

Arbuzov tried unsuccessfully to stop the production before it opened. It has turned out to be enormously popular. Our dinner argument went on: authentic or not, should not the playwright's intention prevail? What should the play-wright/director/stage-designer/actor relationship be? This problem will always be argued.

What is the problem of *Cruel Games* with its two environments which the director had side-stepped? What was Arbuzov's intention? In an interview published by *Smena*, a fortnightly Leningrad periodical, Arbuzov had said: "We often behave without due care of the people close to us . . . We forget that our private life is also the life of the community . . . That is what I should like the spectator to consider." In his theatre review in *Pravda* on 25 April 1979 Dubaso wrote that *Cruel Games* sounds "a warning about carelessness towards immemorial basic consideration such as children, family, love which turns into personal tragedy and which can endanger society. The nucleus of society is family happiness from which starts the young citizen's awareness of actuality; it is not just a private matter but it has national meaning and value. The emancipated Mashka . . . exclaims: 'I'm a geologist and everything else comes after.' But heavy loneliness is the price she pays for her indifference to her child, her husband, to everything that counts in private life . . . And Kai, Nikita, Terenty, not having a normal family life, seek support from each other. The author with his in-born psychological thoroughness shows the difficult and painful development of the individual in these circumstances . . ."

Cruel Games is in complete contrast to Arbuzov's *Tanya* which I had translated and directed with Toynbee Hall students at the end of the war. Tanya starts as a doting wife and drop-out medical student in Moscow until her husband leaves her for a professional geologist, Shamanova; after her baby dies, she completes her medical studies and is appointed to a medical practice at the back of beyond where she saves her husband's baby by Shamanova. That is when Tanya finds herself and wins through. As a doctor in snow-swept Siberia with no private life she is almost a myth.

The play clearly has the opposite moral. But it is a play, not a tract. What strikes me as the essential difference between these two plays is a concern with kindness in *Cruel Games*, which is absent in *Tanya*. It is there in *Once Upon a Time*. Khristofor says: "I think, the whole point is being kind. And being kind means being discreet . . ." In *Cruel Games* it is, I think, a powerful undercurrent that synthetizes the two environments which are moreover treated in the same *genre* or manner.

THE TWELFTH HOUR

The Twelfth Hour was first performed by Meadow Players Ltd. at the Oxford Playhouse, 19 May 1964, with the following cast:

Anna	Judi Dench
Yanina	Olive McFarland
Kirill Karetnikov	James Cairncross
Leonid Svidersky	John Turner
Katenka	Jane Livingston
Orestes Petrovykh	John Moffatt
Ivan Ulybyshev	John Hurt
Ivette	Ursula Jeans
Nikolai Dor	Joseph O'Conor
Nolik	John Barrard
Roman Bezenchuk	James Laurenson
Seryozhka	Larry Jerome
Ryabov	John Standing
Guests	Denzil Vause, Gareth Forwood, Sheila Robbins, Tony Mark Dowse, Susan Hillier, Edgar Masefield, Dalia Hertz
Directed by	Frank Hauser
Designed by	Michael Clarke

Dvenadtsaty Chas (*The Twelfth Hour*) was first produced in Ostrava, Czechoslovakia, on 30 June 1959. It was directed by R. Koval.

It was first performed in the Soviet Union on 5 December 1959 In Kaliningrad where it was directed by V. Tan.

The play was first performed in Leningrad on 31 December 1959 at the Pushkin Theatre with the following cast:

Anna	L. Shtykan
Yanina	V. Koval'
Karetnikov	Y. Tolybeyev
Svidersky	L. Gorbachev
Katen'ka	N. Mamayeva
Petrovykh	B. Freindlikh
Ulybyshev	R. Kul'd
Ivette	G. Inyutina
Dor	V. Chestnokov
Nolik	V. Targonin
Bezenchuk	L. Krymov
Seryozhka	S. Muratov
Ryabov	M. Ekaterininsky
Directed by	R. Suslovich
Designed by	A. Bosulayev

CHARACTERS

NIKOLAY DOR, owner of a sweets factory and a chain of confectionery shops, fifty-five-years-old

ANNA, his daughter, twenty-six

IVAN ULYBYSHEV, her husband, a student, twenty-three

LEONID SVIDERSKY, Dor's colleague, thirty-five

YANINA, his sister, thirty-two

KIRILL KARETNIKOV, a poet, forty-two

ORESTES PETROVYKH, an engineer, forty-eight

ROMAN BEZENCHUK, a postgraduate engineer, twenty-four

KATENKA, Dor's housemaid, eighteen

SERYOZHKA, her brother, thirteen

IVETTE, prima donna of the Leningrad Light Opera Company, forty

NOLIK, her manager, fifty-five

RYABOV, Dor's employee, sixty

GUESTS

The action takes place in Pavlovsk, a Leningrad suburb, on the thirteenth of June 1928 between 8 p.m. and 1 a.m.

152

ACT ONE

Pavlovsk is a holiday resort near Leningrad.

A beautifully equipped summer residence. The flower beds are laid out with early flowers; the paths are neatly sprinkled with red sand. It is a light summer evening, typical of Leningrad.

Under the trees, two women have settled down in deck-chairs. ANNA *is very beautiful, dark-haired, with rather a pale face and a straight fringe right down to the eyebrows. Her friend* YANINA *is a little older, dressed in rather a bright check, her hair cut short in the fashion of the twenties.*

Holding a bottle of brandy, KIRILL KARETNIKOV *stands on the terrace steps. He is a tall, untidy man, in a threadbare blue jacket with a bright red tie.*

ANNA [*reading from a manuscript*]. "Your bunch of pale red roses, they smell of the funeral shroud." [*Pause.*] This poem of mine is rather weak of course.

YANINA. Good or bad, what's the odds! It's all nonsense, anyway.

ANNA. It's funny, I liked it when I wrote it.

KIRILL. It's all rubbish! Your images and rhymes are plagiarized. You should be more explicit. Who are these people? What were they doing prior to 1917?

YANINA. You're quite drunk.

KIRILL. Praise be to Allah! [*Exit into the house.*]

ANNA [*pause*]. You're having a difficult time with him, aren't you?

YANINA. It is nothing, my dear! He writes too little and drinks too much. He cries at night and acts the clown in the morning. [*She lights a cigarette.*] Like the rest of us, he doesn't know what to write about. Horrible Russia all round. A lot of ugly faces . . . He tries to laugh it off and can't.

[*Pause.*]

ANNA. It's so sad here. Sad and deserted. Just a couple of years ago, I remember there were a lot of people in the summer. There was a lot going on. It was fun . . . It's not the same now.

YANINA. To hell with it! I suppose everything's packing up, my dear.

153

KIRILL [*re-appearing*]. It's a funny birthday. Not a soul in the house, only the student-husband, who sits doing calculations on the entresol. There are a couple of cats wandering in and out of the rooms. There's an ominous silence. [*Pause.*] And why isn't Svidersky here? He should be among those present. Well? [*He sighs.*] Actually, Yanina, your brother's a twister. He'll be shot by the secret police one of these days. I'm sorry, Anna, I seem to have upset you on your birthday.

> [LEONID SVIDERSKY *enters by the garden gate. He is swarthy and extremely handsome in a southern way. He has soft, cat-like movements and a melodious voice.*]

KIRILL. Talk of the devil! I was just wondering why you haven't been shot by the secret police.

SVIDERSKY [*to* YANINA]. Why don't you mend his cuffs? They're frayed. [*Kissing* ANNA'*s hand.*] Citizen, may I offer you a fruit-tart from Dor? [*He laughs quietly.*]

ANNA. It's not funny.

SVIDERSKY. Seek and you shall find. It's a *tarte surprise.*

KIRILL [*pointing at* SVIDERSKY]. He disgusts me. I'll remove myself as far as possible. [*Exit into the house.*]

SVIDERSKY. Well, well . . . You paint in the French manner . . . after what do you call them – Dufy, Matisse? At the same time you keep that sot. You're not being very logical, my dear sister.

YANINA. He's talented.

SVIDERSKY. Damn him! He's no good to anyone.

> [*Sound of broken crockery in the house.*]

KIRILL [*appearing at the window*]. Attention, please! I've smashed a decanter. [*Gaily.*] It's crystal, I think.

SVIDERSKY. Idiot!

KIRILL. Put me to bed. Or you'll be sorry.

YANINA [*with a laugh*]. At any rate he's different. [*She goes into the house.*]

ANNA [*after a pause*]. Where's father?

SVIDERSKY. Where do you think? The future of the factory's being decided today. He wanted to come early, but . . .

ANNA. Today? What do you mean?

SVIDERSKY. Look, my love. Times are hard. My friend, your father, is a superb businessman, but he can't be bothered where the "comrades" are concerned. They've raised the taxes. And it's almost impossible for your private tradesman to get raw materials.

ANNA. How silly!

SVIDERSKY. What is?

ANNA. Everything.

SVIDERSKY. Your husband can't be very amusing. You're always so depressed. [*He looks round and seeing that no one is about, he comes right up to* ANNA.] Why didn't you come yesterday? I waited till eleven.

ANNA. It bores me.

SVIDERSKY. That's a lie. [*He kisses her.*]

[KATENKA *comes running out of the house. Dumbfounded, she stares at them.*]

ANNA [*seeing* KATENKA]. What do you want?

KATENKA. I've come to change the tablecloth.

SVIDERSKY. I'm hungry. It's nine o'clock, and we shan't sit down to supper till one in the morning . . .

ANNA [*thoughtfully*].   We'll dine quite soon,
And soon forget
The fresh grilled fish
With fishy smile . . .

SVIDERSKY [*appalled and laughing*]. What is this nonsense!

[KATENKA *removes the tablecloth and goes into the house.*]

ANNA. You're turning us into a laughing stock!

SVIDERSKY. You can't hide anything from the servants. Make her a present of something small and frivolous, there's a clever girl.

[YANINA *comes down from the terrace.*]

YANINA. I've bedded him down on your couch. He has an extraordinary knack of waking up quite sober after a quarter of an hour.

SVIDERSKY. I wish to make a public announcement. Yesterday evening, when a little old lady failed to arrive, I went to the club, where I lost nearly 100 roubles at roulette. I had to borrow my fare home from the porter. [*To* ANNA.] Aren't you moved by my story? Doesn't your conscience prick you?

[ANNA *shrugs her shoulders.*]

YANINA. You don't mean the porters still supply you with cash?

SVIDERSKY. Never for chips, but always for the fare home. [*Pause.*] You do know that your father's not coming home alone, don't you?

ANNA. Is he bringing her?

SVIDERSKY. You must forgive a parent's weakness.

ANNA. I don't know why, but I'm sorry for her.

SVIDERSKY. Well, when she's on the stage, she drives them all mad. But she's as cold as a seal — I swear it.

[ORESTES PETROVYKH *enters through the garden gate. He is forty-eight, dignified, good-looking. He wears a white suit and carries a tennis racquet in a cover.*]

PETROVYKH. Many happy returns of the day, Miss Dor. [*He kisses her hand and turns to the others, speaking rather casually.*] Good evening. [*Again addressing* ANNA.] I've come straight from tennis and didn't have time to change. You'll excuse me, like a good neighbour, won't you? You are attending the reception tomorrow, aren't you? Lyukom is dancing.

ANNA. You're extraordinarily like Felix Yussoupov. Do you remember Serov's portrait of him?

PETROVYKH [*smiling a little*]. I remember Yussoupov himself. He played a very good game of tennis. He was a thoroughbred. My father was a mongrel. It's true that my mother came from a good family. She was the daughter of a governor-general, etc. . . . But she rejected her class. It was very fashionable at the time. In short, my parents propagated reason, goodness, eternity . . .!

ANNA. How about you?

PETROVYKH [*laughing*]. Well, I prefer the ballet! [*Pause.*] Is your father at home?

ANNA. No, father's been detained in Leningrad . . .

SVIDERSKY. How about a game of billiards before the party?

PETROVYKH. With the greatest of pleasure, but . . .

ANNA. You can go with a clear conscience. The ladies will be delighted to have a private gossip.

[PETROVYKH *makes a mock bow and goes towards the house. At the same time* KATENKA *comes running out, carrying a clean tablecloth, and bumps into him on the terrace steps.*]

PETROVYKH. You'll knock me down one of these days, you gorgeous creature.

ANNA. Do watch where you're going!

KATENKA. I'm just unlucky with them. They keep popping up, straight out of the ground. They're so solid and interesting. They don't look where they're going. [*She lays the tablecloth.*]

YANINA. Our engineer's rather entertaining.

ANNA. He's rather cold and supercilious, poor thing. Father thinks quite a lot of him as a business man. He's top boss somewhere. Father believes it's men like him who keep industry going.

YANINA. He's obviously attractive to women.

ANNA. Possibly. He's had a lot of experience . . . But he's not inflammable. Unlike your brother, he's too well brought up.

YANINA. I'm sure you've discovered very different accomplishments in my brother.

ANNA. Yanka, don't be crude.

YANINA. You haven't picked on him for his kindness of heart, I hope. [*She laughs.*] And then your Ivan is such a dear!

ANNA. Ivan has nothing to do with it. Faithful wives went out with the last century. [*Noticing* KATENKA *who is listening carefully.*] Well, Katenka, what are you dreaming about?

KATENKA. Nothing . . . [*She goes slowly.*]

ANNA [*pause*]. You really think Ivan's a dear?

YANINA. Does it surprise you?

ANNA. No, but . . . Ivan's too kind and honest, while your brother's utterly worthless. [*Interested.*] If only one could combine the two of them, something rather amusing might come of it.

YANINA. But that's what you're doing in a sense.

ANNA. Hell, you have a sharp tongue today! [*Pause.*] Poor Ivan's sitting in his room upstairs, calculating something. He's got his finals next week, followed by the labour exchange and unemployment, I expect . . .

YANINA. Does he love you very much?

ANNA [*shrugging her shoulders*]. I expect so, if he could only forgive his father-confectioner . . . He's a young man full of ideals, you know, and the nep-father-in-law must cause a lot of moral suffering.

YANINA. You talk of him, as if you hate him.

ANNA [*thoughtfully*]. That could happen too . . . He's a good little boy, but something about him frightens me. He's kind to people – that will make him ruthless in the end. [*Pause.*] We met a year ago, at a student's party. I read some poetry and it seems the nonsense impressed him. He didn't know who I was and took me for a student. When I was so willing to meet him half way, he felt obliged to marry me at once. It was so touching, I was quite shaken . . . [*With a laugh.*] And that decided it. After we'd signed at the Registry Office, he took me to our pastry shop on the Nevsky Prospect, and over father's pastries, I revealed the terrible secret.

YANINA. How shattering!

ANNA. When he learnt that henceforth he was the heir of Leningrad's most famous firm of confectioners, the poor thing nearly wept in despair.

YANINA. But why did he agree to live here?

ANNA. I couldn't go and live in his hostel, could I? He can't afford a room on his grant. Of course, I know, it's in very bad taste – that I am my father's daughter and he a man without any rights. But I'm not interested in people, persons. I love good poetry, music, painting – in a word everything that's hostile to people. Especially my father and the forces that want him liquidated. And I only prefer my father because his money helps me to publish my feeble verse.

YANINA. But what about Ivan? . . . Why do you want him?

ANNA [*after a pause*]. Yanka . . .

YANINA. Well?

ANNA. Will you believe me if I say that I love him?

YANINA [*thinking it over*]. No.

ANNA [*very non-committal*]. How wise of you.

   [*Enter* IVAN. *He is twenty-three, shy, and has a childish sort of cunning; if he loses his temper, you can't budge him. His clothes are very untidy. He walks down from the terrace into the garden, carrying a new shirt.*]

IVAN. Just listen to them! They're making such a din with their billiard balls, it's very difficult to concentrate. And they've scared the cats. So the cats walked into my room, you know, and sat down beside me. That's why I've decided to stop working.

ANNA [*pointing to* YANINA]. All the same, say how do you do.

IVAN [*to* YANINA]. How do you do! You've painted a most amusing picture. Anna showed it to me. It's true it's rather difficult to guess what it's meant to be, but the colours are very interesting, you know. It's daring, you know.

ANNA. Ivan, why have you brought down your shirt?

IVAN. Well, actually, it's because of the shirt I came down. Katenka came in and said that you said I must put on this shirt. But this isn't my shirt and I want to find out what it's all about.

ANNA. Ivan, you're hopeless! Why, this shirt is my present to you. Don't you understand?

IVAN. Your present? Oh, I see! [*He goes up on the terrace, stops, then walks down into the garden again.*] No, it's no good. Look, it's your birthday today – not mine, and so I ought to give you a shirt – I mean, not necessarily a shirt, but something, anyway. And I only gave you that . . . [*He looks at* YANINA.] Well, you know what I gave you. You're always finding a pretext and making me presents of a lot of rubbish. You know, it doesn't work.

YANINA [*laughing*]. You're marvellous!

IVAN. What about it? And where does she get the money to give me such shirts – silk shirts, you know?

ANNA. But I got it for the book!

IVAN. What, the one published by the author? Why not tell me how much you paid out of your own pocket? [*Angry.*] Why deceive me, you know? You're my wife and, therefore, my best friend. Why do you lie to me? I live here in this house because I love you and, therefore, respect you. But don't thrust other people's money at me in roundabout ways. [*Going up to her and kissing her gaily.*] I love you, but don't let's play the fool.

YANINA. Poor Ivan.

IVAN [*winking*]. How am I poor, if this woman can't live without me?

[*Long pause.*]

YANINA. You know, Ivan, you're rather like an early Christian at the time of the Romans.

IVAN. Get on with you! [*To* ANNA.] Did you hear that? [*Pause.*] What does it mean?

ANNA. Yanina apparently thinks you'll be sacrificed to the lions and they'll end up by eating you.

IVAN. Rubbish, I won't have it! [*Pause for thought.*] Besides, I'm an orphan – who will raise his hand against me?

ANNA [*smiling at* YANINA]. Now isn't he adorable? Don't you want to kiss him?

YANINA. The devil only knows what you're both up to!

IVAN [*kissing* ANNA]. That Karetnikov of yours has gone to sleep on your sofa. [*To* YANINA.] Is it true he sat a whole hour on a lamp-post on Nevsky Prospect, and they couldn't get him down? What a hooligan! Isn't he? Still he writes amusing verse:

"The night. The moon. This century.
Mankind still suffers just the same."

Not bad at all.

KIRILL [*coming out of the house*]. Those lines are sad, and nobody understands that.

IVAN. You awake?

KIRILL. I've woken up. [*Pointing at an empty bottle*.] I can start all over again now. [*To* YANINA.] Do you know what I dreamt about? Envy. She was the thinnest of hags with red hair. All skin and bones. She put her arms around my neck and proceeded to throttle me. [*To* IVAN.] Do you know this hag?

IVAN. Are you envious?

KIRILL. Deeply.

IVAN. Of whom?

KIRILL [*thoughtfully*]. A bass.

IVAN. Who? Who, did you say?

KIRILL. One of our poets has a voice like that. A bass. He sings. It's enough to make one envious.

YANINA. That's stupid.

KIRILL. Do you prefer me? [*Tenderly*.] Oh, you fool.

PETROVYKH [*to* SVIDERSKY, *who follows him out of the house*]. Technique has nothing to do with ideology. It's like the ballet or tennis. You can't mix politics with it. A steam-boiler will always be a steam-boiler. A communist steam-boiler doesn't make sense.

SVIDERSKY. Do you think so?

IVAN. It's not true. Hullo, Mr Petrovykh! You've no proof. What's tennis got to do with it? You just haven't thought this out.

KIRILL. Anna, my dear, your husband's a bit of a puppy.

IVAN [*flaring up*]. What?

KIRILL. Don't get cross. I'm very fond of you.

IVAN [*crossly*]. Well, really, you know . . .

KIRILL. To be a puppy? What could be more delightful!

IVAN. Are you serious?

KIRILL [*thoughtful*]. Quite.

IVAN. Well, I don't know . . .

[*The sound of a car that stops.*]

ANNA. It's father!

KIRILL [*looking past the garden gate*]. She's come too!

[NIKOLAY DOR *enters through the garden gate. He is fifty-five, thickset, heavy, red-faced and has difficulty with his breathing. He wears a dashing grey suit, carries a briefcase and some parcels. He is accompanied by* IVETTE, *prima donna of the Leningrad Light Opera Company, a woman of forty, who does not use cosmetics. She is worried, pale and businesslike.* NOLIK, *the theatre manager, old, small, wearing a pincenez, hurries in after them.*]

SVIDERSKY [*gallantly*]. What a surprise! I salute the idol of Leningrad!

IVETTE. Stop it, Leonid. I'm dog-tired. [*Seeing* KIRILL.] So you're here too!

DOR [*to* KATENKA, *who has entered from the house*]. Take these things to my room. See the driver is well fed. Give him some vodka.

KATENKA. I know, the usual! [*She goes, taking the things into the house.*]

DOR [*kissing* ANNA]. I'm sorry I'm late, but I had some business to attend to. Here's a watch for you. It's gold. The work's old. It's an antique.

ANNA. Thank you . . .

DOR [*looking at her and smiling*]. What a grown-up daughter I have. Shall I tell them your age?

ANNA. You've been drinking again? Why? It's bad for you . . .

DOR. Living's bad for me, my dear.

KIRILL [*to* IVETTE]. It's me.

IVETTE. So I see. [*Kissing* ANNA.] I made your father late. Don't be angry with him. We had to check the takings at the theatre. They've put my husband behind prison bars, so I have to do everything myself. [*She gives her a small box.*] Here's a small stone for you, not expensive, but beautiful . . . Oh yes! I forgot to introduce you – Nolik, my manager.

KIRILL [*clapping his hands*]. But how lovely – Nolik!

[NOLIK *bows to them in silence.*]

PETROVYKH. Last Saturday, I saw you in "Bayader" . . .

IVETTE. Last Saturday? [*Remembering.*] It was a good house.

PETROVYKH. You're as fascinating as ever.

IVETTE. Like hell! I had awful toothache that evening. A filling fell out. [*Looking at her watch.*] Yes, it's time. [*To* NOLIK.] Bring me a glass of water.

[NOLIK *hurries into the house.*]

SVIDERSKY [*going up to* DOR]. Well, what about our business?

DOR. The meeting's not over yet. I found it embarrassing, pacing up and down the corridors, so I left Ryabov there. He'll ring, as soon as they've reached a decision.

PETROVYKH. Are they putting on the pressure?

DOR. Very much so! Fortunately, we confectioners aren't in the front line. We've been spared for the time being. Sausages and so on are done for. But still, it's obvious the end's not far off, for Leonid and me.

IVETTE. Mine isn't far off either. I shall be going to stay with my husband in jail. [*She swallows her powders, washing them down with water brought by* NOLIK.] And here you'll have an operetta called the "Collective Princess". [*To* NOLIK.] Ring the box office and try to find out the exact takings.

[NOLIK *goes.*]

PETROVYKH. Yes, the "comrades" have done an about turn . . . [*Laughing.*] But you're clever. You'll always find a way out.

DOR. I try to. But, as the saying goes, you can't make bricks without straw.

SVIDERSKY [*viciously*]. Y–yes . . . You love our Russian proverbs.

DOR [*sharply*]. I am Russian. My father was a Belgian subject, but I was born and brought up here in Petersburg. [*More softly.*] It's true, I did go to Belgium before the war, but I didn't in any way feel it was my country. Frontiers interfere with trade. A time will come when intelligent people realize that.

PETROVYKH [*laughing*]. So you're a dangerous cosmopolitan!

DOR. Oh, yes . . . like, you know, old Klutz.

KIRILL. Your old Klutz had his head cut off, incidentally. [*Going up to* DOR.] Let's go to that stinking bar of yours, Mr Pastry-cook, and drink to your future. [*Pause.*]

DOR [*to* ANNA, *speaking quietly*]. A clown should know his place.

SVIDERSKY. Karetnikov, you're being tiresome.

DOR. There's no need to be angry, Svidersky. This gentleman, like myself, is due to be liquidated shortly. Ivette, let's go inside.

IVETTE. My legs have gone numb. I must put them in hot water.

SVIDERSKY [*taking her arm*]. My dear, I'd like you to help me solve a problem.

IVETTE. What now?

SVIDERSKY. There's something of the devil in all of us at times, don't you think?

IVETTE. Go to hell! You're a fool, Leonid. [*She goes into the house, followed by* DOR.]

IVAN [*who has remained apart*]. What an interesting person she is.

SVIDERSKY. Yes and very enterprising.

PETROVYKH. She was a marvellous woman.

SVIDERSKY. She still is, if she wants to be.

IVAN. Why did they put her husband in jail?

SVIDERSKY. He was careless with diamonds. Now she runs the theatre instead of him.

KIRILL [*quietly, to* YANINA]. What did her father say to her? [*Pause.*] Well?

YANINA [*after a pause*]. A clown should know his place.

PETROVYKH [*going up to* ANNA]. I must go and change, if you'll excuse me. I'll be back later. [*He bows and goes out.*]

KIRILL. A clown . . . [*thinking it over*]. A clown – how interesting. [*To* SVIDERSKY.] A romantic lead, surely?

SVIDERSKY. You've got a nerve!

KIRILL. Well, it's something.

[KATENKA *comes out of the house.*]

KATENKA. Cook asks when will supper be served?

ANNA. After eleven. There's no hurry. [*To* IVAN.] Ivan, where have you put the shirt?

IVAN. I stuck it under the bench. It was embarrassing, you know. She's an actress, after all.

ANNA. Aren't you a clever little thing.

KIRILL. Yanina, my dear, let's go in and join our host. They might open a stinking bottle or two. [*Viciously.*] Clowns receive crumbs from the high table.

[*He and* YANINA *go into the house.*]

SVIDERSKY. That poetry teacher of yours is ambitious, it seems. What a swine! He's received in a decent house, but his feelings, if you please, have been hurt.

ANNA [*calmly*]. You're handsome but stupid. Women like you for those very reasons. The second reason makes you particularly attractive.

[*She goes into the house.* IVAN *laughs.* SVIDERSKY *shrugs and goes into the garden. The sun has nearly set. A blood-red sunset gradually replaces the golden light.*]

KATENKA [*cautiously approaching* IVAN, *who is sitting on the bench*]. It's terrifying really. Isn't it?

IVAN [*looking round*]. What's terrifying?

KATENKA. The way people live. They deceive each other, they pretend. They're worse than animals.

IVAN [*after a pause*]. Well, yes, you know.

KATENKA. Why have you crumpled your shirt like this? Let me iron it for you.

IVAN [*angry*]. Why do you all go on about this shirt? I never want to see it again. They said it was quiet here, in Pavlosk, you could concentrate. But there's billiards and cats and muddle. [*Pause.*] Katerina!

KATENKA. Yes?

IVAN. Are you my friend?

[*She nods her head in silence.*]

Well, do you pity this Ulybyshev?

KATENKA [*after thinking it over*]. You haven't got any parents?

IVAN. What a diplomat you are! [*Pause.*] Have you any parents?

KATENKA. My mother's dead. My father lives in the country, near Gdov . . . Oh, my father's such a party-man, it's awful! Then I have a brother, he's thirteen. He works at the mill. [*Proudly*.] He's independent. I tell him about everything in my letters. [*Trying to divert him*.] How are your calculations? Doing well?

IVAN [*brightening up*]. I'm getting through my exams bit by bit. In a fortnight I'll be an engineer. But I'm not as young as I used to be. My professor says I have no self-respect and advises me to find some. He assures me it's essential. How can I find it here, when . . . [*He glances round and waves his hand despondently*.]

KATENKA. Keep thinking, as often as you can, how happy you are and how much you know. [*Anxiously*.] Will they offer you a job or is it the Labour Exchange for you as well?

IVAN. I don't know . . . There are a lot of unemployed, but, well, I don't know.

KATENKA. Me too, when I came from the country, I thought I'd get a job at a factory. Nothing doing! Such a lot of unemployed, and I haven't any qualifications. [*Confidentially*.] Only there's a rumour among the people, unemployment's coming to an end soon, honest. And yesterday at the baker's they were saying: the Bolshevik party will pass a decree and build a lot of factories. All owned by the government, the people that is. And one old boy in a railwayman's tunic – buying a white loaf with raisins, he was – well, he spoke up: the truce is over, he said, we're about to start on general reconstruction! [*Pause*.] Perhaps, they're lying, are they?

IVAN [*smiling*]. It doesn't look as if they're lying.

KATENKA. But suppose they send you to another town, what will you do? Will you go alone or will Miss Dor go with you?

IVAN [*immediately downcast*]. I don't know. Of course, she's used to Leningrad. There are all sorts of publishers here, you know, and she has a lot of friends.

KATENKA. Yes, she's beautiful.

IVAN [*cheering up*]. Isn't she? She's amazingly beautiful and very witty, you know. [*Rapturously*.] Sometimes she comes out with something so cutting, the other person just caves in at once . . . [*He laughs*.] You should have seen how she outsmarted that Svidersky just now. You're a fool and so on and so forth, she said. It's enough to make you die laughing. Isn't it?

KATENKA [*gloomily*]. Yes.

IVAN. There's no doubt that she suffers a great deal because of her father and her trivial background . . . She is, after all, a poet, you know, on intimate terms with all that's . . . beautiful. A poet is . . . Can you imagine what a poet is?

KATENKA. Aha! . . . A poet is the kindest person. And he loves people so much, he even talks in verse with them. Well, it's very difficult in verse. I've tried. [*Sadly.*] But I can't.

IVAN. You haven't written verse?

KATENKA [*horrified*]. I have. [*Ready to burst into tears.*] Please don't look at me with such pity! Better give me your shirt and I'll iron it . . . I can do that all right! [*She turns abruptly and bumps into* PETROVYKH, *who, having changed, walks into the garden.*]

PETROVYKH. Got me! Well done! How do you do it, my dear?

KATENKA [*upset*]. God knows, I don't do it on purpose!

PETROVYKH [*seriously, to* IVAN]. She's always there, waiting for me, trying to trip me up. Rather odd, isn't it?

[*Embarrassed,* KATENKA *goes to the table and tries to rearrange the things there.*]

[*Taking* IVAN *by the arm.*] Probably worn out, aren't you? The old man, your professor, is strict. I studied under him too, you know.

IVAN. Did you?

PETROVYKH. Past history now. Do you like our profession? It's enthralling and wonderful, don't you think? The only snag is our bosses don't appreciate us. They don't. They didn't appreciate us before 1917, and now the same thing. In fact, for you and for me, nothing has changed. But there's something in the air again — it's going to thunder. [*Pause.*] A good sunset. As though there's a fire somewhere.

IVAN [*thinking it over*]. Looks like it . . .

PETROVYKH. Yes, if we don't watch out, there will be such a sunset that flames will come leaping up all around us. Don't you agree? Perhaps not. I always thought it possible as a child.

IVAN. You're a man of mystery these days.

PETROVYKH. Really? [*Unexpectedly confidential.*] It's simply that I feel very sad, somehow. [*Looking around.*] It's a lovely white northern light — exactly the same as in my youth. And once again Russia stands at the cross-roads. [*Laughing.*] It's the situation she's usually in and has been for the last three hundred years. Shouldn't we have a drink on this occasion? I feel very warmly disposed towards you, you know.

IVAN. Hm . . . Why should you?

PLATE 15. Judi Dench as Anna and James Cairncross as Karetnikov,
Oxford Playhouse

PLATE 16. Judi Dench and Joseph O'Conor as Dor

PLATE 17. James Laurenson as Bezenchuk and John Hurt as Ulybyshev

PLATE 18. James Cairncross and Ursula Jeans as Ivette

PLATE 19. Scene from Act I, Vakhtangov Theatre, Moscow

PLATE 20. Y. Raikina as Katen'ka, N. Generalova as Serezhka
and G. Abrikosov as Bezenchuk

PETROVYKH. You're married to a beautiful woman. It's touching and endearing.

IVAN. Touching?

PETROVYKH. Lack of experience is always touching. [*Slight pause.*] I suppose you love her, your wife I mean, very much?

IVAN [*serious rather than flippant*]. Madly!

PETROVYKH [*interested*]. And what will you do, if she behaves the way all women behave as a rule?

IVAN. How's that?

PETROVYKH. If she's unfaithful to you.

IVAN. Anna? That's funny . . . [*Very sincerely.*] Why unfaithful?

PETROVYKH. There's nothing wrong with your logic, my friend. Why, indeed?

[*He leads him off into the house.*]

KATENKA [*alone in the garden*]. Everyone knows, everyone's laughing, and he has no idea. Well, I'll go and tell him: why do you put up with it, Ivan Ulybyshev, when she's deceiving you! No, I shan't. What's it got to do with me? [*Listening to a bird singing.*] Thrush, thrush, what d'you bring tomorrow? Bring me happiness and carry off sorrow. [*After a pause.*] Oh Lord, I'm only eighteen and I suffer so much . . . What will happen later?

[ROMAN BEZENCHUK *slips in cautiously through the door. He has curly hair, wears black horn-rimmed spectacles, is enthusiastic and fussy. He wears a cadet's jacket which has seen better days, with a strap across the shoulder and fairly ragged black civilian trousers worn over high boots. He carries a despatch case filled to overflowing and a parcel tied with string, which he holds with as much care as he's capable of.*]

BEZENCHUK [*in a gay whisper*]. Greetings, Katenka! It's what the wanderer says on his return from distant lands. [*He fusses about, not knowing where to put down his things.*]

KATENKA [*delighted*]. Mr Bezenchuk! You've arrived!

BEZENCHUK. Yes, here I am! Is Ivan at home?

KATENKA. He's here. It's Miss Dor's birthday. We've got guests.

BEZENCHUK. What rotten luck! I've only got an hour, that's all. Back to Moscow tomorrow, and after that, well, you won't see me for dust.

KATENKA. But what will Ivan do without you?

BEZENCHUK. That's his business. [*Polishing his glasses.*] There's no knowing with a fool! [*Putting on his glasses.*] How pretty you've grown . . .

KATENKA [*smiling*]. Really?

BEZENCHUK. There's something about you now . . . sort of special. By the way, I've brought you a present from Moscow . . . [*Taking a book from his despatch case.*] It's Mayakovsky's poems. [*Declaiming fiercely:*]

" I trample miles of streets,
Fraught with this hell, where can I go!
You damnable woman! What heavenly Hoffman
Thought you up?"

[*After a pause.*] It's beautiful.

KATENKA. Yes. And I don't understand it.

BEZENCHUK. One can never understand Mayakovsky at first. But afterwards . . . ! [*He clenches his fist and waves it, to show how good it is afterwards.*] Well, how's life? Here and in general?

KATENKA. The confectioner doesn't find business at all sweet. He's full of pre-monitions − very serious and drunk . . .

BEZENCHUK. He's finished! Your firm's being liquidated!

KATENKA. My firm! Aren't you ashamed of yourself?

BEZENCHUK. Ashamed! Me! And where's your class consciousness? It's you who should be ashamed, dancing attendance on a lot of bourgeois exploiters . . .

KATENKA. There you go again, using such words . . .

BEZENCHUK. When you even said that your father's a party man. And how he can put up with your utter irresponsibility, I don't understand it!

KATENKA. It's easy for you townspeople to talk! When mumma died, my. brother and I were left all on our own. I loved my father a lot, you know. Yes, I did. But he was harsh with me, not at all affectionate. [*Thought-fully.*] He took more notice of my little brother. No, I'm not complaining, it's understandable, after all he's a boy. But the point is − everything he did was for society, the people, I mean. I'd say to him of an evening: "Papa, say something, papa. Tell us how you fought against the Whites. Why don't you?" Do you know how he'd answer? "Katerina, be quiet! I've important things to think about." When I grew up, I saw I was a burden to him. So I decided to come up to town to earn my living, especially when he got a job for my small brother at the mill. I came to say goodbye to him. Dad won't let me go, I thought. Not a bit of it. "Go" he said. "It will do you good to have a taste of how the proletariat lives". So I came to Petersburg. And that meant the Labour Exchange and unemployment. [*She sobs.*] That's how it worked out . . .

BEZENCHUK [*unexpectedly at a loss*]. But I only — Katenka, I was only joking, Oh, I always come out with something incredibly stupid! And tears are such a waste. You really mustn't take any notice of such a fool!

KATENKA [*sobbing*]. What fool?

BEZENCHUK. Me, of course . . . No, Katenka, you really mustn't cry. [*Lively.*] And do you realize, right honourable comrade, that we're on the brink of unforgettable changes?

KATENKA. Honest?

BEZENCHUK. There won't be a trace of unemployment left in a year or two. I foresee the reverse, a labour shortage.

KATENKA. That's good, isn't it?

BEZENCHUK. What's good about it! [*Didactically.*] A labour shortage is also bad.

KATENKA. Of course. [*Thinking it over.*] Tell me, are you getting a large salary?

BEZENCHUK. Salary? What salary? No, Katya, you're still wide of the mark. The point is how we transform a sixth part of the world to the new, socialist way of life, and you talk of salaries!

KATENKA. Still, you've got to eat and drink!

BEZENCHUK [*flaring*]. Why? I mean, of course you do, but it's not, as they say, of primary importance. Actually, somehow, you do look at the facts from the wrong angle. [*Shattered.*] It really hurts me.

KATENKA [*suddenly angry*]. And it sometimes hurts me to look at you!

BEZENCHUK. Why is that, if you please?

KATENKA. You're so intelligent, on the whole, but always somehow rumpled and hungry, always in a hurry. But any old nepman can live in complete comfort — he eats well, he drives instead of walking, while you . . .

BEZENCHUK. So what! Do you know what Mayakovsky had to say about it? [*Shaking his fist at* DOR*'s house, he declaims with unusual verve.*] "Eat pineapples and feed on grouse, Your day is done, you bourgeois louse! . . ."

IVAN [*running out of the house*]. Roman! Have you gone raving mad? [*He flies into* BEZENCHUK*'s arms, they kiss.*] Don't you realize the house is full of guests! And you have to go and make this proclamation! [*He laughs, thumps* BEZENCHUK *on the back, who reciprocates and also roars with laughter.*] But it's good, good you've come! Do you know how bored I was without you! Let's go in — there's quite a celebration.

BEZENCHUK. Oh no, I'm not coming in. Your father-in-law and I, you know —
we don't exactly dote on each other.

IVAN. All right, sit down. Tell me about your trip!

BEZENCHUK. Marvellous trip! The government has decided to get the factory
going before schedule! And what's most important — instead of 20,000
tractors a year, it's to produce 40,000 — more than any other factory in the
world! Understand? [*He opens the parcel and with the greatest of care places
a small-scale model of the factory on the table.*] Here you are — the proto-
type, approved, finalized! Now, concentrate your most valuable attention . . .
[*Pointing them out.*] There's the foundry, the workshop, the main con-
veyor . . .

KATENKA. Oh, God . . . Isn't it lovely!

IVAN [*examining it with interest*]. Yes, some installation, you know.

BEZENCHUK. By the way, yours truly, with his own hands, made the cardboard copy of the model. [*He bows.*] Please to love and cherish.

[*The model slips out of KATENKA's hands and falls on the ground.*]

What have you done!

KATENKA. Oh, God! [*She kneels and picks it up.*]

IVAN. Why are you making such a fuss? Your model's intact, you know?

BEZENCHUK. Get to hell out of here — I spent three nights glueing it together!
Actually it is intact.

[*They all laugh with relief.*]

And so, Comrade Ulybyshev, it's known in principle that socialism must be
more productive than capitalism. Now it has to be proved in practice. [*He
roars with laughter.*] In practice! That's the stage we have reached, right
honourable Mr Ulybyshev!

IVAN. You've gone completely dotty!

BEZENCHUK [*hugging IVAN*]. "Eat pineapples and feed on grouse . . ."

ANNA [*appearing at the window*]. "Your day is done, you bourgeois louse! . . ."
A bit of a mouthful, that line.

BEZENCHUK. But it's the meaning, it's wonderful! By the way, good evening.

ANNA. Good evening. Off you go to the kitchen, Katya. Cook's waiting for you.

[*KATENKA goes in silence.*]

Ivan, I'm jealous of that woman.

IVAN [*taking her remark seriously*]. But, my dear Anna, why, how can you ... Only think – she and I ...

BEZENCHUK. She's playing you up, you idiot.

IVAN. Really? [*Thinking it over.*] On the other hand ... Can't I even make you jealous?

ANNA. You can, my dear, but not with her.

BEZENCHUK [*unexpectedly hurt*]. Personally, I'd feel very happy, if a girl like Katenka fell in love with me.

ANNA. Then it's you I'll be jealous of!

IVAN [*to* BEZENCHUK]. That was quick of her ... [*He laughs.*]

ANNA. Where have you sprung from, Mr Marxist? Have you succeeded in putting our sinful universe to rights? Not yet, I suppose! I'm not asking you to supper – you'll refuse anyway. The birthday of a nepman's daughter ... shameful. [*Unexpectedly she bends down towards him and strokes his cheek.*] It's shameful, my dear ... ! [*She disappears from the window.*]

BEZENCHUK [*sighing, as he looks after her*]. What a beautiful wife you've got!

IVAN [*sadly*]. Yes, I know.

BEZENCHUK. All the same, let's get down to business. Three days ago I talked to Gromov about you. He's recruiting the factory staff. I explained how talented you were and he's agreed to take you on, when you've got your degree. In brief, I'm your benefactor – a father figure to you. Please to treat me accordingly.

IVAN. Yes, but don't you see that while you're still at the building stage out there I shan't have any work, you know.

BEZENCHUK. Don't worry, they won't let you sit about twiddling your thumbs. We want to start installing the equipment before the building's complete. [*Pause.*] Why, what's the matter? Why don't you say something?

IVAN. Me? I don't know ... How about Anna?

BEZENCHUK. Have you gone mad? I'm discussing business with you but you're drivelling about –

IVAN. But she's got friends here and various publishers, you know ... She won't come, Roman.

BEZENCHUK. Why then, to hell with her! You'll come alone, which is better still.

IVAN. Will you try to understand that I love her. I love. You know, there does exist this human emotion – love. Of course, I understand that it's something you don't understand, but . . .

BEZENCHUK. You've got yourself thoroughly tied up, you idiot! It makes me sick to look at you. We've been friends from childhood and then, quite suddenly and unexpectedly, you've turned into a sort of parasite. That's what comes of not joining the party. The Whites killed your father, but you live in the summer residence of a nepman. [*With heavy sarcasm.*] You're economically dependent on a capitalist, you son of a bitch!

IVAN. That's a lie. I don't take a penny from him! I'm completely independent, if you must know! And why must you oversimplify like this? Of course, Dor belongs to the other camp, but he's a very interesting person to know. And Anna is kind. All this is an act she puts on.

BEZENCHUK [*mimicking him*]. "Kind" . . . "interesting to know" . . . It makes me sick to listen to this idealized chatter.

IVAN [*flaring up*]. And you're dogmatic! Dogmatic, that's what you are! All that's human is alien to you!

BEZENCHUK. Dogmatic! Me? Will you repeat what you've just said! Go on, repeat it, at once!

IVAN [*taking care not to repeat it*]. Now, love, love is the most sacred, the most beautiful and, you know, the kindest of emotions . . . If you love someone, you don't need anyone else any more. That one person is the whole world for you – only that person exists!

BEZENCHUK [*heatedly*]. The psychology of a shopkeeper! [*Waving his arm in sorrow.*] They've succeeded, the swine! They've infected you! Do you think their hold over us is just economic? Oh, you poor thing! They want to set us an example in morality as well. Their art and their love stink of death, of rotting corpses! Our Mayakovsky loathed the species all his life. No, I wouldn't stay a day here. I'd run away immediately without a backward glance! I'd grab Katenka and run.

IVAN. All right, grab her, if you want to . . .

BEZENCHUK. I'd also grab . . . No, there isn't the time! [*Suddenly angry.*] Please don't distract me with your trifles! I'm not you!

IVAN [*laughing*]. You don't say!

BEZENCHUK. Look, old thing, you've always been rather volatile – the first to start a fight and always after the girls. This kind of nonsense is over and done with now. And still, at this historic moment, you've managed to get yourself deeply involved in some personal mess! It's really revolting!

IVAN. Why don't you put yourself in my place! Then you'll see that . . .

BEZENCHUK. Well, really! That's all I need! To put myself in your place. I've got a place of my own.

IVAN [*pause*]. When must I go?

BEZENCHUK. When you've passed your exams.

IVAN. All right, I'll talk it over with Anna today. At times I feel so disgusted with myself. It's quite extraordinary. But love also means something. You wait and see. You'll find out for yourself.

BEZENCHUK. No thanks. [*Grimly.*] It's beyond my comprehension, brother!

[KATENKA *comes running out of the house.*]

KATENKA [*breathless*]. I've been told to lay the table in the garden. They'll have drinks and snacks here before supper. The master ordered the reserve cognac to be brought up.

BEZENCHUK [*listening to the voices from the house*]. No, I don't want to meet your confectioner.

IVAN. Let's go upstairs to my room . . . No, not here – through the kitchen. [*Gaily, to* KATENKA.] Katenka, do you think Vasilisa will let us through?

KATENKA. Why not?

IVAN. Come on, let's go! Cooks simply adore me!

[*Laughing,* IVAN *takes* BEZENCHUK *by the arm and leads him round the corner of the house.*]

KATENKA [*gazing after them*]. He's laughing, the silly fool. And he doesn't know a thing. If only he'd run for it, poor man.

[ANNA *comes out of the house quickly.*]

ANNA. Where's Ivan?

KATENKA. They've gone upstairs.

ANNA. With Bezenchuk?

[KATENKA *nods.*]

ANNA. What are they up to?

KATENKA. Laughing.

ANNA. What were they talking about?

KATENKA. I didn't hear.

ANNA. Some things it's useful to hear, Katenka. Do you know what I mean?

[KATENKA *nods in silence.*]

And sometimes things happen, it's useful not to notice – not to notice at all, and especially not to talk about them. Do you understand what I mean?

KATENKA [*quietly*]. Yes.

ANNA [*taking a ring off her finger*]. This is a very expensive little ring, but I don't at all begrudge giving it to you. Do you know why?

KATENKA [*barely audible*]. No . . .

ANNA. Because you're a good girl. [*She gives the ring to* KATENKA.] Take it. [*She goes into the house.*]

KATENKA. Oh, God, how disgusting! Shall I throw it away? No, I can't. I'm not rich. [*Depressed.*] If only I could get away from them and their lies . . .

[*The piano is heard in the house.* KIRILL, *just a little unsteady, appears on the terrace. He hears* KATENKA's *last few words, comes up to her and puts his hand on her shoulder.*]

[*With a slight move away from him.*] What are you doing?

KIRILL. Lies. [*Thoughtfully.*] And what are lies? A state of mind, naturally. [*Argumentatively.*] As it was at the beginning, so it is and ever will be.

KATENKA [*quietly*]. It isn't true.

KIRILL. Do you disagree with me, child?

[KATENKA *is silent.*]

KIRILL. How old are you?

KATENKA. Eighteen . . .

KIRILL. Is that all? But you tell lies already, every hour, every minute.

KATENKA [*very quietly*]. No, I always tell the truth.

KIRILL. The truth? [*He puts his finger on his lips.*] Entre nous . . . [*He looks around and speaks quietly.*] The truth doesn't exist. [*Again he places his finger on his lips and rather unsteadily ambles off into the garden.*]

KATENKA [*amazed by his words*]. Doesn't exist? No truth? What a thing to say! [*She looks all around with a new kind of interest.*]

CURTAIN

ACT TWO

The same evening, the same hour, the same place.

KATENKA. No truth . . .

[YANINA *and* PETROVYKH *appear on the terrace, followed by* ANNA.]

YANINA [*continuing the conversation*]. They've invented a lot of rules and live by them. And what's it for? There's nothing more absurd than rules. It's all nonsense, I think. Life and death. Definitely. The lot.

PETROVYKH [*politely*]. You're a brave woman.

[*He helps her into a deck-chair and goes up to* ANNA, *who is dreaming.*]

You've appeared in order to absent yourself again. Where are you?

ANNA [*she smiles*]. Here.

PETROVYKH. I don't believe you.

[*Somewhere near, a string orchestra begins playing.*]

YANINA. There they go . . . And so it'll go on till morning. It's Saturday.

PETROVYKH [*to* ANNA]. Don't you mind the restaurant so near?

ANNA. Why should I? I like cheap effects.

PETROVYKH [*only partly joking*].

> By the window I sat at a crowded ball,
> The violins sang of love and of pain.
> I sent you a black rose, in the golden dawn,
> A black rose in a glass of champagne.

YANINA. My God, how old-fashioned . . .

[DOR, IVETTE, NOLIK *and* SVIDERSKY *come out of the house.* NOLIK *is on and off throughout the following conversation. Every minute he is struck by various ideas on improving the general lot and he spends his time dashing about between* IVETTE *and the telephone. As they enter the lights flicker.*]

SVIDERSKY [*in charge of the brandy bottles*]. As things are, trade is fatal. Upon my word, if Dor and I were invited to work in the circus, we'd feel at home up there on the trapeze. [*To* DOR.] Or wouldn't we?

175

DOR. I don't see anything in common.

SVIDERSKY. Why not?

DOR. We're working without a safety net.

IVETTE. Bravo!

PETROVYKH [*quietly*] . Anna, where are you?

ANNA. I'm thinking.

PETROVYKH. What about?

ANNA. My husband. Is he about to run away, this very moment?

PETROVYKH. Do you mean it?

ANNA. Yes, I do.

YANINA. Karetnikov has disappeared . . .

DOR. Yes. [*He looks at his watch.*] And Ryabov hasn't phoned.

SVIDERSKY. Ivette, my dear . . .

IVETTE. Well?

SVIDERSKY. Love is great nonsense, isn't it?

IVETTE. Leonid, my dear, go to hell. [*She knits.*]

[KATENKA *serves the brandy.*]

SVIDERSKY [*after drinking, he sniffs at his glass and clicks his tongue*]. A work of art!

DOR. A reserve vintage from Erivan.

PETROVYKH. Concocted with great talent. That's how things should be made, with talent and individuality. For my sins, I love craftsmanship in wine, in ballet and engineering.

SVIDERSKY. Now, in our business what matters is the assortment. For Easter Islanders there's no such thing as bad confectionery.

[KATENKA *goes into the house.*]

IVETTE [*noticing* NOLIK *who has re-appeared*]. Well, what are the final takings? Are they working it out still?

[NOLIK *nods sadly.*]

All right, I'll ring them up later myself.

ANNA. Do you love the stage?

IVETTE. I did.

SVIDERSKY [*with a snort*]. But who are you in love with?

IVETTE [*pointing at* **DOR**]. Him.

[**DOR** *kisses her hands.*]

By the way, tomorrow we'll have to use your car to deliver a parcel to my husband.

SVIDERSKY [*persevering*]. Dear lady, why do you love him?

IVETTE. Because he's poor and beautiful.

SVIDERSKY [*roaring with laughter*]. That pest? Now for the last question, my dear. I swear it's the last, upon my word.

IVETTE. Well?

SVIDERSKY. One can't live without women in the world, can one? What do you say?

[*He roars with laughter and is languidly supported by the others.*]

IVETTE. Svidersky, I'm going to bang you over the head with a tennis racquet.

KIRILL [*appearing*]. *Bon soir*! I'm not in the way, am I? And the party's in full swing! [*Raising his glass.*] To Lassalle! [*He drinks.*] Why don't we have supper? I'm hungry.

DOR [*drily*]. Some guests have not arrived!

[*They have all sat down a little apart from each other, and remain silent, not looking at each other, thinking their own thoughts.*]

YANINA. It's a wonderful evening.

ANNA [*quietly*]. I'm cold.

> Transparent spring
> Has clothed Petropolis
> In a green down . . .

PETROVYKH [*to* **IVETTE**]. What are you knitting?

IVETTE. A coat for the poodle.

KIRILL. It's the end! I've fallen in love with you again.

IVETTE. It's too late.

DOR. And where's Ivan?

ANNA. Upstairs.

DOR. Why's that?

ANNA. Bezenchuk is with him.

DOR. That's all we need!

IVETTE [*sighing*]. It's too late. During the epoch of militant communism, I was beautiful. Do you remember, Kirill?

KIRILL. No.

IVETTE. Now I stink of the chemist. Right through.

KIRILL. Memento mori.

YANINA. The surprises there used to be . . . Dear God!

SVIDERSKY. Lelechka went to America.

DOR. How did he manage it?

SVIDERSKY. God's will.

YANINA. I sometimes think the trains don't run any more, not anywhere.

IVETTE. Do you still visit that house in Officers' Street?

KIRILL. No . . . Why?

ANNA [*examining a flower*]. Ivan . . . dear Ivan . . . Dear little Ivan.

SVIDERSKY [*dreamily*]. Yes, America. My grandfather is out there and two cousins.

KIRILL. They'll put them in the electric chair, if they're at all like you, sweetheart!

SVIDERSKY. Now, listen . . .

KIRILL. Quietly, now! I could tear you into pieces!

ANNA. Kirill, will you leave Svidersky alone. Read us some of your poetry. The latest.

KIRILL. I hear and obey. I have to, so long as I'm supplied with brandy. [*Sternly.*] Quiet then. [*Pause.*] Written in the Summer Garden yesterday before dinner. About a revolver. [*Reading very seriously.*]

> When all emotion had subsided,
> The devils brought me a thing of sorrow
> And placed it in my hand.
> Oh, thing of sorrow and of peace,
> Teach me your riddle, while I close
> My eyes and press the welcome trigger.

Crawling into my pink flesh
The iron will leave its tender touch.
A bard he was of different class,
These others are no more, not even
Left a trace. Farewell
The flowerbeds, the aunts and the children,
And you, who watch, barely breathing,
As through the sky, in azure light,
Flies the immortal soul.

[*He is silent for a while.* YANINA, *who has been holding his hand, kisses him quickly.*]

IVETTE [*looking at her watch*]. I'm late again! [*She takes her powders.*]

PETROVYKH [*to* KIRILL, *seriously*]. It's talented.

KIRILL. But it's useless.

ANNA [*thoughtfully*]. Why? It makes its point.

KIRILL. But in spite of our talents, we'll all be kicked out in the end.

SVIDERSKY. Do tell me! Given your attitude of mind, surely it is possible for you to switch over to something positive . . . in the proletarian style.

KIRILL [*seriously*]. Oh, no . . . it's too late. It's too late. [*With a laugh.*] Besides, I haven't been asked. I have not been asked at all.

SVIDERSKY. Is that so important to you?

KIRILL. What do you think! I have my pride. Isn't that so, Ivette?

IVETTE. It's too late. It's too late.

KIRILL. You see, she says so too . . . It's too late. And we had so much – hm? Sunsets on Pryzhka, the Prospect in winter, Sasha Blok, nights in Officers' Street . . . that was something. [*After a pause.*] Please forgive the melodrama. It's not my style. [*He bows and walks off unsteadily.*]

IVETTE. The vodka's corroded him.

[YANINA *gets up and follows him.*]

ANNA. Where are you going?

YANINA. After him. I'm afraid he's going to lie down on the rails again. [*She goes.*]

SVIDERSKY. Well yes, our Byron's not himself today.

ANNA. Do you know about Byron? How surprising. [*She goes into the garden.*]

DOR [*looking at his watch*]. It's gone half past ten. Why doesn't Ryabov phone?

IVETTE. Do keep calm, dear. It has all hung by a thread often enough before, but you've always got away with it.

DOR. All the same, my love, you shouldn't forget that my respite is temporary and that I shall be destroyed. I will be — in accordance with the doctrine.

SVIDERSKY. Well, yes . . . it's a bloody silly doctrine!

DOR. And resistance, as they explained to me at the court of enquiry, is useless. [*Exploding.*] To try and build socialism in a backward country, a country without a motor industry or aviation, a country entirely dependent on the West, it's just rubbish.

SVIDERSKY. That's what I say — it's a joke! It's nonsense! You must admit, the Russian muzhik building a plane or a tractor is a music hall turn.

PETROVYKH. That's where you're wrong! Your Russian is the ideal craftsman, keen, cunning and he can turn his hand to anything. But will the proletariat be able to control industry? There I have my doubts.

SVIDERSKY. That's the whole point! You mark my word! Without us, the experts, the comrades' experiment is not likely to succeed. [*He is not sober.*] Why then, let's move out of the limelight and sit it out . . . Instead of a factory we'll organize a workshop — for the time being. I have some delightful names in mind: "Unbound Labour" for instance . . . or "The Dawn of Freedom." Good heavens, it's not too bad. We'll tighten our belts for a bit. We'll be invisible.

DOR [*with controlled fury*]. To turn into small fry? To go crashing down, step-by-step? To end in the gutter? Is that what you suggest to me, Svidersky?

SVIDERSKY. But you have to hang on to something. You have to believe in something, don't you? All right, you're clever! What do you suggest I believe in?

IVETTE. I'm curious to know what you'll say.

KATENKA [*coming out of the house*]. Cook asks, should mineral water be brought?

DOR. Stop! Be *brought* . . . be *brought*! [*Laughing unexpectedly.*] That's what you've got to believe in, Leonid — the country. Do you see what I mean? In the towns' private enterprise, meaning all of us, is a pitiful minority — only an eighth of the total. But in the country it's the comrades who are the minority. In the country their position is invidious. [*He takes* **KATENKA** *by the hand and strokes her affectionately.*] The peasantry is a clan on its own. Their production is based on private property. You could say it's a capitalist class! [*Triumphant and in good faith.*] And no bread means death to the state.

KATENKA [*flaring*]. Please don't touch me! Really! What next! [*She runs into the house.*]

SVIDERSKY. Do you . . . do you believe in the revolution?

IVETTE. God knows what you're saying!

PETROVYKH. Dor, this is unwise. There are strangers in the house.

DOR [*darkly*]. I hope it's clear to everyone that I cannot love the Communist party.

[IVAN *and* BEZENCHUK *appear in the garden from behind some bushes.*]

IVAN. What's all the panic about? There's your scale model, safe and sound.

BEZENCHUK [*seeing* IVETTE]. Holy Mother of God — fragrant flower of the prairies . . . It can't be her!

IVAN. Will you be quiet!

BEZENCHUK. You live the high life!

IVETTE [*looking at her watch*]. It's past eleven. I must ring up the theatre personally and check the receipts of the snack bar.

SVIDERSKY. What have you and the snack bar in common, you charmer?

IVETTE. I get a percentage from the snack bar.

[*She goes, followed by* NOLIK.]

SVIDERSKY. She's gorgeous!

IVAN [*as he emerges with* BEZENCHUK *from behind some trees*]. We didn't want to disturb you, but the fact is we forgot a parcel here. It belongs to Bezenchuk, and I . . .

DOR. Let me introduce you, Orestes. This is Roman Bezenchuk, my chief enemy.

BEZENCHUK. You flatter me. You have more important enemies. [*To* PETRO-VYKH.] Good evening.

DOR. Do you know each other?

PETROVYKH. Comrade Bezenchuk is my colleague at work. We argue sometimes. I have the impression he doesn't always like me. Isn't that so?

BEZENCHUK. Quite right.

IVAN. Well, that's really, you know . . .

DOR. Quite so! And the subject of your arguments?

PETROVYKH [*after a pause*] . Life.

[*Pause.*]

IVAN. Oh!

BEZENCHUK. My colleague loves to commune alone with his profession. If he had his way, he'd forbid us, poor sinners, at the risk of death to deal with any of the problems that concern only him!

PETROVYKH [*smiling politely*]. It's a bit of an exaggeration, but true on the whole.

BEZENCHUK. Never — let me emphasize this — never have I noticed any desire on your part to share your knowledge of which you have enough and to spare. [*Exploding.*] Why, it's as though . . . Do you want to take over the whole of science?

PETROVYKH. It's sad but, ideally speaking, my fund of knowledge is infinitesimal.

BEZENCHUK [*passionately, as before*]. I think it's criminal, to try and be cleverer than other people at their expense.

PETROVYKH. Well, so I'm already a criminal. You see how quickly things happen for Comrade Bezenchuk.

BEZENCHUK. There's nothing to laugh at. [*Bitterly.*] I still respect you.

PETROVYKH. "Still" sounds rather good! And does it distress you?

BEZENCHUK. Do you know what your teacher said about you?

PETROVYKH. The professor? You make me curious.

BEZENCHUK. Our Orestes shines but doesn't give out any warmth.

PETROVYKH. Is that so?

DOR. Ivan, what are you doing?

IVAN [*having removed his shoe, examining it*]. There's a nail. [*He tries to cope, using a pebble.*]

PETROVYKH. Have you been over the building site?

BEZENCHUK. I'm just back from there.

PETROVYKH. And what are your impressions of the Volga?

BEZENCHUK [*with a laugh*]. It's the end of old Russia.

PETROVYKH [*after a pause*]. The end isn't always a beginning. There's this tricky little word — chaos. As I see it, this little word has found a second home, here, in Russia.

IVAN. Do look, what an enormous nail! [*Showing everyone the nail from the sole of his shoe.*]

BEZENCHUK. Shut up, damn you! [*To* PETROVYKH.] Do you mean, it's beyond our reach?

[PETROVYKH *sees* BEZENCHUK's *scale model and goes up to it.* DOR *is there, next to it.*]

PETROVYKH. Is that it?

BEZENCHUK. That is it.

IVAN [*tearing his attention away from his shoe*]. Hell, it's beautiful . . .

PETROVYKH. It's not bad.

DOR. And do you propose the local peasants should build it? [*Slyly, watching the smoke from his cigarette.*] Pipe dreams.

BEZENCHUK. I understand you. You're afraid to believe it's possible.

DOR [*trying to smile*]. Afraid . . . Why?

BEZENCHUK [*pointing at the scale model, speaking simply*]. This is the death of you, you know.

[*Silence.* DOR, *without moving, looks at* BEZENCHUK.]

IVAN. You never talk like a human being, you know . . . it's always on a cosmic scale.

[DOR *comes right up to* BEZENCHUK *and it looks as though he is about to hit him.* ANNA *appears in the garden.*]

DOR [*sagging unexpectedly and speaking almost jokingly*]. Roman, my dear, you're mixing me up with somebody else. I'm just a poor old confectioner. Humanity loves sucking lollipops. I meet it half way. That's all. [*After a pause he goes to the house.*]

ANNA [*stopping him on the steps of the terrace*]. What's going on here?

DOR. Roman Bezenchuk was having a little joke. [DOR *goes into the house.*]

PETROVYKH [*after a pause*]. Stupid of you, Bezenchuk.

ANNA [*going up to* BEZENCHUK]. What did you say to him? [*Sharply.*] Well?

IVAN [*to* ANNA]. Leave him alone. [*Firmly.*] He's my guest. You understand?

ANNA [*with surprising meekness*]. Yes.

IVAN [*to* BEZENCHUK]. And you're a fool!

BEZENCHUK. Possibly. [*With a sigh.*] I'm outspoken. It's always getting me into trouble.

IVAN. You old maximalist, you!

BEZENCHUK [*not very aggressively*]. Minimalist. Another acid drop.

IVAN. We'll see about that. [*To* ANNA.] I have to talk to you.

ANNA [*not immediately*]. Interesting!

PETROVYKH [*to* BEZENCHUK]. Has it ever occurred to you that the truth is sometimes out of place?

BEZENCHUK. It has. But I've always dismissed the thought.

PETROVYKH. Really!

BEZENCHUK. Adam and Eve invented the lie. [*Again exploding.*] That's all! Their rule is over! [*Suddenly addressing* IVAN *sharply.*] Mind you, I'm not apologizing for anything. The truth! Nothing but the truth! [*He goes through the garden.*]

IVAN. Where are you off to?

BEZENCHUK [*belligerently*]. To your room, upstairs! [*He goes.*]

PETROVYKH [*looking from* ANNA *to* IVAN]. I shan't disturb you. [*He goes.*]

[ANNA *and* IVAN *remain alone.*]

ANNA. Well, say it.

IVAN. What?

ANNA. You wanted to make an announcement.

IVAN. You see, Anna . . .

ANNA. Do you want to leave? You want to go to the hostel.

IVAN. Why do you think that?

ANNA. I'm simply waiting for your decision. [*Thinking it over.*] I've been waiting for a long time.

IVAN. You over-estimate me. I'm not so brave.

ANNA [*with a laugh*]. Can't even Bezenchuk make you do it?

IVAN. I love you. [*Pause.*] I love you, love you.

ANNA. Then why have you closed your eyes?

IVAN. That's how I love you. With closed eyes. [*He laughs.*]

ANNA. Some time I'll open them for you.

IVAN. Heavens! When will you do this dreadful deed?

ANNA. Wait, I'll screw my courage up. [*After a pause.*] Well, what did you want to tell me?

IVAN [*speaking with decision*]. Listen, this is serious. I'll be an engineer in a month's time. No, please don't smile . . . On the Volga they're building the first tractor plant. It's a great task. Roman has so arranged things that they're asking me to go there. Do you see? And I'll go. And you'll go too. You shall go, you shall go, you shall go . . . And there, I'll be a real husband to you, and not a little boy, as here. And we shall start, you know, a new life.

ANNA [*seriously*]. New and bright?

IVAN. Don't you laugh . . . [*Looking at her.*] Stop it . . . What's all this, Anna darling, you aren't crying, are you? But why?

ANNA [*almost calmly*]. I'm sorry for you.

IVAN. For me?

ANNA. Yes, you. [*After a pause.*] And just a little for myself. [*Looking at him.*] Go right away from here.

IVAN [*frightened*]. What's come over you, Anna?

ANNA [*after a very slight pause*]. Do you promise to be a husband on the Volga? [*With a laugh.*] Husband on the Volga. It's a good title for the music hall.

IVAN [*angry*]. What's all this nonsense? Stop it at once! [*Pause.*] I don't understand what you really want.

ANNA [*speaking flatly*]. I want you to be here. Right here. I want you to sit on this little bench. I want you to myself. That's all. I want you to be mine. At my beck and call. I don't want you to go anywhere. [*She looks at him in silence.*] That's what I want.

IVAN. The way you talk — it's rather frightening.

ANNA. Ivan, my dear! [*Seizing him by the hands.*] You don't need me any more, do you, Citizen Ulybyshev?

IVAN. Do stop it . . . [*After a pause.*] First I want an answer to what I've been saying. Seriously . . .

ANNA [*unexpectedly businesslike*]. All right, Ivan, I'll think about it. About the Volga. And now go to your Bezenchuk. [*Affectionately.*] We'll be having supper soon, do you hear?

IVAN. I'm going. But you're a strange woman. [*He goes then turns again.*] You'll drive me mad, the lot of you . . . [*He goes into the garden.*]

ANNA [*thoughtfully*]. In clear Petropolis where dumb Persephone sits high we'll die.

> [PETROVYKH *emerges from behind some trees. Café music can again be heard in the distance.*]

PETROVYKH. Are you bored?

ANNA [*turning around*]. A little, as usual.

PETROVYKH. How can I amuse you?

ANNA [*smiling*]. As best you can.

PETROVYKH. Have you ever tried telling the truth?

ANNA. Never. It would be awful, I should think.

PETROVYKH. Not so very long ago, the maximalist was being very noisy about it. Shouldn't we try it too? In case it amuses you?

ANNA. I hate truth.

PETROVYKH. You're very dogmatic.

ANNA. All right, let's try it. [*With a touch of defiance.*] Are you fond of my father?

PETROVYKH. You see, even as a child, I didn't care for sweets.

ANNA. Then why do you come here?

PETROVYKH. I take pleasure in your company.

ANNA. A good beginning.

PETROVYKH [*bowing*]. There you are!

ANNA. What do you like about me?

PETROVYKH. It's difficult to make you out at first.

ANNA. A rickety virtue. And what do you dislike about me?

PETROVYKH. You're careless in your choice of lovers.

[*Momentary silence.*]

ANNA. A man is a poor judge in such matters, especially if he's . . .

PETROVYKH. An interested party?

ANNA. You're a brave man.

PETROVYKH. It's simply that I'm too old. I have nothing to lose.

ANNA. You're a flirt, apparently.

PETROVYKH. It's characteristic of men my age. [*Pause.*] Do you love your husband?

[*Silence.*]

Have you dropped out of the game?

ANNA. And what do you think?

PETROVYKH. Don't torture the boy. Let him go. I could weep for your Ivan.

ANNA [*almost desperate*]. I love him!

PETROVYKH. Yes. And you're preparing a cruel revenge.

ANNA. Why?

PETROVYKH. Because he will leave you. And you know it. [*Pause.*] I guessed as much.

ANNA [*not immediately*]. How pathetic I must seem to you!

PETROVYKH. A woman in love always seems pathetic to the outsider.

ANNA. I can't stand his superiority. One of these days I'll tell him the whole truth about myself . . . to make him weep and cry out in pain.

PETROVYKH. Rubbish, my dear! He's a fine young fellow, really. Don't break his heart.

ANNA [*as though speaking about somebody else*]. I'll probably do it all the same. [*As though complaining.*] It's difficult to control oneself.

PETROVYKH. In that case – poor old Ivan. [*Pause.*] Although one does have to pay for everything.

ANNA. I suppose I could have been nicer. [*With a hint of a smile.*] My childhood keeps coming back to me, more and more, and my mother. If I'd stayed with her, I'd be different, quite different, don't you think? After all, there was some good in me. Yes, there was! [*Looking at* PETROVYKH.] I don't like your game.

PETROVYKH. I only wanted to help you . . . to know yourself.

ANNA. He who knows himself should die. He has nothing to live for.

PETROVYKH. That's interesting!

ANNA [*addressing him sharply*]. Do you love me?

[**PETROVYKH** *laughs.*]

Answer me.

PETROVYKH. It's a rather complicated question. After all, I'm already old. [*With unaccustomed heat.*] But as for envy, yes, envy . . . The sight of a beautiful woman teetering off to meet her lover infuriates me. [*With a laugh.*] It's funny, but. in such situations I almost believe that I've been robbed.

ANNA. Poor little thing . . . You have to shout for help quite often, obviously.

PETROVYKH. Not as often as all that, unfortunately. There are hardly any beautiful women left. As for love – does it exist in our time? There's beastliness and debauchery all around. I'm tired of taking part in it. I've had enough.

ANNA. Tiredness doesn't improve a man's looks.

PETROVYKH. What can I do about it? [*After a pause.*] Are you making fun of me?

ANNA. A few moments ago, for some reason, I was afraid of you, but now . . . The stand you're taking – of the man who's out of line – it's just funny. You must admit, there's a touch of lip service about it.

PETROVYKH [*rather spitefully*]. I see, you're enjoying my truth game, aren't you?

ANNA. And I expect there's a central board where, like a lackey, you stand to attention before all the influential brutes. Of course your weary epicureanism exacts a hefty salary, doesn't it?

PETROVYKH. I didn't think you'd be so hurt by my reluctance to go down on my knees to you, my dear. [*Slightly superior.*] As for my servility, aren't you jumping to conclusions? Mm? Why shouldn't one eat a little humble-pie, so as to strike an unexpected blow later? The blow will be struck, that's obvious. Historically, it's inevitable. Well, now you can go and report all this to Number 2 Gorokhovaya – the Leningrad branch of the Secret Police. [*He bows and goes out.*]

ANNA [*alone*]. The poor peacock's tail is ruffled. And how he fascinates! [*With a laugh.*] It's a drama!

[DOR *comes out of the house, notices* ANNA *and goes to her.*]

DOR. Are you alone? On an evening like this?

ANNA [*with a rather comic intonation*]. Sit down, father. [*She looks at him searchingly.*] Do you want to have a little chat too?

DOR [*laughing suddenly*]. Why, are they being impossible? [*After a pause.*] Look, my dear, I wouldn't really advise you to encourage Svidersky. He's a nasty piece of work, you know.

ANNA. No, it's nothing . . . a bit of fun.

DOR. Oh, well.

ANNA. What shall we talk about?

DOR. Let's talk about death.

ANNA. Let's! [*With a laugh.*] Is there anything new to be said about it?

DOR. Bezenchuk has just promised it to me. Rather metaphorically, it's true. From a marxist point of view.

ANNA. Why didn't you throw him out?

DOR. I didn't want to offend your Ivan.

ANNA. You're lying.

DOR. You're right. [*He laughs quietly.*]

ANNA. Why are you laughing?

DOR. What a miserable creature man is. How has God endowed him? With cowardice, first and last. I ought to have boxed Bezenchuk's ears. Instead, I made up to that swine – put on a show as the ailing old man . . . [*Parodying himself.*] I'm just a poor old confectioner, Roman, my dear . . . I could have killed him. Instead, I side-stepped the issue as usual . . . It was here, here that I stood and faced him, I stood and hated him. Him? Yes, but I hated myself more! For my meanness, helplessness, my clowning.

ANNA. Don't upset yourself. We're all the same.

DOR. Don't you love people?

ANNA. No.

DOR. And you're right. Man is the most cunning of all the beasts. When I look at the two-legged animal, made in the same image as myself, I always think that it wants to deprive me of something. [*Putting his arms around her.*] Don't love people.

ANNA. I don't love them.

DOR. And if you should fall in love, fear him more than anyone else.

ANNA [*looking round*]. Really?

DOR. He won't spare you because you're fond of him. He'll trample on your feelings and laugh. That's how your mother treated me. Then she went off with a beggar. It was more amusing with him.

ANNA. Oh, you poor thing.

DOR. No, why? I'm eternally grateful to your mother. She left you to me.

ANNA. You've had little joy from me. [*Bitterly*.] Only Ivan's enjoying himself. For the moment.

DOR. Your Ivan's crazy. It's boys like him who put up the suicide rate.

ANNA. Why do you always jeer at him? Why do you do it?

DOR [*after a pause*]. I'm jealous of him, my child.

ANNA [*thinking it over*]. What about Svidersky?

DOR. Well, you've had fun with lots of others, but Ivan.

ANNA. Aren't I having fun with him?

DOR [*sighing*]. It's no fun with him.

ANNA. How observant you are.

[*Silence.*]

DOR. Leave him. Let him go his own way. Otherwise . . .

ANNA. What?

DOR. He'll break your heart. He'll turn you into a beggar. He'll age you. I see everything, you know, and the way you look at him . . . [*Whispering*.] There are times when I want to drive you out of the house, both of you. [*Almost groaning as he speaks*.] Why do you want Ivan — there are plenty of others?

ANNA. Why do you want me?

DOR. You're like your mother — you're beautiful. [*He looks at her for a long while*.] If you want me to, I'll drop everything: the factory and the business and Svidersky. We'll go off together to the end of the world. It must have an end somewhere! I could feast my eyes on you from early morning — how you wake up, how you go to wash, a towel in your hand, how you pour the tea out . . . There's no one but you!

ANNA. What about money? You'll be bored without, my dear.

DOR. I have three diamonds . . . And what diamonds! They'll see us through.

ANNA. I'm not talking of that. You have to coin money, and go on coining it! Without that hobby you won't last a week. You'll die of boredom.

DOR [*looking at* ANNA *lovingly*]. How well you know me . . . [*Affectionately he embraces her.*] At least do what I say, let me be better than I am. Telling lies, my dear, is the only pleasure there is. We're only happy when we tell lies.

ANNA [*smiling to herself*]. That's funny.

SVIDERSKY [*appearing in the window*]. Hasn't Ryabov telephoned yet?

DOR. No.

SVIDERSKY. I don't understand it. [*He disappears.*]

DOR [*unexpectedly*]. If I become a beggar, you'd throw me over, Annette. [*Pause.*] Will you throw me over?

ANNA [*she's too lazy and unwilling to lie*]. Nonsense.

DOR. What use am I to you, my child? Your mother left me even when I was rich.

ANNA. If you'd been poor, she might have stayed.

DOR. She might have . . . It's possible. But you take after me. You love money.

ANNA. I do love it. I can use it. Very well. So don't lose it. Please. Do you hear?

DOR [*looking at her*]. It's terrifying.

ANNA. What?

[DOR *brings out a revolver and places it on the table before him.*]

And what on earth's that?

DOR. A revolver.

ANNA. What for?

DOR [*laughing*]. I don't know.

[ANNA *goes to* DOR. *Takes the revolver and examines it.*]

ANNA. It's lovely. Did you pay a lot for it?

DOR. Quite a lot.

ANNA. Let's shoot Bezenchuk. That would be fun.

DOR [*looking at at his watch*]. It's after eleven, and no news from Ryabov. It looks like the end, my child.

ANNA. Do you think so?

DOR. He's too fond of me to come and tell me to my face that I am a beggar now.

ANNA [*shcking the revolver*]. Is it loaded?

DOR. I'm godfather to his son. Yes. [*Gaily.*] You can shoot yourself through the heart.

ANNA. The heart?

DOR [*smiling*]. Right here.

ANNA. Give it back! At once! [*She takes it from him.*]

DOR. Little idiot . . . One can always shoot oneself in the end.

ANNA. Today's my birthday. We'll assume you've given me this lovely present. Together with the little watch. Agreed? [*She embraces him.*] And don't argue with me today. All right, my dear? [*She kisses him with affection.*]

DOR [*looking at her in some surprise*]. It didn't occur to me that you cared so much for me.

ANNA [*placing the pistol in her handbag*]. There's quite a lot that doesn't occur to you.

[KATENKA *enters.*]

KATENKA. Cook is still asking, when are we having supper. The joint will be overdone, she says.

DOR. Some guests still haven't arrived. Tell her to deal with it. [*He goes towards the house, then turns back to* KATENKA.] Are you angry with me?

KATENKA [*with a wave of the hand*]. That's all right!

DOR. You're a sensible girl. [*He gives* KATENKA *some money and goes into the house with* ANNA.]

KATENKA. Oh, how disgusting! [*Thoughtfully.*] And standing in the park there are beautiful, sad statues. [*Very quietly.*] Oh dear, the world is so sad to live in, so sad . . .

KIRILL [*appearing*]. Are you meditating?

KATENKA. Why did you say that truth – that there's no truth?

KIRILL. The truth, my little friend, may exist. Only we don't believe in it.

KATENKA. You don't? And who're you?

KIRILL. Rhymesters of sorts. But I shouldn't let it upset you, Katenka. They'll exterminate us soon. Like bed-bugs.

KATENKA. Why?

KIRILL. Because we're in the way of socialism. Sad, isn't it! It can't be helped. There'll be others to replace us. More stable, more correct, in appearance. They'll build nice little houses and write verse saying that truth exists. They'll have grasping paws like this, and later on they'll start eating each other. The poor cannibals! Finally, they'll be exterminated as well. Like the bed-bugs.

KATENKA. And what will happen then?

KIRILL [*angrily*]. And then will come the dawn of happiness and justice.

KATENKA. How wicked you are.

KIRILL. Don't think I'm joking. I expect this notorious dawn will really come. It would be just stupid if it didn't, you know. I'm worn out, my little friend, and have a headache. [*Pause.*] You see, there's a man who bothers me. He also writes little verses. He's called Vladimir Mayakovsky. And this chap, Mayakovsky, bothers me. I can't forgive him.

KATENKA. Forgive him? What for?

KIRILL. His faith. That truth exists. I envy him. Don't you see?

KATENKA [*thinking it over*]. I'm sorry for you.

KIRILL [*with satisfaction*]. I'm not sorry for myself. I'm certain that I'm good for the dung-hill. [*Raising his finger.*] That's quite something!

KATENKA. I think you're always play-acting.

KIRILL. Up to a point, dear heart. [*With unexpected affection.*] You're a sensible girl, Cinderella. If I were a prince, it's your slipper I'd find. Although it's unlikely to give you any pleasure. You see, I'm observant. I know who your heart aches for. But that's going to be our secret. All right?

KATENKA [*sighing noisily*]. Keep quiet! Don't talk about it! [*She quickly runs into the house.*]

KIRILL [*thoughtfully, looking after her*]. She's run away. I must be right. Oh, Ivan, you fool . . .

[SERYOZHKA, *thirteen-years-old, enters the garden through the gate. He is dressed like a peasant.*]

SERYOZHKA [*after a look round*]. Hullo!

KIRILL. Good evening to you.

SERYOZHKA. Who are you? The host?

KIRILL. A guest.

SERYOZHKA. I see! You're drinking wine.

KIRILL. If I'm offered any.

SERYOZHKA [*listening to the music*]. And the canteen is next door.

KIRILL. Yes, all the amenities! [*Looking at the boy with interest.*] Where do you come from?

SERYOZHKA. The outskirts of Gdov.

KIRILL. You live on the land?

SERYOZHKA. No, I'm a miller.

KIRILL. An important job. And what are you doing here?

SERYOZHKA. I'm looking for my sister. Is this Citizen Dor's villa?

KIRILL. It is.

SERYOZHKA. Then I've found it! My sister lives here as a housemaid. For thirty roubles all found.

KIRILL. Katenka?

SERYOZHKA. Do you know her?

KIRILL. I love her.

SERYOZHKA. What?

KIRILL. Don't be cross. You misunderstand me. I'm her friend.

SERYOZHKA [*looking him over*]. Your coat looks shabby. Who are you?

KIRILL. A man.

SERYOZHKA. We're all men. What kind of man are you? A workman, an employee or some sort of nepman?

KIRILL. I'm a man of private means.

SERYOZHKA. Father didn't tell me about them.

KIRILL. And who's your father?

SERYOZHKA. He was a Communist.

KIRILL. Was?

SERYOZHKA [*firmly*]. Was. [*He puts a very great deal into the word.*]

KIRILL. And now?

SERYOZHKA. He's been killed. [*Without the slightest self-pity; on the contrary, with great firmness.*] I'm an orphan now.

KIRILL. Does Katenka know?

SERYOZHKA. Not yet. [*Removing his cap.*] I came to tell her.

KIRILL. Have you buried your father?

SERYOZHKA. Last Sunday.

KIRILL. But why didn't you write to her?

SERYOZHKA. Auntie Marusya – father's sister – said not to. She'll come to the funeral, she said, and lose her job in town. One's got to be careful about jobs these days. There's unemployment.

KIRILL. A wicked woman, this aunt of yours, isn't she?

SERYOZHKA. Marusya? No . . . [*With a wave of the hand.*] She's just hard-up. So am I. I live on my earnings.

[*Silence.*]

Do you know what a peasant's life is like?

KIRILL. No.

SERYOZHKA. It's misery. [*Rather low.*] The point is, father wanted to . . . change it all.

KIRILL. But who . . . killed him?

SERYOZHKA. The enemy.

KIRILL. Whose enemy?

SERYOZHKA. Ours. [*Slight pause.*] He died for the Communist party.

[KIRILL *sits down on the bench and remains silent for a long time.* SERYOZHKA *comes up to him, and* KIRILL *strokes his head.*]

KIRILL [*not loud*]. Well . . . hold on, son.

SERYOZHKA [*after a pause*]. In the evening I got back from the mill and saw father sitting in the hut, writing something in a notebook. He was enjoying himself. "What are you laughing about, dad?" I said. "Have you won a thousand roubles?" "No less", he said. "We're going over to collective farming." "What will happen now?" I asked. "Now begins the future". He was pulling my leg. I sat down to have some tea and he went out of the hut. That day I'd eaten some roach at the mill, so I was thirsty towards the evening – something awful. I sat there drinking my third cup of tea. There was a shot in the woods. It was too dark for hunting. It was evening. I thought about it and began pouring out my fourth cup. The men came into the hut. [*After a pause.*] They were carrying my father. He was dying. He was shot point-blank with a fowling piece. They laid him down and he looked at me. "I shan't see you, Sergei, in your prime", he said. "But a shot won't alter things. Your life has begun." Then the men brought Nikolai, the murderer. I remember five years back he used to play knucklebones with father. He was a wild man and handsome. And last summer he married Zinka Solodukhina and great riches. Father said to him: "Why did you shoot me, Nick? It was mean of you!" "Shooting was too good for you", said Nikolai. "You think I've sold my youth for nothing, don't you?" Then the men began beating him up but Fedya, the policeman, arrived and took him over. "Don't you beat him up", he said. "The government will deal with him. The people who persuaded him to do this will also face the firing squad." Then everyone went away. Only I and Nina Nikolayevna from the pioneers' camp stayed behind. And when it began to grow light, father opened his eyes and said for the last time: "That's it . . . I tried for the people's sake, now it's your turn. Make a success of it. Act within the law." We buried him three days later. In the rain. With flags.

KIRILL [*after a long silence*]. And what do you intend to do now?

SERYOZHKA. Now I must take his place.

KIRILL. What is his place?

SERYOZHKA. He was party member. [*Pause.*] Don't you understand?

KIRILL. Well then . . . [*Quietly.*] Live your life. Don't give way.

SERYOZHKA. Is my sister inside?

KIRILL. Yes. Shall I call her?

SERYOZHKA. No. I'll find her myself. [*He goes into the house.*]

KIRILL [*listening to the music, which is still playing*]. Oh, my head, my head . . . [*Confused.*] I appear to be completely sober. [*Getting up and thoughtfully repeating* SERYOZHKA's *words.*] "That day I'd eaten some roach at the mill, so I was thirsty towards the evening — something awful . . ." [*Clenching his fists.*] I'm worthless . . . Shit art!

YANINA [*coming into the garden*]. There you are! And I was looking for you at the station. I'm quite worn out.

KIRILL. Oh yes?

YANINA [*taking him by the hand*]. You're so restless today. Let's go home. Would you like to?

KIRILL [*slowly*]. Why? They'll be serving supper now and I'm greedy.

YANINA. I very much want to get down to work really early tomorrow. For three days now I've been stuck, I don't know why.

KIRILL. Stuck, are you? A fig to that!

YANINA. Kirill, what are you saying? Everything in our life is worthless. Everything, that is, except work. It's our last stand — you've said so yourself.

KIRILL. Rubbish! It's you who are worthless. You always were and always will be. Don't cry. I'm the same. We're all the same! [*His anger breaking through at last.*] We wanted to pocket art, to possess it in private, so that art should belong only to us . . . What idiotic pretensions! What's the image of your soul? A daub! A fig in a black square.

YANINA. Kirill, be quiet. [*Trying to kneel before him.*] I beg you, my dear . . .

KIRILL [*roaring*]. You silly idiot! Don't you really feel that time has got you by the nose? [*He roars with laughter.*]

YANINA [*getting up, swaying*]. Swine! [*She slowly goes into the house.*]

KIRILL [*raising his eyes and looking up*]. God, forgive me . . . if you exist.

[*The telephone rings.* SVIDERSKY *can be seen in the open window. Like some tiger he hurls himself towards the telephone and mumbles something.* DOR *comes running out of the garden and throws himself towards the window and* SVIDERSKY.]

DOR. Well, what is it? What is it? Tell me!

SVIDERSKY. Quiet! It's Ryabov.

CURTAIN

ACT THREE

The same evening, the same hour, the same place. SVIDERSKY *and* DOR *are at the telephone.*

DOR. What is it? Tell me!

SVIDERSKY. Quiet! It's Ryabov. [*He listens for a time and then hangs up the receiver.*]

DOR. Well?

SVIDERSKY. The meeting's over.

DOR. Go on.

SVIDERSKY. He didn't wish to give away secrets on the phone. He wants to see you personally.

DOR [*in despair clenching his fists*]. To wait till tomorrow.

SVIDERSKY. He's coming by car. He'll be here in forty minutes.

[*Pause.*]

DOR. Do you think there's any hope?

SVIDERSKY [*with a laugh*]. Hope . . . What's it worth today?

DOR. Let's be logical. [*Thinking it over.*] The fact that he wants to see us personally is a positive sign, I should say. Wouldn't you say so? After all, he could have told me by phone if the business had crashed. Well? What do you think?

SVIDERSKY [*weighing up the facts*]. Hell! On the other hand – it's very likely. You may be right!

DOR. I'm beginning to feel hopeful! [*He laughs.*] Our old boy wants to come and show off in person, how once again he's twisted them round his little finger . . . It's like him.

IVETTE [*coming out of the house*]. The bar takings amount to 800 roubles. Not bad! They've eaten all the sandwiches!

DOR. Ivette, there's a chance that Ryabov has got away with it.

IVETTE. I never doubted it.

PETROVYKH [*appearing in the garden*]. Dor, I congratulate you!

198

[YANINA *and* NOLIK *come out of the house.* EVERYONE *shakes hands with* DOR.]

DOR. No, no, this is premature. It's a bad sign.

[*A new group of* GUESTS *enter the garden through the gate. All greet* DOR *noisily. The women kiss* ANNA *who has appeared.*]

SVIDERSKY. At last! We're dying of hunger!

GUESTS. We were held up. Business, you know. Business!

DOR. We'll go and eat now. But first a glass of the special! [*Pointing to* ANNA.] To Anna. The only one.

[*All drink and greet her. There is a lot of noise.*]

And now, another drink, for a special occasion . . . Shh! . . . a secret.

A GUEST. Really?

DOR. Shh . . . [*In a whisper.*] Apparently, yes.

IVETTE. Oh, darling! . . . You drink good brandy.

DOR. You're alight! [*Looking at her in delight.*] At last! . . .

SVIDERSKY. To our host! May he never run dry!

[*New applause.*]

DOR. Just a moment. I'd like to say a few words. We're all living and working in nightmare conditions. And yet we, the businessmen and tradesmen are the rock and the foundation. Woe to the nation, if this is not understood. But if the country put us in charge, we could provide the money. [*Significantly.*] My meaning is clear.

A GUEST [*in the silence with tears in his eyes*]. Bravo!

PETROVYKH. I must protest.

[*Almost an unreal silence sets in.*]

It's unlikely that the businessman would be able to control industry. Please forgive me for saying so, but he's too petty and egotistical.

SVIDERSKY. Well, congratulations!

PETROVYKH. Unfortunately, it's the engineers who must take charge of industry and, therefore, the state.

[*Murmurs of disgust.*]

DOR. What childish pretensions! It's your talent – our organization. Other combinations are out.

PETROVYKH. I beg to differ. Planning and scientific management are the business of the intelligentsia, that is, the people capable of thinking constructively. I regret it still hasn't been understood here in Russia, in spite of the change of power. Instead of being placed at the head of industry, we're still subjected to controls.

SVIDERSKY. How absurd! The intelligentsia is pure nonsense in Russia. You mark my word, Yanka knows. She says it was Merezhkovsky, who invented the intelligentsia.

KIRILL. What, are you insulting the intelligentisia? There's a black eye for you!

SVIDERSKY. How dare you! You're drunk!

KIRILL. Hist, popinjay! [To the others.] You're all silent. [To PETROVYKH.] Bravissimo, Orestes! From the sidelines I heard your defence of the lowly and innocent but constructive thinkers. Well then, let's drink, my engineer, to the salt of the earth that's dirt cheap. [Raising his glass.] To Kirill Karetnikov! Vivat! [He drinks.]

DOR. You shout, you do nothing but shout all the time. [Controlling himself.] I'm sorry but I rather think we've had enough of you!

KIRILL. That's also true. You've had enough of me. But I've had more than enough of myself. [To DOR.] It's time to leave the stage, confectioner. You know, I only really exist because of you. Let us take hands like little children and let us vacate the place. [Pointing to PETROVYKH.] But not to him. He's rather thin-blooded.

IVETTE. Now why are you shouting here, you great big fool ... [It looks as though she is about to burst into tears.] No, it's too late.

KIRILL. Do you feel for me? And I'm sorry for you ... Where's that volcano? Extinct ... tut-tut!

SVIDERSKY. Upon my word, we ought to throw him out and stop all this.

YANINA [throwing herself towards KIRILL]. Please don't touch him. You don't know him.

KIRILL. I bear witness that your last hour is come.

[In the silence the clock in the house is heard striking.]

Twelve o'clock! For whom does the bell toll? For the private man leaving the stage. [In a deep bass.] Adieu, mon plaisir. Quiet please. I'm not only speaking of tradesmen. Who am I? A private person! [Pointing at YANINA.]

Who's she? [*Pointing at* **PETROVYKH.**] And him? Or her? [*Pointing at* **IVETTE,** *then glancing at* **ANNA.**] And her, over there? We're all private people. Private men and women – some in the arts, some in love, some in service. It's like the cooing of doves. And our, our little world is more lovely than anything on earth. [*Desperately.*] But we've been told to pack up! People don't want to tell lies any more, or to swindle, or over-charge, and so they're driving us out . . . The clock struck twelve. It's closing time.

[*Suddenly the lights go out. Enquiring, frightened whispering replaces the silence. But there is no blackout – the night is too light for that. Everything just appears ghostly and grey.*]

VOICES. Who turned out the lights? The fuse has gone! A breakdown at the power station, probably.

DOR. It's nothing! They'll bring the candles on in a moment. But first I must reply to –

KIRILL [*his bass drowning the other voices*]. Candles won't help. Darkness is darkness. On this question the power station agrees with eternity. We've used up all our credit. There will be no light. It's the end. Disperse yourselves.

[*Candles are brought on. There's a sharp change. The highlights and flickering shadows – all waver in an endless, moving pattern.*]

DOR [*clutching a candle in his trembling hand*]. All this ranting is a lie, Karetnikov, a dream, a vision! And I shall prove it. You can deprive me of my factory, my confectioner's shops, but is there really a power capable of purging the human being of the passions, the indestructible passion for personal possession, for privacy, by which a man lives as he locks the sacred door of his house . . . You fancy that people are tired of lying, swindling, over-charging. You poor innocent! For the poor two-legged animal, that's the whole point of living! Hand my factory over to the state, and from tomorrow the assistants, the workers, the salesmen will begin to swindle and cheat each other and the comrade director more than anyone else. But he won't panic. A sensible man will dip into the pocket of the state without a qualm! Why? Because he'll be controlled by his acquisitive instinct – a sacred instinct which transforms our life and makes it beautiful . . . No, we'll go on fighting. Mark my word – to quote Leonid, mark my word. We can beat a temporary retreat. We can even disguise ourselves. But to destroy us, impossible, since no decree can annul the essence, that lives in our very pores and all the cracks of the human heart and spirit. I raise this glass to our strength, to our tenacity. However black today may be, here's to our indestructible future!

[*There is an explosion of delight and shouts of approval. The bottles flash, toasts are drunk, champagne flows, all in the wavering candlelight. In the house someone has noisily struck up on the grand piano.*]

SVIDERSKY [*beside himself, running up the veranda steps and calling out*]. To supper . . . to the table!

IVETTE [*starting a popular song of the period*].

> When midnight chimes overhead
> The guests have all gone to bed.
> You see a crack in the door,
> Someone's awake in this
> House of the Dead.
>
> And soon the corridors sound
> With footsteps moving around.
> You mustn't even whisper,
> This is the song the phantoms
> Of midnight sing.

[*Holding hands, they all join in the refrain and, carrying the candles they weave their way into the house.*]

> If you drink you will die just the same,
> If you love you will die just the same,
> If you don't you will die just the same,
> So let's drink and make love.
> What you miss you will find in the grave,
> What you have you will lose in the grave,
> We shall all meet again in the grave,
> So let's drink and make love.

[*The* GUESTS *file into the house.* KATENKA *remains in the garden looking after them.*]

KATENKA. Oh, God, how frightening . . . And a bit funny . . . As though they aren't people at all.

[BEZENCHUK *quietly emerges from around the corner. Listening to what is going on in the house, he crosses the garden cautiously.*]

[*Bumping into him.*] Oh! Who's that?

BEZENCHUK. Katenka!

KATENKA. Mr Bezenchuk, is it you?

BEZENCHUK. Katenka, it's good, it's wonderful I met you!

KATENKA. Why don't you go in to supper?

BEZENCHUK. I can't stand their ugly faces.

KATENKA. But you're hungry.

BEZENCHUK. Not very. Ivan gave me something to eat . . . Poor Ivan! He's gone down . . . into the underworld.

KATENKA. You must excuse him, he has to. After all, he's the husband.

BEZENCHUK. Husband! He isn't a husband, he's a fool. [*After a pause.*] As for me . . . You know, actually I was looking for you.

KATENKA. For me?

BEZENCHUK. The last train leaves in an hour. Hardly any time left. Moscow tomorrow. It's possible we shan't meet again.

KATENKA. Mr Bezenchuk, don't say that.

BEZENCHUK. Please, you don't have to add Mister. I'm Roman, Romka for short — that's all. All right?

KATENKA. Yes.

BEZENCHUK. Now then, I've been thinking a long time, Katenka, and I've come to the conclusion that I must make you an offer . . . A purely business offer, of course. To hell with this house! Come to us, to Tsaritsyn, to the building site. Why waste your youth on these wild animals . . . You know the work there is out there? It's marvellous! And you'll get proper qualifications. You'll be of social value to us. Well, why don't you answer?

KATENKA. It would be fine, of course . . . [*After a pause.*] What about Mr Uly-byshev? Has he decided? Is he going too?

BEZENCHUK. Looks like it. Imagine the great life we'll have together!

KATENKA. If I were to get my little brother over from the country? Can he get settled there?

BEZENCHUK. We'll fix up the little brother too. I'll get you into the hostel and we'll study together in the evenings. You're going to the factory school.

KATENKA. I'd rather we went to the pictures together, the three of us, of course.

BEZENCHUK. They're going to build a circus out there. Gromov promised on oath. But, of course, the main thing is we'll be in the vanguard. We'll dedicate our life, completely and utterly, to build socialism. [*Slight pause.*] Does that mean, you're willing? Truly? What a night. Unforgettable, isn't it? It's aston-ishing, the lights out, music playing in the distance . . . I was sitting up there in Ivan's room, reading a poem. "Listen! They light the stars, it means — somebody needs them. It means — every evening there will be one star at least alight above the rooftops!" Beautiful!

KATENKA [*barely audible*]. Very.

BEZENCHUK. Katya . . . do you see me clearly.

KATENKA. No . . .

BEZENCHUK. I can see everything . . . To me you look as though you're all aglimmer in the dark. Are you dreaming of something right now, are you?

KATENKA. I don't know. I feel as though I'm floating up above somewhere and seeing everything, suddenly, everything all around . . .

[*Drunken shouts can be heard from the house.*]

BEZENCHUK. Hear them? They're still hoping for something to happen. They don't know they're doomed. Irrevocably. For ever. Oh, they'll go to the attack again – in different guises, carrying other flags. The poison of their private morality may even influence the hearts of the more unstable fighters. But historically, historically speaking they're doomed, though all the battles lie ahead! Yes, ahead – the unknown thirties, forties, fifties . . . How much there is in store for us! [*Deeply moved.*] Look, the hour of dawn approaches. A new day begins. Our day, Katenka . . . I give you my word, I've never been so worked up before. And I expect I look a fool, but what can I do, I'm totally happy . . . Yes, yes, just that. The world with all its contradictions seems to me astonishingly harmonious. I'd say even beautiful. And you, Katenka, you are my deepest sleep, my awakening, my strength. What strange, extraordinary words? . . . Yes, yes, I expect this is exactly how people felt in the Renaissance, when they smashed their damnable, dark strongholds of the Middle Ages. And I understand the strength of their love . . . And Dante and Petrarch and all the others! Here's your hand – kind, small and strong. I'll kiss it, however comic or silly it looks. How often I've laughed at Ivan and now look at me! [*He kisses her hand.*] I shan't be here tomorrow and I'm telling you I love you because I don't feel tied any more, not in any way. I have nothing more to lose. I'm off on my way, all of me, I'm all on the road. And I'm always with you, wherever I am. Always.

KATENKA [*quietly*]. Roman, my dear, don't . . . Don't talk like that. [*Almost a whisper.*] You see, I belong to someone else.

BEZENCHUK [*not immediately*]. But why?

KATENKA. I don't know. That's how it is. And I shall be true to him – for ever.

BEZENCHUK. You love someone?

KATENKA. Very much. [*Long silence.*] Do forgive me.

BEZENCHUK. Then why did you let me . . . ?

KATENKA. You talk so well, it's marvellous! It's more beautiful than in the theatre. I'm sure I'm quite, quite different now, ever so much better, because of your words.

BEZENCHUK [*pained*]. I shall probably never be able to say them again.

KATENKA. You will. After all, I'm not the only girl in the world.

BEZENCHUK [*obstinately*]. No. I shan't be able to repeat this. Not to anyone.

KATENKA. Roman, my dear, there was nothing between us, you know.

BEZENCHUK. That's what you say. [*Desperately.*] But it seemed to me I'd lived the whole of life with you – happy, sad, endless! [*Smiling sadly.*] It's always the same with me. I think it all up but actually there never was anything. [*Hurt and passionate.*] Nothing? No! You may not be mine now, but surely tonight won't stop being beautiful because of that? Surely all I felt won't vanish? No, please, that would be so unfair. We shan't forget this night, you and I. We'll preserve it in our hearts always. Isn't that true?

KATENKA [*quietly*]. Yes, my dear.

IVAN [*appearing in the garden*]. Katenka, are you there?

KATENKA. What's wrong?

IVAN. Vasilisa is waiting for you in the kitchen. Off you go.

BEZENCHUK [*aggressively*]. Look here, what an idiotic way to talk!

IVAN. Will you shut up! [*To* KATENKA.] Katenka, my dear, your brother's here. He's looking for you.

KATENKA. Seryozhka?

IVAN [*very upset*]. Please, will you try to . . . No, I can't. [*He sits down on the bench, his head in his hands.*]

KATENKA. Where is he? In the kitchen?

IVAN [*without raising his head*]. Yes.

KATENKA. Oh, God . . . [*She runs into the house.*]

BEZENCHUK [*raising him from the bench*]. Talk!

IVAN. They've killed her father.

BEZENCHUK. The kulaks?

IVAN. Yes.

[*Long pause.*]

BEZENCHUK. Then why have you left her alone?

IVAN. Romka, it's frightening, isn't it?

BEZENCHUK. And what did you expect?

IVAN. When you read about it in the papers, it's not the same. But here and now . . .

BEZENCHUK. This is not the time for discussion. Let's go to her.

[BEZENCHUK *takes him by the elbow and they go almost running behind the house. A drunken din can be heard from the dining room – shouts, and insistently the song, again and again. The shadows and the candles are on the move inside the house.*
  Against the background of the approaching song, SERYOZHKA *appears leading* KATENKA *by the hand.*]

KATENKA [*bewildered*]. What's the matter with you? Where are you taking me?

SERYOZHKA. This isn't the place, it's too noisy. Let's go a bit further. [*He leads her into the garden.*]

[*The moment they disappear, dancing* GUESTS *file out of the house. Led by* DOR, *they circle the garden in the flickering candlelight and again go back into the house, leaving* SVIDERSKY *and* ANNA *near the bench.*]

SVIDERSKY [*breathless with laughter*]. Your father's possessed by the devil. Listen, he's leading them a dance round the house again. Upon my word, he'll wear them out. What an old rascal! I've never laughed so much!

ANNA. In clear Petropolis where dumb Persephone sits high, we'll die.

SVIDERSKY [*looking at her cautiously*]. Been drinking?

ANNA. Yes. We must hurry.

SVIDERSKY. Where?

ANNA. To the gates of eternity, my beloved.

SVIDERSKY. Having fun, my sweet?

ANNA. Control yourself, you fool. Look at the night. As white as a shroud all around us.

SVIDERSKY. Well yes, the night . . . Actually there is something kind of dramatic about it. We're on board ship in a storm . . . They're singing again. The ship's sprung a leak and we're all sinking to hell.

ANNA [*listening*]. I expect that's how the rats squeal, when the ship sinks. [*Sharply.*] Are we any better than they are? [*She embraces him.*]

SVIDERSKY [*frightened, he suddenly sobers up*]. What's come over you, Annette?

ANNA. Yes. I should be pitied. There was, there was a time I was almost human . . . a long time ago when I was a child. It's possible. But it's so frightening, it's so frightening.

SVIDERSKY. What is?

ANNA. To live without hope.

SVIDERSKY. This is all nonsense. [*He kisses her.*]

[IVAN *appears in the garden and sees everthing.*]

IVAN [*foolishly raising his arms*]. What are you doing?

SVIDERSKY. Oh, hell!

ANNA. Well, now you've found out, my dear. It's the end. The end.

IVAN [*to* SVIDERSKY]. I'll kill you!

SVIDERSKY. How will you kill me? What with? Idiotic!

ANNA [*in despair*]. Ivan, here's a revolver. Shoot him! Do something irrevocable!

SVIDERSKY. You little moron!

ANNA. Shoot!

IVAN [*tears in his eyes*]. How do you mean – shoot! What nonsense. They'll take us all to the police station. [*Falls down on his knees.*] Mother in Heaven, it's pure music hall.

ANNA. Music hall? Really!

IVAN. And Petrovykh said . . . It means he knew. It means they all knew. [*On his knees, he stretches out his hands to her.*] Who are you, tell me, Anna. Why, why are you like this?

SVIDERSKY. I expect I'm not wanted here. [*To* IVAN.] Pull yourself together, Ulybyshev, it's all so trivial. [*He embraces him and whispers in his ear.*] But if you finally do decide to shoot me, give me a shout. I'll be in the billiard room. [*He goes.*]

IVAN. Nothing makes sense. [*He looks at* ANNA.] I believed in it so much – in love, you know. But it turns out to be a music hall joke . . . [*He weeps.*] A lot of nonsense.

ANNA. No, it's no music hall joke. You want to get off lightly, my dear. Go on crying! These aren't tears? I thought you could do better. [*She takes his hands.*] Listen, my husband, during the six months we've been married, as well as Svidersky, there were also Yurka Stilyanudy, Kira Lyutov . . .

IVAN [*looking at her in terror*]. Why, why are you telling me this?

ANNA [*not immediately*]. I'm telling you this out of pity. To shock you and to make you go for ever. So that you don't crawl back on your knees to forgive me.

[*IVAN looks at her for a long time and then, afraid, puts his hands over his eyes.*]

[*A statement.*] You don't like me. That's understandable. [*With a laugh.*] Are you leaving, my dear?

IVAN. Remember how kind I used to be? Till you die, remember that. [*He runs into the house.*]

ANNA. Well, now there's nothing more to wait for. You're played out . . . my sweet.

[*A very tall and thin old man enters by the garden gate. He wears a boater and carries a cane. It is* RYABOV. *Listening to the noise, the singing, the odd shouts, for a moment he stands swaying, then slowly sinks down on the steps and begins to weep bitterly like a child, who cannot be consoled.*]

RYABOV. It's finished. Dear God, it's all finished.

ANNA [*running up on to the terrace and opening the doors into the house, she calls out almost in triumph*]. Father, Ryabov has come!

[*The* GUESTS, DOR, SVIDERSKY, PETROVYKH, KIRILL, YANINA *and* IVETTE, *all come running out of the house, with candles in their hands.*]

DOR [*his collar undone, his tie askew*]. At last! [*Suddenly laughing.*] And what the hell are you doing there on all fours?

SVIDERSKY [*in a whisper*]. He's crying.

DOR [*shouting*]. Ryabov!

RYABOV [*in a thin voice*]. Dear Mr Dor, in accordance with the decision taken today, our business is in liquidation as from the first of July of this year. The whole property, of which an accurate inventory will be made, has been requisitioned by the Leningrad Workers' Cooperative.

[*A long silence.*]

PETROVYKH. It was to be expected.

[*The electric light comes on.*]

KIRILL. Let there be light. From us to you with knobs on!

RYABOV [*breaking out*]. Mr Dor, I have been with you for thirty years! What am I now going to do with myself? I counted on, I was certain of being rewarded for my affection, my doglike devotion. God, what now! [*Sobbing.*] What does it mean – was I deceived? [*He seizes* DOR *by his coat.*] Deprived of everything?

DOR [*throwing him off*]. Be quiet, you idiot . . .

SVIDERSKY. Just a moment! Is this decision final?

DOR [*angrily*]. They don't need eclairs and meringues. Expensive! At best they'll arrange for an issue of oatcakes. Quite right! Well, that's that. [*Approaching* ANNA.] I'm sorry this happened on your birthday. Forgive me, my dear.

ANNA. What? Have they scotched your tail, daddy? [*Desperately.*] It's you, you we have to blame for everything! Nepman. What a funny word. [*Looking at* DOR *with hatred.*] Damned nepman!

PETROVYKH [*coming up to her*]. You deserve a good thrashing.

ANNA. No. That's not enough. [*She runs off into the house.*]

DOR. Well, it doesn't matter now . . . [*to* IVETTE]. And when are you leaving?

IVETTE. I'm not easily scared. I'll wait a bit.

[BEZENCHUK *and* KATENKA *enter the garden.* SERYOZHKA *stops a little way behind them.*]

DOR [*on seeing* BEZENCHUK, *he is momentarily possessed by anger*]. So you're here too? Come to laugh over me, you and your brigade of *sans culottes*. You think you've won?

BEZENCHUK [*calmly*]. Speak up, Katenka.

KATENKA. Mr Dor, I can't possibly stay with you any more. We've had a misfortune and my brother's come to fetch me.

DOR. You're running away too? [*Pointing at* BEZENCHUK.] With him? In a hurry to make good? [*He pours out a glass of cognac and hands it to* KATENKA.] Have a drop of brandy, Katyusha. It's special from Erivan. As for you, Ivette, my dear, put on her apron. Pick up the crumbs from the table, every single one of them.

BEZENCHUK. What a filthy thing to say.

SERYOZHKA [*running up to* DOR]. You haven't the right to jeer. [*Trying to find the words.*] Exploiter! At home it's people like you who shoot people! I know you!

DOR [*hurling himself at* BEZENCHUK]. Now, where's that magic castle of yours? [*He snatches the scale model from him, throws it on the ground and treads on it.*]

KATENKA. Don't you dare!

BEZENCHUK [*guessing right*]. It means they've shut up shop! It's understandable.

KATENKA [*picking up the scale model and trying to put it in order*]. You think we can't manage without you? That we shan't be able to carry on. Is that it?

DOR. Bitch!

IVETTE. Aren't you ashamed of yourself – in front of the servants! You're being thoroughly neurotic! [*She slaps his face.*] Do come to your senses!

KIRILL. What a girl!

DOR. And where's Ivan? He wants to take my daughter away . . . [*Rushing about in despair.*] She'll go away now . . . with them.

IVAN. [*Running out of the house, with a travelling bag*]. Let's go, Romka . . . Quick, let's get out of here!

[*There is a shot. Silence. Only* SERYOZHKA *instinctively throws himself towards* BEZENCHUK *aware that he will be his friend for years to come.*]

SERYOZHKA [*hugging* BEZENCHUK]. There's shooting!

DOR [*as though coming to his senses*]. My pistol . . . Anna, my darling!

[DOR *runs toward the house. The appearance of* NOLIK *on the steps of the terrace stops him.* NOLIK *is silent. He is terrifying.*]

[*Quietly.*] What's happened?

NOLIK. Miss Dor looked in the mirror and she said: "What, my sweet?" She gave me this note, then she winked and shot herself with a revolver.

DOR. My dear child! [*He runs into the house.*]

PETROVYKH [*to* SVIDERSKY]. Get a doctor at once! The second house on the right . . .

[SVIDERSKY *runs out through the garden gate. Some of the* GUESTS *follow* DOR *into the house.*]

YANINA. But why so . . . pitiless?

IVETTE. The note! [*She takes the note from* NOLIK *and reads it.*] "Let me shoot myself. Good luck, Ivan , my dear." Good God . . .

[*Automatically she looks at her watch and drops all her pills. Slowly she enters the house, supported by* KIRILL.]

PETROVYKH [*going to* IVAN, *who stands alone*]. Go to her. Ulybyshev, why are you standing here?

IVAN [*staring with unseeing eyes*]. You knew as well. Go away . . . I hate you too, you know.

PETROVYKH. Well, that's logical. [*To* BEZENCHUK.] She was careless in her life. Much too careless. [*He goes into the house.*]

[SVIDERSKY, *accompanied by a* DOCTOR, *goes into the house.* KATENKA, SERYOZHKA, BEZENCHUK *and* IVAN *remain in the garden.*]

KATENKA. What a thing to happen!

IVAN [*firmly*]. It had to happen.

BEZENCHUK [*exploding*]. Are you out of your mind? How can you talk like that? Why, even I am sorry for her!

IVAN [*with a laugh*]. You poor thing, what do you know? It's all a game. Have you watched roulette? It's a game. Even her death.

KATENKA. How can you, Mr Ulybyshev? After all, a living human being.

IVAN. Really?

[KIRILL *comes out of the house.*]

BEZENCHUK. Is she alive?

KIRILL. She'll recover. Her aim was very erratic. She wasn't sober.

IVAN. You see? It's a game . . .

SERYOZHKA [*impatiently*]. Why are we standing about? Shall we go?

BEZENCHUK. Let's go. The last train's due. [*Looking around.*] Look, it's quite light. [*Suddenly anxious.*] Well, so starts our famous journey . . . [*He laughs.*] Through the twentieth century!

SERYOZHKA [*admiring him*]. Not so fast . . . I'm coming with you.

BEZENCHUK. Of course! And with me, little brother, you'll do all right!

KATENKA [*to* IVAN]. Let's go . . . come, give me your hand, Mr Ulybyshev.

IVAN. Katenka . . . [*Not immediately.*] I don't think I shall ever be kind again. No, never again.

KIRILL [*coming up to* SERYOZHKA]. Good luck, miller. Live your life to the full.

SERYOZHKA [*pointing at* BEZENCHUK]. He and I . . . we'll do our best.

BEZENCHUK [*to* KIRILL]. What's keeping you here? Come with us.

KIRILL. It's too late. [*Thoughtfully.*] I'm like a used coin. The letters don't stand out, I'm all blurred. [*To* KATENKA.] Don't take on – things will work out your way. [*With a wave of his hand at them.*] Well, off you go!

BEZENCHUK. We're going . . .

[*They go.*]

KIRILL. And perhaps, I might . . .

[YANINA *appears out of the house.*]

YANINA [*approaching* KIRILL *and sitting down meekly beside him*]. Kirill, it's all so awful . . .

KIRILL. Oh, Yanka, I'm sorry for you. Here you sit, with your painted face, cropped hair, kindly, silly . . . You're thinking up something, working something out . . . And none of it's worth a bean now.

FINAL CURTAIN

The Twelfth Hour

The Twelfth Hour was the first play by Aleksei Arbuzov professionally produced in Britain. I used the second act in Russian-by-Radio broadcasts on the BBC Third, as it was then known. Later Arbuzov and I met when he came over as a tourist and on 26 March 1964 he wrote a letter to Frank Hauser who had decided to put the play on at the Oxford Playhouse.

First, about Chekhov's influence, Arbuzov wrote in the letter, as understood by the Moscow Arts Theatre there was a minimum in *The Twelfth Hour*. But there was no denying the influence of *Chekhov through the prism of Meyerhold*. (Refer to Meyerhold's letter to Chekhov regarding *The Cherry Orchard*, published in the Chekhov Volume of Literaturnoye Nasledstvo.)

The setting was Leningrad "or rather Petersburg . . . always a fantastic enigma of a town, a somewhat unreal ghostly symbol, offspring of the incomprehensible white nights." Gogol in Nevsky Prospect and Dostoyevsky in *White Nights* gave expression to the Russian intelligentsia's idea of Petersburg, Arbuzov went on. Meyerhold followed in this tradition in his production of Lermontov's *Masquerade*.

Meyerhold's theme which ran through all his productions was *The Feast At The Time Of The Plague*. That is the dominant mood of *The Twelfth Hour*: "a tragi-comic harlequinade of masks, the fantastic white night, the mysterious semi-darkness and wavering candlelight, the line of dancing half-drunk guests and the pointless shot." The writers and painters closest to the mood were Hoffmann, Blok, possibly Edgar Allen Poe, and Magnasco, Bosch, possibly Blake. Arbuzov added that his favourite English play was Shaw's *Heartbreak House*.

The play should go crescendo with a slow, slightly elegiac opening and an explosive ending, excluding the final three interchanges of dialogue. In the increasing attack and speed of the overall tempo (as in Ravel's *Bolero*) there should be changes in rhythm; there should also be visual contrasts, for example, white night dusk and a blood-red sunset.

Arbuzov continued: "I remember 1929 was for our country as important as 1917, because 1929 was the end of Old Russia. With collectivization and the first great constructions of the five year plan, it seemed as though the whole of Russia was on the move. The stations were full of people on their way to unknown destinations. Young people were mad with enthusiasm. The old way of life, its supports and structure had all collapsed but as yet there was no new way of life. It was like a disturbed, gigantic ant heap. All that lies outside the play. But it should live in the play," he wrote.

I should explain, since it is not generally known, that NEP stands for New Economic Policy, an emergency measure introduced by the Soviet Government of 1921 to restart the economy in the post-revolutionary chaos. In theory everything belonged to the people but during NEP, private or capitalist enterprise was encouraged by subsidy. The play opposes community interests with private, exclusive values in art as well as in industry and manufacture at a time of extreme tension when nepman was also a term of abuse.

Arbuzov ended his letter to Frank Hauser with a detailed description of the individual characters. They were very real and had "psychological edge and depth", those who belonged to the future as well as the past. When young he had met a woman like Anna whom it took some time to forget. He recommended that the youthful Don Quixote, i.e. Bezenchuk, should have a sense of humour.

The fascinating production problem of *The Twelfth Hour* is the balance between the reality of the people Arbuzov has created and his overall design of a grotesque "danse macabre". In Frank Hauser's production, the characters were more human than grotesque. I remember Arbuzov was very surprised, especially by the passion of the political arguments. He mentioned this to me sixteen years later: "It's funny, the Russian actor playing Bezenchuk was mostly interested in his love scene with Katenka." In a later conversation after I had watched with great interest his *Six Loves* on Moscow television, he mentioned the difficulty young Russian actors had in understanding some of his plays, especially his early plays where private and public life was chaotically and passionately one and the same thing.

LOVELY TO LOOK AT!

An optimistic comedy in two parts

Moyo Zaglyadeniye (*Lovely to Look At!*) was first produced in 1973 at the Dagestan Gorky Russian Theatre of Drama. It was directed by B. Vinogradov and B. Levin.

The play was first performed in Moscow on 5 June 1976 at the Miniature Theatre. It was directed by B. Shchedrin, designed by E. Emoiro and the music was composed by D. Atovmyan. It was billed as "An Optimistic Comedy".

There are no cast lists or photographs available.

CHARACTERS

VASYA LISTIKOV, twenty-six-year-old employee of a large institution; a remarkable young man

DARLING 2, his solicitous wife, twenty-three

SEVA POLONSKY, Vasya's close friend and colleague, who displays a lot of energy at thirty

DARLING 3, eighteen-year-old student, lovely to look at and madly in love with Vasya

SERGEY SERGEYEVICH, her unhappy father, nationally famous television announcer of the central network

AVENIR NIKOLAYEVICH, extremely widely-read intellectual and librarian of the Frunze district, about forty-five

AKIM LISTIKOV, Vasya's father, a sincere and uncompromising old man

GENNADY, Akim's second son, a limp young man

ALICIA, Akim's daughter, who will most probably make her mark in the arts soon

ALEKSANDRA ALEKSEYEVNA (AUNTY SASHA), a very nice woman of fifty and a capable lift operator

VALENTINOV, her nearest and dearest, an ex-alcoholic

AURORA IVANOVNA VALOIS, of uncertain age, a departmental head in Vasya's institution

[*The play should be played with great flamboyance.*]

ACT ONE

Scene One

The remarkable young man, **VASYA LISTIKOV**, *is rushing home from work. He carries a worn dispatch case and a shopping bag with groceries. He feels cheerful and lighthearted. Spring is on the move and there doesn't seem to be anything to worry about. Swinging his dispatch case, he partly dances and sings as he approaches home.*

VASYA.   You're alive, so what's the fuss?
Life's a pleasure you enjoy.
See the people going past,
Surely some of them are nice!
Meeting fools is not too bad,
Silly people make you laugh.
Just beware of dreary bores,
Know that only death is worse.
No, don't fuss, old man, don't sulk.
Look, it's lovely weather now.
Even if it were to rain,
Leaping puddles can be fun.
You're alive, so what's the fuss?
Life's a pleasure you enjoy.
See the people going past,
Surely some of them are nice!

[As he hurries home, enthralled by everything, **DARLING 3** *appears in the garden of the seven-storey block where he lives. No words can describe her. Youth and beauty are so combined that young men cannot tear their eyes away from her. At the same time, the lift operator,* **AUNTY SASHA**, *still a very nice woman, is sitting on her bench by the entrance. She notices* **DARLING 3**, *who approaches her shyly.]*

DARLING 3. No? . . . Isn't he home?

AUNTY. He'll be here soon. It's about his time.

DARLING 3. I brought you some chocolate with raisins. For tea.

AUNTY. Sit down. *[Makes room for her on the bench.]* I don't eat chocolate. *[Thinks.]* Valentinov can have it.

219

DARLING 3 [*anxious*]. Who is Valentinov?

AUNTY. A man.

DARLING 3 [*suddenly*]. I'm so unhappy!

AUNTY. Calamity! You are so comely but he's married.

DARLING 3. I only want to see him as he comes home, wearing his cap, swinging his shopping bag with the bottle of yoghourt in it. [*Thrilled.*] He buys different sorts of yoghourt! I noticed him first from the window through my binoculars. He was lugging home five bottles of mineral water in the rain. He's so handsome. I have looked at the world through binoculars as a child and ever since. I'm very shy. Long ago I knew that personal contacts were not for me. No! . . . So I even chose to study ancient Greek, you know. I can be frank only with you. You're a lift operator, and of course, you understand me. Thank you for letting me sit here and take a little peep at him. I live in the house opposite, and tomorrow without fail I'll bring you some chocolate mousse.

AUNTY. All right. Valentinov will eat it.

DARLING 3 [*clapping her hands*]. It's him! It's him! . . . He's coming . . . [*She rises and goes a little to the side.*]

VASYA [*running in*]. Aunty Sasha, I salute you! Has Darling arrived? The point is I must have forgotten my key. I can't get into the flat. And obviously I'm doomed to wait for her here, in your pleasant company. [*He sees* DARLING 3, *looks at her puzzled, waves to her and shrugs.*] Unless my memory plays tricks, I'm sure we haven't met.

DARLING 3 [*almost fainting from the thrill and the embarrassment of it*]. No . . . No . . . Thank you for your kind attention.

VASYA. Aunty Sasha, I'm very worried. The third cashier at our store is away sick for the second week. We have queues and we fight over all sorts of things. Today I nearly dropped a bottle of yoghourt. [*Turns to* DARLING 3.] But you have to concentrate to choose 200 grammes of cheese, you know. [*A little stern.*] I still don't think I've ever seen you before.

DARLING 3 [*quietly*]. Probably not.

VASYA. Never mind, would you like a lemon waffle? [*He takes a small package from his shopping bag and holds it out to her.*] Try it, please.

DARLING 3 [*half-fainting*]. Oh, thank you . . .

AUNTY. I'm having roast veal tomorrow. I shall be fifty.

VASYA [*with insight*]. I shall be delighted to wish you many happy returns of the day. I always like sitting here with you, when I lock myself out.

AUNTY. Vasya, you're a dear! You're a hero! If only more people were like you.

[DARLING 3 *moves a few steps away either because she is embarrassed or because she wants to look at* VASYA *adoringly from afar.*]

VASYA. I always try and save Darling in every way I can from doing the shopping. She comes home from work very tired. But I am very curious to see what's available from day to day. I feel quite thrilled when certain groceries appear.

DARLING 3 [*aside*]. Dear God! Dear God! What a darling he is with his shopping bag! I can see a bunch of tulips and two small cucumbers and there must be something fascinating in that little pink parcel. It's touching how he loves her, his Darling . . .

[AURORA IVANOVNA VALOIS, *a woman of uncertain age, approaches moving slowly.*]

VALOIS. Glad to see you on duty, Aleksandra Alekseyevna. Listikov, what are you doing here?

VASYA. Waiting for my wife. I can't get into my flat without her. Allow me to present you with two tulips from my bunch.

VALOIS. Listikov, you're sucking up to me.

VASYA [*in despair*]. No, why? It's with all my heart. You're the head and my senior colleague, therefore near and dear to me. Why shouldn't I give you two tulips?

VALOIS. I think I believe you. You're a well brought-up and nice man, even if you are only twenty-six. [*Smells the flowers.*] Pretty little flowers. [*Looks attentively at* DARLING 3.] I've never seen you here before.

DARLING 3. I simply came to see how people come home from work . . .

AUNTY. She's a very earnest student and the daughter of the famous Sergey Sergeyevich.

VALOIS. You mean, him?

AUNTY. The same.

VALOIS. I think that's very interesting. And I'll be going home now.

VASYA. No, wait! . . . I should like to take advantage of our unexpected meeting. [*Passionately.*] Give us back our Stripikov. Soon it will be a year since his posting to distant Ustegorsk. It is our advance post, I know that. But it is the back of beyond. I could weep for poor old Stripikov, who plays an excellent game of volley ball. But as he writes in his letters, there's no one to play volley ball with. I shan't even mention the symphony concerts he was used to as a boy and ever since. And, of course, I'm not saying that their one-room flat is far too small for him and his clever wife. My friend has laboured in the back of beyond for a whole year. Please put his case to the powers that be.

VALOIS [*after a pause*]. You have made a very good speech. I have listened to you with great interest. You have now risen in my estimation. It gives me great pleasure to have responsive members of staff. You can be certain that I shan't forget you.

VASYA [*thrilled*]. What about Stripikov?

VALOIS. I shan't forget him either. I find you very congenial.

[*Unhurried she goes into the house.*]

AUNTY. Well said, Vasya! It's profound.

DARLING 3. I don't know you at all. I don't know your Stripikov. But I felt happy listening to your generous and heartfelt words.

VASYA. And I am tremendously inspired. Stripikov's family is tired of waiting. And we, his colleagues, will be glad to greet him as he returns to our ranks. Yes, though I have forgotten my key, tonight has started awfully well. [*Looks round.*] But what's that? There's a man coming whom I don't like at all. It would be mean to run away. He lives quite far and he's bound to be upset if I'm not at home.

[AVENIR NIKOLAYEVICH *emerges. A faint smile hovers on his lips. As usual he is filled with hidden sadness.* AUNTY SASHA *and* DARLING 3 *watch what happens from afar.*]

AVENIR [*smiling sadly*]. It's me.

VASYA. No doubt. [*Cautious.*] But it would be very interesting to know what brings you here?

AVENIR [*he's full of poison*]. Once again it's my desire to alleviate somehow the grief of your poor wife.

VASYA [*politely*]. My ex-wife. It's most important I should explain that Lyudmilla and I were divorced two years ago.

AVENIR [*with a sad smile*]. Lyudmilla! . . . Can you speak the name of the woman, you so recently and tenderly called Darling, with such provoking indifference?

VASYA. But I can't call her Darling after I've married another Darling! [*Heatedly.*] Believe me, I greatly valued Lyudmilla's unique personality. After all, I did marry her . . . Darling has always meant to me . . .

AVENIR [*furious*]. How dare you call her Darling? Who gave you the right to speak of her with such provoking familiarity?

VASYA [*heatedly*]. Yes, yes, of course, you're right. I have many failings. But I keep trying. No doubt I shall mend in due course.

AVENIR. In due course! Oh, yes. That's a long way away. In the meantime, I have come to the conclusion that you must give her back the napkin with the cat on it which you took two years ago. I found out this week that she associates her happiest moments with that napkin.

VASYA. But my mother gave the napkin to me.

AVENIR [*passionately*]. Moreover, you really should not walk on the right-hand side of the Boulevard, where her favourite bakery is. You realize, don't you, that every meeting with you has a traumatic effect upon us? She buys her black bread and high-calorie rolls there, only there at the bakery.

VASYA [*faintly*]. It's awfully sad, but I'm having a pair of corded trousers made there, only there by the tailor.

AVENIR. If you had the slightest decency, you would have arranged long ago to have your corded trousers made somewhere else. [*Unbearably sad.*] I'm madly in love with your wife. I'm a simple Soviet librarian, but I'm madly in love with her. For two years every day I have brought her books and watched her suffer and develop and stay awake all night. Believe me, I'm utterly worn out, I blame myself all the time. Oh, life is monstrously complicated, painfully complicated. There's only one thing left for us, Comrade Listikov, compassion. And secret suffering during the long, sleepless nights.

VASYA [*deeply moved*]. But why should you suffer? Why not confide your secret to her? Tell her you love her.

AVENIR [*with sad exclamation*]. What? Crudely snap the fine threads that bind me to her? And you can sink so low as to suggest that to me? No, I'm a plain, simple Soviet librarian and I'd rather carry my cross in silence. In silence, do you hear?

VASYA [*depressed*]. I hear you.

AVENIR. Will you give the napkin back?

VASYA. I will. [*Stepping back to the bench where* AUNTY SASHA *sits.*]

AVENIR. That's better, that's better, Comrade Listikov. [*He laughs bitterly.*]

VASYA [*to* AUNTY SASHA]. He's a remarkable man and the best librarian in the district. But he can be heavy going.

[DARLING 2 *comes running briskly towards the house.*]

DARLING 2 [*seeing* AVENIR]. What! You here again? But I've done what you asked and I don't go to the Garden Ring Road, now I know the traumatic effect it might have on Lyudmilla.

VASYA [*casually, as it were*]. You know, Darling, today he wants the napkin with the cat on it. [*Searchingly.*] Let's give it to him.

DARLING 2. All right, we'll give it to him. But why aren't you at home?

VASYA. I'm waiting for you, my sunshine. I forgot my key.

DARLING 2. You'll drive me mad. You've got the wrong tie on again and, of course, no clean hanky! Go and have a shower at once. I must have a serious talk with you. [*To* AVENIR.] I'll try and find the napkin with the cat on it. You mustn't despair.

[*Briskly she runs into the house.*]

AVENIR [*bitterly to* AUNTY SASHA]. And he swopped his wife for that creature. God, how blind people are!

VASYA [*gesturing and bowing in embarrassment*]. Please don't upset yourself.

AVENIR. But I'll be back. [*Smiling sadly, he goes.*]

[VASYA *attentively looks at* DARLING 3, *finally shrugs and runs into the house.*]

DARLING 3 [*in despair*]. Dear God, what is this? He sees me many times a day, but keeps shrugging and being puzzled and running away! Is that Darling of his so very superior to me that he can't even remember me?

AUNTY [*suddenly fierce*]. Well, I don't like her! . . . I said so to Valentinov, I don't like this Darling of his and that's that. Our Vasya is a man with advanced views. He should have love and affection. Instead, she bullies him all day – go and have a shower, why are you wearing the wrong trousers? He should be hugged but instead she removes his socks and rushes off to launder them. Well, she is not affectionate, she's cold.

DARLING 3. While I . . . I . . . Aunty Sasha, if only I had him, how I'd hug and kiss him and never stop.

[*The elderly and absurdly splendid* VALENTINOV *comes marching through the garden towards* AUNTY SASHA.]

VALENTINOV [*briskly*]. Well, Sasha, what's for supper tonight?

AUNTY [*exulting and frightened*]. Oh, dear God, here's Valentinov. Now, Darling, take a good look and remember – that's Valentinov.

DARLING 3. Hullo! [*She stops, frightened.*]

AUNTY [*gazing fondly at this man*]. He's from the House of Writers.

VALENTINOV. I do all their repairs. [*He winks and laughs like a child.*]

AUNTY. Come, I'll give you something to eat, Semyon.

VALENTINOV [*merry and stern*]. Pull yourself together Sasha, and don't call me Semyon? We haven't been married for seven years. I'm not your Semyon. I'm Comrade Valentinov.

AUNTY [*not at all upset*]. Dear God! I can't even make a joke. Come along, Valentinov.

[*They go out arm-in-arm.*]

DARLING 3. And I'm left alone. Completely alone. But I'm nice. I'm pretty. I'm a dear.

Music. The Gallop.

BLACKOUT

Scene Two

The action is immediately transferred to VASYA's *small flat where he lives with his* DARLING 2.

VASYA [*running in happy*]. Well, here I am home at last! Home is one room but I love coming home! Darling and I built it together. It was like a fairy tale. We joined a cooperative and moved in at last. But where is Darling? Probably in the bathroom doing my laundry. I'm a happy man!

[*Enter* DARLING 2 *in a very feminine little dressing-gown.*]

DARLING 2. Go and have a shower at once. You're covered with dust. Here are your clean shirt and your socks.

VASYA. In a moment. I'll just take the groceries out of my shopping bag. And the tulips must be put in water . . . I gave two of them to Comrade Valois. She walked past, you know, and I enjoyed giving her two flowers.

DARLING 2. You'll drive me mad.

VASYA. And let's hurry up and find that napkin with the cat on it and send it to Darling. Avenir suffers so much, it hurts me to look at him.

DARLING 2. My dear Vasya, perhaps you should go back to her?

VASYA. Darling, I can't. She was always telling me she was sacrificing her life for me. All the time I felt sort of embarrassed. Uncomfortable sort of. And then every day she said I'd drive her mad. [*Smiles happily.*] That's when I met you, Darling.

DARLING 2 [*touched*]. Oh, dear God! If you like, I'll go and shake the rug on the balcony? You aren't ill, are you? Perhaps I should put a mustard plaster on your chest?

VASYA. Certainly not. I'm quite fit, Darling.

[*Enter the thirty-year-old* **SEVA**, *businesslike but very handsome.*]

SEVA. You here? All the better.

VASYA. Just a moment, Seva, how did you get in?

SEVA. Yesterday I put your key in my pocket, quite without thinking.

VASYA. We're so absent-minded, it'll be the death of us. I forgot my key because I'm absent-minded. You took it because you're absent-minded. We must pull ourselves together.

SEVA. Quite right. I could do with a bite of something.

DARLING 2. There's sausage. Vasya has just brought some.

VASYA [*good-natured*]. Only leave some for me. [*Affectionately.*] I know you! [*Happy.*] After my shower and Seva's tea, we'll go to work on our new method of accountancy.

SEVA [*eating sausage*]. Well, we'll sort that out later . . .

DARLING 2. We'll see.

VASYA [*enthusiastic*]. We should stop being irresponsible! We should work at our new method of accountancy every evening. You realize, they're relying on us, they're waiting for us. We mustn't weaken. Remember, this work has brought us three together. It has forged our friendship.

SEVA. That's true enough but I'd rather not advertise my involvement.

VASYA [*stern*]. Why not?

SEVA [*with a diplomatic smile*]. Comrade Kapetchenko took a summary glance at our method and was not duly enthusiastic. And Kapetchenko will be our next departmental head.

VASYA [*with insight*]. Honestly, I'm very worried by your opportunism. Our job is to stand firm in the face of Kapetchenko's civil service stupidity, and to persuade him by our actions. Now I'll go and take my shower, Darling.

[*He goes.*]

SEVA [*looking after him*]. He's a really splendid chap!

DARLING 2 [*sadly*]. Yes. [*Pause.*] Would you like more sausage?

SEVA. Certainly not. We'll leave some for Vasya.

[*He gets up, looks fondly at* **DARLING** 2 *and kisses her with confidence.*]

DARLING 2 [*after a deep breath*]. Have you got a clean hanky? I could wash it for you.

SEVA. You know, there's no point in waiting. We must tell him everything today. Decently and frankly.

DARLING 2. But supposing it has an awfully traumatic effect on him?

SEVA [*proudly*]. We'll be telling him the truth. He'll appreciate that.

DARLING 2 [*rather doubtful*]. He may not appreciate it.

SEVA [*heatedly*]. I swear he will. You've been married two years and you don't know him. He's a marvellous chap, quite super, you know.

DARLING 2. If he is, why am I leaving him?

SEVA [*trying to explain it to her*]. You've fallen madly in love with me. That's the point. [*Kisses her again.*] Got that?

DARLING 2 [*affectionately*]. I think you will lose this button on your jacket. Give it to me, I'll sew it on properly.

SEVA [*listening*]. He's coming back. Pull yourself together and tell him everything immediately. In the meantime, I'm going out for a breath of air. And remember, there's nothing worse than lies. [*Disappears on the balcony.*]

VASYA [*entering*]. I like taking a shower after the day's work. I feel easy and cheerful. Where's Seva?

DARLING 2. In the meantime, he's having a breath of air.

VASYA. Look, Darling, I'm very worried by his materialistic outlook. It keeps breaking out. It wasn't noticeable before.

DARLING 2 [*embarrassed*]. Yes . . . Before it didn't break out so often.

VASYA. There, you see, it breaks out more often now. Seva hasn't any real enthusiasm, any courage, I mean, all those qualities he used to have.

[**DARLING** 2 *tries to say something.*]

Kapetchenko has brushed our work aside and now, you see, Seva's afraid! First, it is not a fact that Kapetchenko will be our departmental head. Romanov may be appointed. He's shown a very lively interest in our work.

[**DARLING** 2 *again tries to tell all.*]

These reshuffles ought not to influence us. Our job is to prove to everyone that our new method of accountancy is progressive and up-to-date.

DARLING 2. Dear Vasya, I don't love you any more.

VASYA [*smiles*]. What?

DARLING 2. I don't love you any more.

VASYA. What do you mean – you don't love me? You loved me a moment ago. Now you don't. It doesn't tie up. Stop making silly jokes. Besides, it isn't true. [*Worried.*] Now, please!

DARLING 2. No, it is true.

VASYA [*smiles and winks at her*]. You're telling lies!

DARLING 2 [*in despair*]. You'll drive me mad. I've decided to fall in love with a normal man.

VASYA. No, wait! It can't be. Together we decided never to part.

DARLING 2. So what! All that's finished now.

VASYA [*very quietly*]. Is it true? Are you going to leave me?

DARLING 2. What else can I do?

VASYA. Well, now . . . Well, now . . . [*Tries to raise his morale.*] You mean, I could have the top window open all night?

DARLING 2. Of course, my dear . . .

VASYA [*sadly*]. Well, you know, it's worked out very well . . . Who would have thought . . . [*Flaring up.*] No, wait . . . Why? Why have you stopped loving me?

DARLING 2. That's what happened. Please forgive me.

VASYA. No, no, I understand up to a point. I have so many failings, I'm quite surprised sometimes. I suppose you met a remarkable man and fell deeply in love with him. Who is it?

SEVA [*entering*]. Me.

VASYA [*very surprised*]. Him? [*Looks at SEVA with interest for a long time.*] Why? [*Shrugs.*] It's very unexpected. [*Hurt.*] I must say straight out, you have both surprised me very much. [*Pause. Looks at them again.*] I hope you aren't joking?

SEVA. No, really, Vasya! To joke about such matters would not be nice! [*Briskly.*] Now, let's keep calm and sort it all out. No panic.

VASYA. Well, it's a good idea.

SEVA. First of all, you're my best friend and you can always trust me. No one can help you more than me.

VASYA [*rather doubtfully*]. Do you think so?

SEVA. Well, of course! [*Decisively.*] Take a look at Darling. Well, take a close look at her. You see?

VASYA. What exactly?

SEVA. She is not right for you. What's more, she'll destroy you.

VASYA. Are you quite sure?

SEVA. Absolutely. You're a romantic, a seeker of what is new, a restless soul. As for her — take a closer look a her — she has no social interests whatever.

VASYA [*worried*]. I think you're exaggerating a little. Darling is rather an unusual woman.

SEVA [*passionately*]. I tell you she has no spiritual passion at all! She's earth-bound and she's entirely indifferent to the communal activities of daily life.

VASYA. Wait! Why did you fall in love with her then? I hope you have fallen in love with her?

SEVA. You see, I'm funny that way. The things I want from life are different from what you want, romantic that you are. [*With great spiritual anxiety.*] Besides, you yourself know, love is vicious!

DARLING 2. I say! . . . I don't think that's quite right.

VASYA. Yes, really, Seva . . . I know how much you care for me, but you must behave like a gentleman to Darling.

SEVA. Now, come, Vasya, I love her, and that gives me the right to be frank about her failings.

VASYA. I'm glad to hear you say that. Love and lies don't go together. God knows!

SEVA. That's why we decided to be frank with you. I hope you appreciate our sudden impulse.

VASYA. Certainly. [*Thinks and grows rather sad.*] Your impulse was well-timed, on the whole. [*Very warm and sincere.*] From time to time I have also thought I wasn't right for Darling. I'm complicated and difficult, full of contradictions. I'm restless and inconstant and I doubt if I could make her happy. But Darling is . . . she's so . . . Well, she's so nice.

DARLING 2 [*with deep affection for him*]. I think you're losing your voice. You should have some hot milk and soda.

VASYA. Nonsense! I'm worried about something else. In this new situation shall we be able to go on with our method of accountancy?

SEVA. I don't mind going on, as long as Kapetchenko doesn't find out.

VASYA. Well, I'm disappointed in you, Seva, I'm disappointed by your new calculating approach. Darling, you must take him firmly in hand and protect him from all that's superficial and bad.

DARLING 2. All right, darling, I'll try.

[*Long pause. All remain silent and look at each other.*]

VASYA [*bewildered*]. Well, all right, what shall we do now?

DARLING 2. I don't know.

SEVA. I think . . . In a sense, we'll have to go our different ways.

VASYA [*humbly*]. Considering everything.

SEVA. Move out and move in . . .

VASYA. You have my key, on the whole . . .

SEVA. Up to a point . . . Of course, I could take Darling home. It would give me very, very great pleasure. You know, we have a large four-room flat. Unfortunately my father's an inveterate woman-hater and the arrival of a woman in our place would undoubtedly have a traumatic effect on him. But any shock to the nervous system at his age has a lasting effect.

VASYA. I agree. There's no point in upsetting your father. He's only just recovering from a very bad bout of angina.

DARLING 2 [*sincerely*]. The more I think, the more convinced I am that Vasya should go back to his father. Why shouldn't they clear for you your nice old nursery, which they turned into a dining room with great speed.

VASYA. That's what I was thinking, Darling. There's nothing quite the same as the place where you were born. I miss my father very much and my brother and sister have been too long without me. Of course, I must go and see them today and warn them of my unexpected return.

[*He puts on his cap.*]

SEVA. I'm very glad, everything has turned out very, very well.

VASYA. Yes, but one thing is very, very bad. I love her very much. [*Looks fondly at* DARLING 2.] Very much.

SEVA. Aren't you funny . . . Why do you love her?

VASYA [*embarrassed*]. Well, I do . . . [*Goes to* DARLING 2.] You know, Darling, to stop loving you now, today, would be like losing everything I value. I'm sorry, I don't promise to stop loving you at once. It would be rather difficult, my pet. [*Pleased at reaching the right conclusion.*] Yes, the whole trouble with love is, we want the person we're in love with, to be what she can't be . . . Well, she can't.

DARLING 2 [*now very much at a loss*]. I don't understand! You'll drive me mad!

VASYA. That's what Darling used to say. Well, all the best. [*He goes, deeply upset.*]

Scene Three

The set changes immediately. We're in the room of VASYA's *childhood. Among other things, we see his brother* GENNADY *and his sister* ALICIA *there.* GENNADY *is listlessly draped over the back of an old armchair.* ALICIA *has come to rest in a wooden rocking chair in a fantastic pose. The conversation between brother and sister is fairly futile.*

ALICIA. Coward!

GENNADY [*feebly*]. Leave me alone.

ALICIA. Spineless egotist!

GENNADY. It's all rot, you know.

ALICIA. Rot. No doubt. But you're a man, up to a point, and you could tell father the truth.

GENNADY. I've done with illusions. I've had them.

[*Enter* VASYA. *He looks round the familiar room and smiles.*]

ALICIA. That you?

VASYA. Hullo.

GENNADY [*without changing his awkward pose*]. Long time no see!

VASYA [*in the grip of the past*]. The excitement one experiences in the places with happy memories of one's youth. The tears I shed in my infancy downstairs in the hall. The fights I fought as a child in the backyard. It's so surprising to see the empty birdcage still hanging in the corridor. And mother's little old brolly stands by the phone as usual. [*With insight.*] It's good.

ALICIA. I'm not clear what you're excited about. Our flat is depressingly old-fashioned.

VASYA. Really?

GENNADY. It's a rotten flat. Rotten furniture. Everything's rotten. Off with their heads.

ALICIA. At last you've spoken up like a man.

GENNADY. But you can't change anything. I've done with illusions. I've had them. The older we get, the more father's character deteriorates. Imagine, after his birthday, he decided to begin our education all over again.

ALICIA. We're adults. It's intolerable.

GENNADY. It's the end. I'm bored with his pronouncements. Let him say what he likes. I shan't say a word.

ALICIA [*to* VASYA]. You've come at the wrong moment. When he sees you, father will start telling us all over again what a wonderful example you are.

VASYA. You're always joking. I'm glad Dad has a good opinion of me. [*Cheerful.*] And what if I am wonderful?

ALICIA. Out of the question.

GENNADY. You're mediocre.

VASYA [*good-natured*]. Children, I think you exaggerate. How are you?

ALICIA. Awful! I take antibiotics all day — drugs and more drugs. I come home very late. Nothing helps.

VASYA. That's amazing. [*To* GENNADY.] And how are things with you?

GENNADY. Exhausted, old boy, utterly exhausted . . . I only left the sanatorium yesterday.

VASYA. Was it all right?

GENNADY. Foul! I felt I was being ordered about. Breakfast at nine, dinner at two, supper at seven! And you're supposed to submit to that, I don't know why. As if you were a machine, a robot! It's intolerable! I had five more days there but I ran away.

VASYA. No, things don't seem to be going right for you.

[*Enter* VASYA's *father,* AKIM LISTIKOV, *a brisk though frail old man.*]

AKIM. Hullo, Vasya! I'm glad to see you at home. Pity you don't visit us more often. Many curious things happen here. Take your brother. He fell out of his chair, broke his head and was in great pain. The heart surgeons sent him at once to a sanatorium. Then your sister decided to get married. She got off lightly with shock only. She wrote a poem about it saying she disagrees. She disagrees with absolutely everything. The poem won't be published. And the young man's gone for good. [*Points at his children.*] They have now assumed their favourite attitudes and they are waiting for something. I'd love to give them a thrashing but I don't want to appear in court. They're capable of reporting me to the UN. Sit down, Vasya, I'll go and change into my slippers and I'll be back immediately.

VASYA [*looking after him and shaking his head in a significant manner*]. He doesn't stoop. He's strict.

ALICIA. It's disgusting! He absolutely ignores the fact that we're grown up.

AKIM [*returning*]. In brief, I'm glad to see you, Vasya, in good health. You're my hope and stay. These layabouts draped over their armchairs are no good to themselves or to our society.

VASYA [*with faith in the triumph of what's good and true*]. Papa, I respect you a lot but you shouldn't exaggerate. Why, they aren't layabouts! Take Gennady. He finished his studies. He's a laboratory assistant somewhere. At the same time he plays the trumpet with an amateur group called "Smiling Through". Now, Alicia is studying at the institute to write poetry and she's bound to learn, since she's taught there by our splendid poets. Her love cycle, "Trembling", is guarantee of that. It was published in Youth Magazine under the headline: "Attention, Alicia Listikova!" So wouldn't it be better to believe they mean well and to rejoice in their success?

AKIM. Vasya, you respect me, I respect you. But don't you start lecturing me. You're too young. This drip depresses me from morning to night with his quite idiotic appearance and behaviour. As for Alicia's tremblings, I mean her disgusting poem, it's a disgrace to our name! I'm a master carpenter and I've had a lot of trouble in my life. I was beaten, I went hungry, but I never wrote poems like that! Now people pay attention to me and respect me. I even go to our famous Bolshoi Theatre and listen to "The Demon" and "The Mermaid," operas like that. I'm excited by "The Inspector General," in the astonishing performance of the oldest actors of our country, all of which makes me happy. But as for playing the trumpet in a quartet called "Grinning Away" – no, never! Only you, Vasya, with your energy and love of life, have brought me consolation. The ferment of the Listikovs lives on in you and I'm glad. True, you had your off-moments. You married in a great hurry. What did I tell you? Look at the problem from every angle! But no: "I'm madly in love with her." All right! Our combined efforts got you a flat to live in happily and crazily. Then another no! Three years later he left his wife! Somehow he found out he'd stopped loving her. I was very sad and angry with you, Vasya. But you convinced me you were justified. Once again, you have a decent wife and a good flat. At work you're on velvet. You don't play any trumpets or describe your tremblings in verse. So honour and glory to you,

Vasya. Come and see us more often. You might have some influence on your brother and sister.

VASYA [*thrilled*]. Thanks, Papa. I'm thrilled by what you've said. I feel I can spread my wings. Because my troubles aren't over. All my difficulties lie ahead. I must tell you that at this moment I'm going through awful tragedy. I may crack up, but I'm full of optimism. In spite of the bitterness I feel. [*With deep emotion.*] Papa, you've asked me to come and see you more often. I'll take you at your word. Why come and see you? I could come and live with you permanently. Let me stretch out here, on my old, long-forgotten sofa and I'll be the happiest of men.

GENNADY [*shifting his stance at last*]. That's interesting.

ALICIA [*coming to life*]. Yes, something new.

AKIM. Just a moment, Vasya, you've suggested something quite impossible about this sofa. What do you mean, you want to stretch out on it permanently? You have a well-equipped flat of your own!

VASYA. I must confess to you without holding anything back, Darling doesn't love me any more.

AKIM. What's that about?

VASYA. I suppose, it's about her falling in love with Seva Polonsky, my best friend, a very talented and determined man. [*Significantly.*] We're collaborating on a piece of work, I mean, our new method of accountancy. All three of us have worked on that together, nights too. [*Pointing at his brother and sister.*] Well, you said my enthusiasm was an example to them.

GENNADY [*raising his head*]. More than once.

ALICIA [*gloating*]. I remember something of the kind.

AKIM. Now then, quiet! We'll discuss this in greater detail. [*To* VASYA.] You've allowed your obviously silly wife to fall in love with some Seva or other. I'm asking you — what good are you?

GENNADY. Exactly!

ALICIA. Let's have his answer!

AKIM. Quiet, I said! If a man isn't loved any more, it follows he is without interest. That's one. Now, two. We'll assume, you really don't amount to anything and your Darling has fallen in love with a different type. But what's the connection between her feelings and your proposal to occupy this sofa? Why should you wish to deprive us of our dining room? What's the link with your Darling falling in love with that scoundrel Seva?

VASYA. But Papa, you realize, they must settle down. Believe me, I feel my grief deeply but I have a great regard for what they feel. Without hesitation I've given them my living accommodation, hoping that in the long run we'll all be infinitely happy.

AKIM [*terribly angry*]. Now, get out! And never set foot in this house again!

[*Very long pause.* VASYA *finally realizes that it isn't a joke and that he must leave the house where he was born. He goes towards the door.*]

[*After him.*] I don't grudge the sofa. I don't grudge the dining room. But it's bitter for a father to know that his son is an absolute fool. No, you are no Listikov, you're a mess.

VASYA [*on reaching the door, he turns and, looking at his father, he addresses him with great spirit*]. That's marvellous, Papa! I tell you frankly, I love the way you condemn me in anger. Very good of you, very bright of you. I'm simply thrilled. It's the only way a truly loving father should behave. I thank you with all my heart. But rest assured of one thing – I am a Listikov, and nobody else. [*He leaves the house where he was born with great dignity.*]

GENNADY. Well, the nerve! Wanting the sofa.

ALICIA. Schizophrenic! Bluebeard!

AKIM. Now then, quiet! [*Long pause.*] Well, I don't know, he may well be a Listikov? [*He remains deep in thought.*]

Scene Four

Sunset. VASYA *returns to his former home. His walk is less assured and springy and it is all because he is very deep in thought. That nice* AUNTY SASHA *is sitting once again on her bench by the gates.*

AUNTY. Good evening, Vasya. The sun is setting and today, Friday, is nearly over! The town is less and less noisy. [*With deep sympathy and great interest.*] Where have you been? You're so depressed, so sad.

VASYA [*shaking himself free of the burden of his thoughts*]. Not at all! I had a glass of mineral water at the corner and it suddenly occurred to me that life is extraordinarily fascinating in spite of our troubles. How I'd love to get on a train and go right away. As for going away on a ship!

AUNTY. You have a lovely way of talking about everything. Thank you.

VASYA. It's wonderful when a hard-working and honest woman like you celebrates her fiftieth birthday . . . These celebrations go unnoticed but they are full of social significance. It's a great pity that our national press takes no notice of these festive occasions.

AUNTY. Thank you, my dear, for your heartfelt words. I wish you'd say it all to Valentinov.

VASYA. I shall. Where is he?

AUNTY. Over there, drinking tea on my balcony, as usual. He doesn't take vodka or coffee now. He's very sober.

VASYA. But I don't get it . . . Is Valentinov your husband?

AUNTY [*cheerfully*]. Why, no . . . He divorced me. He divorced me seven years ago.

VASYA. Why is he always hanging about here?

AUNTY. He can't live without me.

VASYA. Then why did he divorce you?

AUNTY. Well, you know, Valentinov is stupid.

VASYA. Why did you have anything to do with him?

AUNTY. What do you mean, why? I love that stupid Valentinov.

VASYA [*thinks*]. Yes, life is beyond my understanding. All we can do is rejoice that some of its manifestations are beyond the bounds of reason. For instance, Darling has fallen out of love with me and, because of that, Papa has thrown me out. I don't even know where to spend the night.

AUNTY [*throwing up her hands*]. Fallen out of love! With you! But how could she? With a remarkable person like you!

VASYA. I don't understand it.

AUNTY. Well, I never liked her, well, ask Valentinov . . . Don't worry, Vasya. Any one of our lovelies will fall in love with you. All you do is look at her. That's all and she's yours.

VASYA. Why did Darling fall out of love with me?

AUNTY. That's an old muddle . . . The whole problem is a muddle. And it's gone on for so many years! At the time of the personality cult too. As for France!

[*Enter* VALENTINOV *pleased with everything.*]

You could ask him. He's seen everything, and lived through it all. Look, Valentinov, his Darling has fallen out of love with him!

VALENTINOV. Well, if you don't leave them in time, they're bound to fall out of love with you. Take me, for instance. Why did I divorce her seven years ago? I was afraid she'd leave me.

AUNTY. You're an awful liar. You divorced me because you went to work in the House of Writers. You told me I wasn't good enough.

VALENTINOV. That's so. I said that. It's true when I began working for writers, success went to my head. After working for five years, I stopped drinking. You know why? I hadn't grasped my opportunities before. I nearly died, you know. Now I'm sober and I'm building myself a holiday house. By the reservoir. Why should the writers care? There's always something going wrong in the House of Writers. [*He winks.*] And I repair it.

VASYA. Everything you say, Comrade Valentinov, is compulsive listening. Unfortunately, it doesn't help me in my complicated predicament. I'll say goodnight and go home. Though that expression has now gone out of date. I wish you both success in your work and your private life. [*He goes out slowly.*]

VALENTINOV. Listikov, with this story of his, has knocked me out. There it is – an indescribable example of the inconstancy of women. To think that sometimes you grumble at me.

[DARLING 3, *hiding in the shadows till now, at last appears centre stage.*]

DARLING 3 [*going to* AUNTY]. I've been watching him. He was so downcast out there in the street, he hadn't even got his shopping bag . . .

AUNTY. Now, Darling, don't be a butter-fingers. His wife has left him. He doesn't belong to anyone now.

DARLING 3 [*pressing her hands to her bosom*]. Dear God!

AUNTY. A woman-tenant here said to me, when a man's been deserted, you can catch him with your bare hands.

DARLING 3 [*the excitement is almost too much for her*]. Now . . . Now . . . my hour has come. I'll go and change into a short-sleeved dress and go and have my hair done. [*She runs out.*]

VALENTINOV [*thoughtfully*]. Listen Sasha, I have a suggestion. Let's address each other by our surname for the chic of it. In the House we have an amazing writer who addresses his wife that way. It sounds great – way out.

Scene Five

The scene changes immediately to VASYA's *room, which isn't his any more. It's bursting with activity.* DARLING 2 *and* SEVA *are in the process of moving the furniture. They're working away cheerfully and easily, occasionally embracing each other to get on with the job with renewed energy.*

SEVA [*looking at the changes*]. I think the table would look better here.

DARLING 2. The divan would probably be better on that side.

[*Energetically they move the divan.*]

SEVA. Have you told your mother about the changes in your private life?

DARLING 2. I'm afraid, darling. She's very fond of Vasya.

SEVA. It's difficult not to be fond of our sunshine. When it was obvious you were quite wrong for him, I didn't know what to do with myself.

DARLING 2. I'm very upset too, Seva.

[*They kiss firmly and move the divan again.* VASYA *enters, sees what his friends are doing, and in silence, briskly, he joins them in moving the furniture.*]

SEVA [*to* VASYA]. Further left, left, old thing.

VASYA. But you go to the right.

[*Finally the work is done and they all look at it with satisfaction.*]

SEVA [*to* VASYA]. Well, what do you think?

VASYA. I think it looks nice. A good idea. Well done!

DARLING 2. I'm very glad you like it.

SEVA. I suppose everything's all right with you. Have you seen your father?

VASYA. I have. No doubt of that.

SEVA [*firmly*]. No serious complications, I hope?

VASYA. Well . . . Papa couldn't get over it.

SEVA. What's the position?

VASYA. Well . . . The room must be done up a bit, renovated here and there . . .

DARLING 2. Darling, for the time being you can sleep on the little sofa by the door.

VASYA [*moved*]. Thank you very much, Darling. I always knew you were a real friend. [*Pause.*] Though I'm not clear what I should do now.

SEVA. Think of something. Darling and I must have a talk.

VASYA [*delighted*]. Wait! I completely forgot, I must go and see your mother, Darling! She's going out to a very grand birthday party and again she has absolutely no one to leave the child with.

SEVA. Child? How old is it?

VASYA [*thrilled*]. Just eight months.

SEVA. What? [*To* DARLING 2.] Your mother has a baby?

DARLING 2. But he isn't my mother's at all.

SEVA. Whose then?

DARLING 2. My mother's domestic.

SEVA. Domestic? Where is she then?

DARLING 2. Vasya, where is she?

VASYA. Alena? The Conservatoire. Today they have the first performance of a new symphony by Shostakovich. Seva, you must realize, her extra-mural course at the institute is very involved and she has no time at all for the child. [*Passionately*.] But can you blame her for falling in love with Igor? Can you blame them if she has a child?

SEVA. Of course, they aren't really to blame but . . .

DARLING 2 [*thinking it out*]. You know, Seva, I suppose now it's your turn to look after the child.

SEVA [*horrified*]. What?

DARLING 2 . Get dressed! Mother will tell you how to feed Arkady and how to stop him crying.

VASYA [*in despair*]. No, please . . . What's the point? I've thought this out. Please don't deprive me at least of him. It would be inhuman. Arkady is a remarkable infant. He and I have established real contact.

DARLING 2. Well, if you insist . . .

SEVA. No, wait . . . Why does he insist? He wouldn't, if it weren't worth his while . . . There must be something to it. [*Decisively*.] Right! I'm going to this Arkady! I want to see him as well.

VASYA. Pull yourself together.

SEVA. I'm not handing over what's mine!

VASYA. Isn't Darling enough for you? At least let me have my Arkady.

SEVA [*he is a decent man*]. Well, all right, after all you are my best friend.

VASYA. Thank you, Seva, you're behaving like a real man.

SEVA [*shyly*]. Yes, all right . . . It's nothing . . .

VASYA. Besides, you obviously want to be alone together. [*Pause.*] Well, I'm off. [*Puts on his cap.*] The sun has set. I like this time of day when the shadow of evening imperceptibly draws down over the quiet side streets. From the open windows of small houses, you hear laughter, unknown voices and music in the distance . . . And the thought that life is still surprising and wonderful never leaves me for a moment. [*He looks round and notices* DARLING 2 *and* SEVA *for the first time, as it were. He raises his cap and smiles at them.*] Goodbye. [*He goes out.*]

Scene Six

He is now crossing the courtyard. Neither VALENTINOV *nor* AUNTY *nor* DARLING 3 *are there. It is still light in the early spring twilight, but some of the windows are lighting up.*

AUNTY [*sadly appearing at the window*]. Where are you going, Vasya?

VASYA. To see my Arkady.

AUNTY. God be with you. [*She disappears.*]

VASYA. What a warm evening. I'm sure some people are already bathing some-where in the Silver Forest? Others are enjoying themselves in rowing boats. [*Giving rein to his dreams.*] And someone in a train has sat down and is now unpacking his food hamper — roast chicken, cooked by his mother or his darling wife . . . At Khimki someone is going somewhere by steamer. The ship's hooter hoots, all rush out on deck, wave their hats, the seagulls fly all around and everywhere they're selling ice-cream. At the airport . . . But no, I don't know about that as yet; I've never flown in an aeroplane. It all lies ahead of me! [*Pause. He is even more carried away.*] And on an evening like this is it bad on Leninsky Hills? Lovers wander below by the parapet, talking of everything, about to embrace each other. They are happy! [*Amazed by a sudden thought.*] Supposing someone's waiting for me out there, on a bench above Moscow River? [*He moves down to the apron-stage and carefully looks at the audience. Music. He declaims to music.*]

> Oh Darling, you with whom I may,
> I may, yes, fall once more in love,
> Are you amongst the audience here
> And with a ticket you have bought?
> Oh, Darling, wait, no hurry now —
> I still adore my darling wife.
> I know, I am alone and sad
> But Darling, wait, don't hurry now.
> Oh Darling, better wait a while.

Till I am out of love with my
Own Darling, nothing can be done.
Oh Darling! Better wait a while.
Oh Darling! Better wait the day
When I have ceas'd to love at last.
Oh Darling, we'll be happy then . . .
Perhaps. It may be so. Who knows!

[*With a wave of his hand, he goes. The touching music grows more lively.*]

CURTAIN

ACT TWO

Scene One

A quiet and cosy little room in semi-darkness. There's a cradle, but it is empty. The infant is in VASYA's *arms.* VASYA *is singing softly to him, and ingratiatingly walking about the room from corner to corner, waiting with interest for results. The child falls asleep and* VASYA *lowers him carefully into the cradle.*

VASYA. What unexpected bliss — he's gone to sleep! Dear, kind Arkady . . . It can't be the last time I'm here! Surely I'll see my friend again! [*Bends over the child's cradle.*] He's asleep and he doesn't suspect that our parting is irrevocably close! But I seem to be awfully hungry. It's funny today wherever I went no one gave me any food. Somehow we never got round to it. Though we might have if things had been different. [*He glances at the little bottles put out for* ARKADY.] Darling's mother is so kind. She left Arkady a very fine selection of little bottles. I don't think he'll feel deprived if I have a couple. [*With great satisfaction he drinks the contents of one little bottle.*] Shredded carrot, no doubt of that. It's surprisingly good. Shall I have another? [*He empties another little bottle with equal satisfaction.*] Excellent juice, sent us from torrid Algeria, I suppose, after she threw off her colonial chains for ever. [*Looks at the sleeping infant.*] The impact a child makes in early infancy with his unclouded face, his manly gaze and his happy condescension in forgiving our idiotic behaviour. The many ways we are swindled out of our happy condescension is enough to make one weep. When we complain about things and wring our hands at night . . . Oh no, I can't bear it. He has wetted himself! Just think, my beloved friend has played the dirty on me! [*Thinks.*] Well, what does it matter? He's human; a young thing still without discipline. It isn't as if he were a bee or a highly evolved ant. Wait a bit and he will destroy all that's human in himself and he won't make any mistakes then. After all he is the king of nature. [*Automatically, he takes a third little bottle and drinks it.*] Is this the third bottle? While he's quietly asleep, I'm being beastly to him. [*Looks into the cradle.*] He smiled . . . He must have seen me and gone to sleep again. [*Bending over the cradle,* VASYA *softly sings a lullaby.*]

> Sleep, my darling friend Arkady,
> Clever child of times atomic,
> Clever child of times atomic,
> Sleeping godlike, stern and gentle,

242

Much is going on inside you,
You're digesting and maturing,
You're digesting and maturing,
Lying, dreaming – leaping, dancing.
Neither men-revisionists nor
Women dogmatists nor
Cretins, louts, nor trouble-makers
Haunt your nights of sleeping, dreaming.
Sleep my wise Arkady, soundly,
But remember Jumping-Jack-O,
But remember Jumping-Jack-O,
He would never lie down ever.

[*The bell goes.* VASYA *jumps up immediately.*]

The bell! . . . Who could it be?

[*He goes out and returns at once with* DARLING 3. *She is both blindingly beautiful and half-dead and alive.*]

DARLING 3. Hullo . . . Good evening.

VASYA. Well hullo . . . But who are you?

DARLING 3. What? Don't you remember me?

VASYA. No, should I? . . . I've seen you somewhere, of course. Yes, your face is terribly familiar . . . I know! Many years ago we grew up together in the same kindergarten.

DARLING 3 [*in despair*]. Not at all. We did not grow up together in kindergarten.

VASYA [*stern*]. Then, why do I know you almost too well?

DARLING 3. We meet every day near your house.

VASYA. Why?

DARLING 3. I don't know. I haven't the slightest idea.

VASYA. Someone must know?

DARLING 3. Obviously! I live in the house opposite and today I was around, when you gave me a lemon waffle.

VASYA [*pleased*]. Why, of course! . . . It never occurred to me you were the young woman I never recognized when we met! How did you get here?

DARLING 3 [*after pause, very gentle and just as nervous*]. May I tell you the whole truth?

VASYA. My God, has something awful happened to Darling?

DARLING 3 [*dryly*]. I expect she's alive and well.

VASYA. Thank you for your good news. Now, tell me the whole truth.

DARLING 3. Aunty Sasha told me, you went to look after a baby temporarily deprived of its parents. And then quite by chance I suddenly remembered, a long time ago I used to bath and put my youngest sister to bed. So I decided to come and help you!

VASYA. That's excellent! But why did you decide to come and help me?

DARLING 3. I . . . I simply can't imagine.

VASYA. Very curious. What's your name?

DARLING 3. Darling.

VASYA. What a funny name . . . [*Tries hard to remember.*] I know someone else by that name . . . Ah, yes! . . . Yes, of course.

DARLING 3. What's that young man's name?

VASYA [*significantly*]. Arkady.

DARLING 3. He seems to have an excellent appetite. Look, he's already had three little bottles. We could put the rest away. I don't suppose he'll want any more today.

VASYA. You don't know this Arkady. He has a gigantic appetite! On one occasion, he and I drank . . . I mean, I did . . . I mean, he did . . . [*Trying to get out of it.*] I mean, we both did.

DARLING 3. Judging by your interesting comments, you must be very fond of children.

VASYA [*proud*]. Yes. I am definitely sorry I haven't got one of my own.

DARLING 3. I sympathize deeply. Besides, I've always thought that in our country an increased birthrate was most desirable and that it was entirely up to — each one of us.

VASYA. Please, believe me, I appreciate what you say very much. Though, considering your age, I hope you have no children?

DARLING 3. As a matter of fact, I'm learning ancient Greek. I still haven't found any other hobbies.

VASYA. Most probably your husband will find the other hobbies.

DARLING 3. It is just that surmise which has prevented me from marrying. Mutual hobbies are only possible with a mutual out-look.

VASYA [*has a good look at her*]. You look as though you are growing up under the supervision of your parents?

DARLING 3. Up to a point. It's true, my mother's on tour in Bolivia. [*Significantly.*] But my father's Sergey Sergeyevich.

VASYA. Which Sergey Sergeyevich?

DARLING 3. The Sergey Sergeyevich.

VASYA. Oh, really? Our chief accountant?

DARLING 3. Certainly not. The television announcer.

VASYA [*very grim*]. Television is my worst enemy. It stops me concentrating . . . [*Walks about the room.*]

DARLING 3 [*with a secret adoring look*]. He is so splendid! I'm sure he'll drive me mad! [*After a pause.*] But why don't you ever recognize me though we meet nearly every day?

VASYA. I'm always thinking of my wife. Other women's faces don't exist for me.

DARLING 3 [*not overjoyed by his frankness*]. Your wife! I heard she was leaving you.

VASYA [*casually*]. I heard the news too. But her falling out of love with me is her business. I can go on being in love with her.

DARLING 3 [*confused*]. Will that go on for a long time?

VASYA. Obviously until I get bored. [*Thinks.*] Don't you see . . . Love is a completely unknown phenomenon. Well, what can people who aren't in love say about it? And those who are – they're mad.

DARLING 3. You're right, it is bad.

VASYA. It couldn't be worse!

DARLING 3 [*with inspiration*]. If I thought I could help you, I'd do anything without hesitating.

VASYA. I must not be helped. If I am to suffer, and obviously there is scope for that, well then, let me get on with it. Man must experience everything![*With panache.*] Let us suffer if we must! Right! We'll cope with that as well!

DARLING 3. Well, why not, we'll cope. But where are you going to live?

VASYA [*cheerfully*]. Nobody knows! I've given them everything! I hope they're happy.

DARLING 3. And you?

VASYA [*reasonably*]. Without my Darling, I can't be happy anyway.

DARLING 3. Please, excuse me, but I can't take any more. [*She faints.*]

VASYA [*catching her*]. Now, that's all I need. She's fainted! What, the hell, I thought nobody had fainted for a long time. Fainting went into a decline after the October Revolution. The grim days since have made us tough. What's that? Arkady's waking up! What shall I do? Holding this Darling, obviously I shan't be able to rock Arkady to sleep!

[*Dragging* DARLING 3 *to* ARKADY'*s cradle.*]

I don't know who to put where? [*He can't tear his eyes away from* DARLING 3.] How pretty she is . . . Simply lovely. Just as well, I love my Darling, or I'd fall hopelessly in love with this one and ever after suffer madly from un-requited love. Yes, excellent – I love my wife . . . [*Frightened.*] No, no longer mine. She belongs to another. And that's the snag. I love another man's wife. Listikov! It's amoral! My God, Arkady! [*Shouts at* DARLING 3.] Now, really, you must come round or we'll be lost!

DARLING 3 [*coming round*]. What? What's happened?

VASYA. Arkady's awake!

DARLING 3. What Arkady?

VASYA. The one who had been asleep in his cradle.

DARLING 3. Why didn't you say so before? Arkady's awake and you don't say anything. Look at him thrashing about. We must feed him at once. But his little bottles are cold! I'll go and warm them. [*Picking them up and running to the door.*] Try and calm that young man. [*Runs out.*]

VASYA [*looking after her*]. All the same, this Darling is an awfully nice young woman. It's hard for me to call her by that name. There are unnecessary associations . . . But look! My dear Arkady's turned over and gone to sleep again. [*Faint knock at the door.*] What's the meaning of that? Someone's scratching at the door.

[VASYA *goes to the door. It opens a little and the pale, sad face of* AVENIR NIKOLAYEVICH *pokes in.*]

What, you again?

AVENIR [*bitter*]. Yes, it's me again.

VASYA. How did you get here?

AVENIR. Your wife gave me this address. Your wife – it sounds tragic!

VASYA. Now you want something else from me.

AVENIR. Comrade Listikov, I've been wandering alone in the streets of Moscow. I walked past various stalls deeply depressed by our earlier conversation. Though the bustle of life went on all round me and the happy laughter of children came from all sides, I could not get over a sense of deepest grief.

VASYA [*cautious*]. But we'll give you back the napkin with the cat on it.

AVENIR [*angry*]. It isn't a matter of napkins, Comrade Listikov! [*With great fervour.*] My prime aim is to arouse your remorse and to make you suffer at the thought of what you have done!

VASYA. What an extraordinary statement!

[*The door opens and* **DARLING 3** *enters with a little warm milk and porridge.*]

DARLING 3. Here we are, it's ready. [*Sees* **AVENIR**.] What? Have you got here too?

VASYA. Darling, the point is . . .

AVENIR. What? Another Darling? Comrade Listikov, you must stop!

DARLING 3. Why should he stop? Certainly not! We must feed our Arkady!

AVENIR. Your who?

DARLING 3. Arkady. There, asleep in his cradle.

AVENIR [*wrings his hands*]. A baby! Unhappy baby! Listikov, you have surpassed yourself.

VASYA [*calm*]. Why do you think that?

AVENIR. One Darling wasn't enough for you. You found another. That wasn't enough for you either. You had a third and on top of that you got a child! While your first Darling lives in the torments of loneliness, and your poor second Darling innocently gives me this address, you are enjoying yourself in no uncertain manner with this third Darling, rocking this unhappy baby to every side! My God, the bankruptcy of this generation!

DARLING 3. If you don't clonk him on the head, Vasya, I shall.

VASYA. If you do, I'll think you deplorably aggressive. Pull yourself together. Avenir Nikolayevich is the best librarian of the Frunze district.

DARLING 3. Really? I should never have thought so.

VASYA. Nevertheless, he is. [*With solemnity.*] Avenir Nikolayevich, it isn't our child. We're only keeping an eye on him in our free time.

AVENIR. What is your relationship with this new Darling?

VASYA. We meet in an atmosphere of utter frankness and mutual understanding.

AVENIR. Listikov, don't prevaricate. I can see perfectly well the dumb adoration with which this young woman looks at you.

VASYA. You've gone mad! Why should she look at me with adoration? See how beautiful she is! Me next to her! . . . She isn't that silly . . . [*To* DARLING 3.] Why don't you tell him?

DARLING 3 [*to* AVENIR]. You're mean, that's what you are! [*With inexpressible tenderness.*] You should pity him. His wife has just left him.

AVENIR. What? Honest to God?

DARLING 3. She left him.

AVENIR. How very unexpected! [*Thinks quickly.*] I hope you aren't going back to your first Darling? Who will share my suffering during the long autumn evenings?

VASYA. I shan't deprive you of that, Avenir Nikolayevich. I'm not going back to her. I love my Darling.

AVENIR. Do you really love her so much?

VASYA [*proud*]. Too much!

AVENIR [*astonished*]. So madly?

VASYA [*with dignity*]. Too madly.

DARLING 3. Ah! [*Faints.*]

VASYA. What? Not again? That is too much . . . [*To* AVENIR.] You see what you've done to this poor innocent creature.

AVENIR. How awful! I'll never forgive myself! During the long, rainy nights I shall remember this evening.

VASYA. Good, that will come later. But now our determined Arkady seems to be waking up again. This is his moment. Now he'll come into his own.

AVENIR. In what sense?

VASYA. He has opened his eyes. With a long-suffering air, he raises his left eyebrow . . . Avenir Nikolayevich, with the remaining bottles off to the kitchen with you! Warm them up, if you have a heart.

AVENIR [*seizing the bottles*]. I'll do anything! How mean and pathetic I am! During the long, stormy nights I shall remember this! [*Runs out with the little bottles.*]

VASYA [*gazing fondly at* DARLING 3]. How lovely she is. No words to describe her. Oh, if only I weren't in love with my wife!

[*A gentle, barely audible melody is heard.*]

Scene Two

Night in the garden of **VASYA***'s house. The light by the entrance is out. The bench is empty.* **VASYA** *and* **DARLING 3***, both tired, wander slowly through the garden.* **VASYA** *carries a bunch of flowers.*

DARLING 3. Well, we got here. [*Sighs.*] That's that.

VASYA [*sincerely*]. I don't know how to thank you, Lyudmilla Sergeyevna. You calmed Arkady's rage when he woke up. You coped with Avenir, whose grief is apparently boundless. Finally, you were instrumental in getting this beautiful bunch of flowers. I'll give it to Aunty Sasha. It will add a touch of colour to her modest festivities.

DARLING 3. But when shall we see each other again?

VASYA. Soon, I think. Should Arkady be taken away from us, I'll try and find something else of a similar nature.

DARLING 3 [*pause*]. Do you ever go to the cinema?

VASYA. No, I don't go to the cinema, because I'm always busy with important things.

DARLING 3. Oh, I'm sure you lead a full life. That's why I think I'll go to bed.

[*Sadly waving her hand,* **DARLING 3** *goes towards her house.*]

VASYA [*dreamy*]. Aunty Sasha will be fifty tomorrow morning, when we're all enjoying our Saturday. My bunch of flowers will just come in handy. Of course, it would be a good idea to surprise her and convey the flowers to her rather earlier . . . An idea! What if I were to climb the drainpipe to her balcony and leave the flowers on her window-sill? Anonymous gift! I can just imagine how pleased and surprised she'd be. That's settled! [*Holding the flowers in his teeth, he climbs up the drainpipe and after a few complications, he reaches the balcony.*] The drainpipe hasn't collapsed and I have reached my destination! [*In the light of the moon, with tender solemnity he places the flowers on* **AUNTY SASHA***'s window-sill.*] Sleep well, dear friend! I associate so many cheerful and exciting moments with you. Happy I went up in your lift while my dear Darling waited for me at home. It's sad but a great gale has swept it all away. Though you, Aunty Sasha, an honest working-woman, are still peacefully asleep behind this window. When I think of you I always realize the hard role of women, which is only now beginning to improve and very slowly. My darling Mum . . . Devotedly she worked all her life, so that we, her three children, should be cheerful and happy. With jolly yells, Papa brought us up; but Mamma mended and darned and ironed our clothes, cooked breakfast and dinner and supper, swept the flat, washed the floors, windows and pots and pans, went to market and stood in the queues; and she also managed to work at the post office. She had just one small weakness. Once a month she went to the circus which she loved more than anything else with the exception of us and Papa, of course. My darling Mamma, things aren't going too well without you and I miss you very, very much. [*He sings the song about his mother.*]

A quiet evening, home alone
I hear the dripping kitchen tap
And I believe it's you in there,
With hot spaghetti waiting me.
A quiet morning, I awake
And hear the empties clink next door
And I believe you're off to buy
A yoghourt in our shop for me.
A quiet night and half awake
I hear the creaking bedroom floor
And I believe it's you beside
My bed to kiss goodnight to me.
On holiday beside the sea
I hear the shingle slide behind
And I can see the tiny trunks
And funny tow'l you brought to me.

[**VASYA** *waves his hand in the direction of* **AUNTY SASHA**'s *window and carefully begins climbing down the drainpipe. But this time his luck is out. The lower part of the drainpipe breaks away and he goes crashing down to the ground. The windows in the house fly open and the startled inhabitants are not slow to comment.*]

VOICES. Hooligans! . . . They broke the drainpipe. Police! He deserves ten days inside! There he is hiding in the entrance. Miserable alcoholic! What a generation! . . .

Scene Three

The garden disappears. Back in **VASYA**'s *room, poor* **DARLING** 2 *wakes up and sees her ex-husband.* **VASYA** *looks awful. His trousers are torn and his jacket has seen better days. Enchanting music is heard throughout the following scene.*

VASYA. Hullo! It's me.

DARLING 2 [*in bed, half-asleep, looks him over*]. But how awful . . . Why do you appear to me in my dream looking so peculiar?

VASYA. I'm sorry, Darling, it isn't a dream, it's real. Our daily round.

DARLING 2 [*grumbling*]. It must be a dream. You can't tear your trousers like that when you are wide awake, now can you?

VASYA. Apparently, Darling, though I shouldn't have thought so.

DARLING 2. What are you talking about? I'm terribly sleepy and I don't understand . . . Go and have a shower at once.

VASYA. Are you talking in your sleep? Or are you really suggesting I should go and do it? The recent events have had a very traumatic effect on me. I fell almost from the first floor. There were people chasing me.

DARLING 2. There you are . . . And you say it isn't a dream I'm dreaming. Either get out of my dream or go to bed. I've made up your bed over here on the little divan by the door.

VASYA. Wouldn't it be better to put me further from you? I'm in a very traumatic state as it is.

DARLING 2. You are making long speeches again. You'll drive me mad.

VASYA. You all promise to go mad, but nobody does.

DARLING 2. If you say another word, I'll wake up.

VASYA. Well, all right, all right . . .

DARLING 2 [*pulling the blanket over herself*]. Today has been very difficult.

VASYA [*rubbing his bruised side*]. No, I wouldn't call it easy. [*Without undressing, he stretches out on the divan, apparently worn out.*]

DARLING 2 [*falling asleep*]. Judging by everything, divorce is not all that simple. Many different problems come up . . .

VASYA [*falling asleep*]. Yes, you're right, without a doubt . . .

DARLING 2 [*in her sleep*]. Seva, Seva . . . Vasya's really quite something in his own way . . . Don't you think so?

[VASYA *snores.*]

[*Tenderly.*] Frankly, he's a hundred times better than you.

VASYA [*suddenly wakes and jumps up*]. Eh? What? . . . Darling, are you awake?

DARLING 2 [*grumbling*]. Well, what do you want now?

VASYA. Were you dreaming of me?

DARLING 2. No, I was dreaming of Seva. Why do you ask?

VASYA [*exulting*]. Because I was dreaming of you.

DARLING 2. I hope I didn't take any liberties.

VASYA [*thinks and then decides to say no*]. No. You can go fast asleep, Darling.

DARLING 2. That's good. Sleep well.

VASYA. Thank you. Look after yourself, Darling.

[*They stop talking. Quiet music.*]

Scene Three

The morning is at its height. The birds are singing cheerfully in the trees and shrubs. AUNTY SASHA *comes out of the house, her hair done, wearing an expensive dress.*

AUNTY. The shock I've had this morning! I woke up and I was fifty. The worst of it is, I was forty-nine only yesterday ... It is not a celebration. I don't even want to roast the veal. The one nice thing, Valentinov made me laugh in the night ... He hasn't forgotten. He keeps thinking. That's good ...

[VASYA *comes out of the house, limping slightly.*]

Vasya's up! Why are you limping? Have you got pins and needles?

VASYA. Something like that. [*Cheerfully he admires the flowers on* AUNTY SASHA's *window-sill.*] What interesting flowers you have on your window-sill.

AUNTY. Thanks to those flowers, Vasya, an essential part of the drainpipe has broken off. [*Pointing.*] You see how ugly it is. Sort of naked. It's all Valentinov's doing. I'm sure of that. Only a hooligan like him would think of climbing up the drainpipe to my window! But I'll tell you a secret: I'm very flattered. [*She goes into the house.*]

VASYA [*after a pause, sincere*]. Still, it's very interesting the way it has worked out. Even surprising. Yes, life, in all its variety, never fails to please.

[*Enter* VALENTINOV. *He's sullen but he carries a big parcel.*]

Comrad Valentinov, may I congratulate you on Aunty Sasha's birthday.

VALENTINOV [*bleakly*]. Yes? Think so?

VASYA. What a strange mood you're in. Why the bitter laugh?

VALENTINOV. I'm very angry. What hooliganism! They say a man went climbing up to Sasha's window at night. [*Sees the broken drainpipe.*] You see, there you are! The people are not telling lies! I was going to give her this as a surprise. [*Indicating the parcel.*] But she has men climbing down from her windows at night.

VASYA [*with a touch of childish cunning*]. Well, you divorced her, you know. She's a free woman now and has a right to everything.

VALENTINOV [*swaying with anger*]. What do you mean, she has a right to everything, when I eat at her house, dinner and supper, don't I? We have a lot in common.

[AUNTY SASHA *comes out of the house. At the sight of* VALENTINOV, *a woman-in-love awakes within her and she crosses the garden with allure.*]

AUNTY [*happy with* VALENTINOV]. Oh, oh, Valentinov, you are a one . . . Well, you made me laugh, all right.

VALENTINOV [*somberly*]. Birthday greetings to you. Why are you smiling?

AUNTY [*anxious*]. Why are you so serious?

VALENTINOV. I was very happy and I even had a present for you. I looked forward to giving it to you. But now I give it to you without any pleasure or excitement. [*He hands her the parcel.*] Here's two kilos of the best butter. It will keep a long time if you put it in the fridge.

AUNTY. Well, fine, thank you for your present. Let me give you a kiss.

VALENTINOV. You can take the butter but I won't have any kissing. You're a loose woman. Men come climbing down from your window! Look, they've broken the drainpipe.

AUNTY. All right, Valentinov, all right! Do you think I don't know the joker?

VALENTINOV. Then tell me at once – I'll knock his block off.

VASYA. Comrade Valentinov, you'd be acting like a hooligan. Perhaps someone with good intentions climbed up the drainpipe to place a bunch of sweet-smelling flowers on the window-sill.

VALENTINOV [*with contempt*]. You don't say . . . You don't find fools like that!

AUNTY. Now that's enough! All right, you've had your fun. Do you think, I don't know it was you? [*Again gives him a smile full of promise.*] Oh, you are a one! . . .

VALENTINOV. Me? Who am I?

AUNTY. The man who came up the drainpipe to see me.

VALENTINOV [*furious*]. Don't you try to make a fool of me, Sasha. [*Threatening.*] We're going in now. I must have a serious talk with you. [*In the doorway.*] I didn't divorce you seven years ago, so that men should go climbing up drainpipes to visit you at night.

[*They go into the house in their different states of mind.*]

VASYA [*alone*]. Obviously I should have confessed to everything. But Valentinov inspires me with great caution. I'm beginning to think I'm a bit of a coward?

[SERGEY SERGEYEVICH *and* DARLING 3 *come around the corner.*]

DARLING 3. There, you see, you see he's perfect!

SERGEY. Who, Darling? The one on the bench?

DARLING 3. Where does someone like that come from? He's remarkable . . . Look at him, waving his arms and turning this way and that . . .

AUNTY [*anxiously appearing in her window*]. Vasya, come running up! Quickly! Make peace between Valentinov and me and hurry! [*Disappears.*]

VASYA. Coming! [*Runs to the entrance and disappears.*]

DARLING 3 [*pulling her father by the sleeve*]. Daddy, you're my joy and solace. Although you are Sergey Sergeyevich, a man loved by all the nation, you have been tireless and cherished me whilst mummy has been popularizing our national art of the ballet. And so I have grown up as an unusually model child. I'm now eighteen, but no young man can boast of anything. Nothing at all. Well, aren't you delighted with me?

SERGEY. Surely you have noticed, I'm always delighted with you!

DARLING 3 . In that case, do all in your power and make Listikov unite his life with mine.

SERGEY. But, my dear, I know nothing about him.

DARLING 3. I have a feeling I shall be happy with him. I'm in love for the first time! If he isn't my husband, I shall leave immediately on a new gigantic building project.

SERGEY [*in despair*]. Brief me on how to begin.

DARLING 3. Daddy, I have an awful confession. I tried to seduce him all night but he never noticed. I suppose I haven't acquired the technique and I keep losing my head.

SERGEY [*embracing her*]. My poor child . . .

DARLING 3. Tell him how I love him and explain to him that I'm not so bad. I don't think he knows that. If it doesn't work, well, then . . . then . . .

SERGEY [*horrified*]. Then what, my dear?

DARLING 3 [*choking and whispering*]. Go all the way, do you hear? Describe our flat. Tell him about our furniture! He's homeless. It might work . . . [*In despair.*] And tell him about our garage. [*With a shriek.*] You see how I love him. Love has dredged from the bottom of my heart all that's wicked and awful, and I'm ready now for almost everything! [*Whispers again.*] Tell him how nice it is to have a holiday house.

SERGEY. But I can't tell him lies, my dear . . . You know perfectly well it's awful to have a holiday house.

DARLING 3. For my sake, tell him it's nice . . .

[*VASYA appears. He goes to* DARLING 3 *and looks at her closely for a long time.* DARLING 3 *seizes up in horror.*]

VASYA [*remembering*]. Oh, yes! [*Shakes hands.*] Good morning!

DARLING 3 [*extremely anxious*]. Now, Daddy, this is Vasya with whom I spent a fabulous night by the cradle of a remarkable child.

[*For some time* VASYA *and* SERGEY SERGEYEVICH *bow and scrape before each other with great tact.*]

But I must be going. Now be good, both of you. Please.

[*She goes, dying of anxiety. For some time* SERGEY SERGEYEVICH *and* VASYA *look at each other smiling.*]

VASYA [*gallantly*]. I heard, you're Sergey Sergeyevich.

SERGEY [*modestly*]. Yes. I've been him for a great many years now.

[*There's another amiable pause.*]

Have you known Darling long?

VASYA. I saw her three years ago for the first time. Abruptly I changed my life and married her soon after. I was the happiest man on earth.

SERGEY. What? Do you mean that?

VASYA [*intoxicated*]. I was happy!

SERGEY. You say, you married her?

VASYA. I have no reason to deny it.

SERGEY. It's beyond me! And you took the risk? You know that three years ago she was only fifteen.

VASYA. S 'rely not! I'd never have thought it. I think you're making a mistake.

SERGEY [*mildly*]. That would be rather difficult. I am her father.

VASYA. What? You too? What about Fedot Nikolayevich?

SERGEY [*tactfully*]. He wasn't there.

VASYA. He was. I swear!

SERGEY [*horrified*]. He was not.

VASYA. Just a moment, somehow I've lost the thread . . . What are we talking about?

SERGEY. I'm talking of my daughter, Darling, who has just introduced us.

VASYA. Oh, yes — she's also called Darling. [*Obstinately and significantly.*] But I was talking of my wife, Darling, who has left me for my best friend, Seva Polonsky. Or rather she did not leave, he came instead. That's what complicates matters.

SERGEY [*ingratiating*]. You should see our flat! There's some awfully ancient furniture standing in the corners . . . We bought two carpets. The fish in the aquarium darts about. So does my wife, who usually goes away for half the year.

VASYA. How long does she stay when she returns?

SERGEY. She mostly returns in order to go away again . . . We have a wonderful Saxony dinner service for twelve. And one enormous bronze candelabrum.

VASYA. Only one? That hurts, I suppose.

SERGEY. Not at all. The thing's unique. Imagine a huge candelabrum like that . . . My wife dotes on it every time she's back. [*Recollecting himself.*] Yes! I quite forgot to mention it, we have a car.

VASYA. You don't say! . . . [*Tries to get away.*]

SERGEY [*catches him up*]. A wonderful Volga, pale blue, which has only done fifteen hundred! There's a chauffeur to go with it. True, he's rather mercenary, but he's quite a character, on the whole.

VASYA. It's all very interesting but I must go and see my great friend, Seva Polonsky.

SERGEY [*in despair*]. No, wait! We have a holiday house on the canal! [*Fiercely.*] Two floors, two verandas, six rooms! [*Grabbing* VASYA *who's trying to slip away.*] It's been done up in an indescribable colour! There's a remarkable dog kennel. [*He could burst into tears.*] We're trying to grow strawberries . . .

VASYA [*confused*]. Please, don't upset yourself . . .

SERGEY. Listen to the most important thing of all. The holiday house has a garage. It's well heated.

VASYA. I'm glad for your sake, believe me.

SERGEY. True, it doesn't come cheap. Black-market coal has gone up a great deal of late. And it is not easy to get hold of.

VASYA. I sympathize with you very much, but . . .

SERGEY. Maintenance is a real problem. The fence is always falling down. It's almost impossible to get a caretaker. Every week something else needs repairing. Nobody wants to dig the garden. The heating is permanently out of order. The roof never stops leaking.

VASYA [*pained*]. But that's awful.

SERGEY. I don't know why but the chauffeur cheats me. I'm sure he does. He keeps selling me my own tyres. And there are constant hallucinations with petrol tins.

VASYA [*passionately*]. It's a kind of hell! Believe me, my heart bleeds for you.

SERGEY. No, wait! . . . [*Confused.*] That is not what I meant. [*Goes all the way.*] The point is, my daughter is in love with you.

VASYA. What? She with me? It's impossible. Why should she?

SERGEY. That's what I asked her, though I put it more tactfully. But she won't listen to me. I love Listikov, her lips murmur at night.

VASYA. She'll drive me mad! . . .

SERGEY. Yes, yes, quite mad.

VASYA [*meditative*]. How absurd it all is. She is in love with me and my own Darling isn't. Everything has to be upside down!

SERGEY. Do I understand that you refuse to fall in love with my Darling?

VASYA. Please don't be angry but I still love mine. And it's rather difficult to fall in love with someone else.

SERGEY. But your refusal will kill her. She'll go away to distant parts and be a newsettler.

VASYA. Wait a moment . . . [*Takes serious stock.*] It's the beginning of June. I might be able to do something towards the end of the next quarter. I can't promise, of course. After all, love is love. But as any honest man would, I must certainly try and help you out of this awful mess.

SERGEY. What are you talking about?

VASYA. Well, your holiday home, of course. Your chauffeur and tyres, your fence that keeps falling down, and your leaking roof. I'm not heartless and I realize the traumatic effect it has on you. [*Enthusiastically.*] Wait! I think I've found a way out. If you find the holiday house so trying, why don't you give it away?

SERGEY [*catching his enthusiasm*]. To whom?

VASYA. I don't know! Anyone, if it's that bad. Give the car away too. To hell with it!

SERGEY [*quietly plaintive*]. But how can I give it away? You're a strange man. That holiday house is mine.

VASYA. Have you got a son-in-law?

SERGEY [*spreading out his arms ruefully*]. No. [*Interested.*] Why do you ask?

VASYA. I simply thought how painful it would be if he had to cope with your house, car and chauffeur. I don't envy him!

SERGEY [*feebly*]. No, why . . . [*Hopeful.*] And the bronze candelabrum? It's quite something.

VASYA [*with a terrible realization*]. Stop! Now I think I know what your game is! How mean of you! You decided to marry me to your daughter in order to throw upon me the burden of your house, chauffeur and well-heated garage. Sergey Sergeyevich, it is unworthy! And you were prepared to sacrifice your poor child for this. Shame! Go away . . . At once!

SERGEY [*in despair*]. But I assure you . . .

VASYA. Silence! [*With great inner strength.*] Now I know how right some people are to mistrust our artistic intellectuals! Oh, how right they are!

[SERGEY *in horror backs out of the garden.*]

[*After a pause.*] Well! That man has upset me! I even forgot how nice the weather is today. [*He smiles again.*]

[AURORA VALOIS *comes out of the house.*]

VALOIS. Here you are, Listikov. I've been looking for you everywhere. It surprises me that I need you.

VASYA. Really?

VALOIS. I need you more than ever.

VASYA. Why do you need me more than ever, Comrade Valois?

VALOIS. Yesterday I was shaken by what you said about Stripikov. I immediately consulted another colleague. She was equally shaken but she found a way out by transferring him back to Moscow and you to Ustegorsk. Without delay!

VASYA. That's impossible!

VALOIS. I appreciate your indignation. Ustegorsk is very remote without cultural facilities. In short, I have already made a copy of your refusal to go there. [*Thrusts a piece of paper at him.*] Sign here.

VASYA. But why? Why should I refuse to go? I've never been there. No doubt there will be a lot of new impressions waiting for me at Ustegorsk. I can only welcome your colleague's insight.

VALOIS [*rather cross*]. You've agreed very quickly, haven't you? I find this suspicious. Perhaps you'd better stay. I'll consult my colleague. Besides, I'm used to you. You're a pleasant and valuable young man.

VASYA. No, no, to be where I haven't been, that's perfect! Tell me, when do I leave?

VALOIS. Our representative flies there in a few hours. [*Exulting.*] Are you ready to fly out of Moscow today?

VASYA. Certainly. Why, I've never flown in an aeroplane. [*Enthusiastic.*] Spreading my wings! Finding myself up here, on top. That's what I've been missing of late.

VALOIS. Well, I'll go and get a ticket for you. Well, fly away, leave us. It makes me happy and sad. [*She goes.*]

VASYA [*alone*]. First thing in the morning, what luck! I'm lucky again.

DARLING 2 [*appearing in the entrance*]. Vasya, come quickly . . . Seva's dying, I don't know why!

VASYA. How awful! [*Aside to audience.*] Not so lucky now.

[*Taking DARLING 2 by the hand, he runs into the house with her.*]

Scene Four

VASYA *and* DARLING 2 *anxiously run into the familiar room where* SEVA *is feeling very sorry for himself.*

VASYA [*dashing to the divan where SEVA lies in his agony*]. Seva, don't leave us! Hold on, old man! Look at the nice weather we're having!

DARLING 2. Remember how we love you . . .

SEVA [*glancing somewhere up to the ceiling*]. Kapetchenko wasn't appointed! That miserable fool Kapetchenko was turned down! Darling, change the cold compress on my forehead. Romanov was appointed. [*Clutches at his heart.*] I think I'm going to die again.

DARLING 2. Stop it at once, do you hear?

VASYA. You're a fool, Seva. Believe me – we should always look down on our trials and tribulations from somewhere above!

SEVA. You don't understand! For two years I've been setting up this edifice. I took on the gigantic though not impossible task of getting myself appointed assistant head of the department. First, I had to guess who would be the Head. I reckoned on Kapetchenko with his stormy and rapid rise, his whole powerful image of the blunt, down-to-earth man. I put my money on him and made a complicated chart of his advancement. Before he could be Head, Arbuznikov had to be promoted. That was only possible if Filaterov stayed put, which could only happen with Kosykh's promotion, which was impossible without a corresponding demotion of Svetlana Drozd, which implied the promotion of Maurice Bogoslavsky. It was enormous work! A titanic business! So what happened? I managed the lot. They promoted Arbuznikov, they stopped Filaterov, they advanced Kosykh, they demoted Drozd, and finally promoted Bogoslavsky. But as head of our department, they did not appoint Kapetchenko but that sensible man, Romanov! [*In dumb despair he collapses on the divan.*]

VASYA [*to* DARLING 2]. It's astonishing, the nonsense he's been wasting his time on!

SEVA [*tossing and turning again*]. For two years I lived in the orbit of that fool Kapetchenko. I took my leave when he did. By accident, as it were, I turned up at the same sanatoria. Like an idiot I went picking mushrooms with him. I sat holding a fishing rod and in the evening we sang Ukranian songs for two voices. For two years I suffered and worked it all out to he last detail. And what happens? [*Again he collapses on the divan.*]

VASYA. I'm sorry, Seva, but I don't know why you gave two years of your life to these mean intrigues.

SEVA. For one thing, not to be transferred to some Ustegorsk or other instead of Stripikov.

VASYA [*smiles in sympathy*]. Well, you must postpone your hopes of that.

SEVA. Why?

VASYA [*with a sense of great superiority*]. You see, I'm being sent to Ustegorsk. I'm awfully sorry for you, old man. You have suffered for two years. You're still suffering. While I have lived happily with a song in my heart and now I'm off to the back of beyond, infinitely curious to find out what it's all about!

DARLING 2. But you were always sorry for Stripikov.

VASYA. I'm not Stripikov! I take an enormous interest in the world around us. And in natural phenomena as well.

SEVA. Enough! [*Clutches at his heart.*] While you're babbling away, I expect Romanov is having me sacked. I'm sure he hasn't forgotten how, to please Kapetchenko, I sat on his new hat in public.

DARLING 2 [*with inspiration*]. Our method of accountancy! Romanov always showed great interest! [*Forcibly.*] Vasya, you mustn't go.

VASYA. Too late! For the last hour Comrade Valois has been kindly rushing from one booking office to another in search of a plane ticket for me.

DARLING 2. We must finish our work! And to save Seva, we shall announce that he and he only is the author of the method.

VASYA. That's wonderful! Darling! I'm full of admiration at your selfless love for him. All right, I'll stay and we shall save this Seva.

SEVA [*embarrassed*]. You know, chaps, something else has occurred to me. In the present circumstances I really don't think I should marry Darling.

VASYA. What do you mean?

SEVA. Everyone knows, that sensible Romanov adores his wife. The police fined him for hooliganism, when he kissed her on the underground escalator after they'd been married for fifteen years. They're often seen dancing for hours together at the Café National. Doesn't that mean that Romanov favours family stability? How can I behave in basic contradiction of his outlook!

DARLING 2. But you said, I was madly in love with you.

SEVA. Well, sweetie, I could be wrong.

VASYA. No, wait! [*He's very shaken.*] Did you really say what you've just said? [*To* DARLING 2.] And could you come back to me after all that's happened?

DARLING 2 [*at a loss*]. But if Seva made a mistake and I'm not madly in love with him, then . . .

VASYA. Silence! [*Turns to* SEVA.] But how awful, it seems you're a heel. [*Almost exulting.*] I'm surprised I never noticed it before! To turn down Darling! . . . [*Looks tenderly at* DARLING 2.] Turn you down! My best friend, Seva Polonsky? Even my love for you, Darling, begins to fade. One can't go on loving a woman, who's in love with an obvious heel. Seva, I'm right, aren't I?

SEVA [*business-like*]. Broadly speaking, you are right. But in this particular case, you're wrong. I should know whether I'm a heel or not. I definitely know I'm not. [*Gives an embarrassed smile.*] It's simply that one doesn't want to remain a nonentity.

DARLING 2. It's funny, you know, Seva has a button missing on his sleeve and I don't want to sew it on. [*Runs to the door.*]

SEVA. Where are you going?

DARLING 2. To see Comrade Romanov! They mustn't take our Vasya away! [*She runs out.*]

VASYA. No, no one has any power over me now!

[ALICIA, GENNADY *and* AKIM *appear and stand in the doorway.* AKIM *holds out his hands to* VASYA. *They're all motionless with emotion.*]

[*Astounded.*] Papa!

[*Stormy tears pour down* AKIM's *face, he is unable to speak and only shakes his head expressively.*]

What does this mean? I can't possibly guess!

GENNADY [*fairly prosaic*]. Look, old thing, I don't know why but he's forgiven you. See the embarrassed way he holds his arms out to you.

ALICIA. Even I feel touched. He made us move the furniture all night. You ought to be pleased. The dining room's gone. We've prepared the nursery for you again.

AKIM [*whispering with elation*]. Vasya, come back!

VASYA. It's amazing! [*Falls into his father's arms.*]

GENNADY [*approaching the recumbent* SEVA]. Hullo! [*Slaps him on the shoulder.*] What are you doing here, old man?

SEVA. Not so loud . . . I'm dying.

ALICIA [*offering him a cigarette*]. Why don't we all go to Laura Luntz tonight? They have a new gimmick. They drink tea.

VASYA [*freeing himself from his father's embrace*]. I'm happy!

AKIM. Vasya, you have passion. You do some silly things but you are a Listikov! Come, let's get down to business. [*Points at his son and daughter.*] Let's deliver them from cynicism.

[*Just then* AVENIR *pokes his head round the door and looks around the room with a pained smile.*]

VASYA. What, you again?

AVENIR. I don't know what you'll feel about this. Last night your ex-wife decided to stop suffering and to get married.

VASYA. To you?

AVENIR. No, no, apparently some other man. But I'm bearing up. If she married me, the fine threads uniting us would be bound to break. But now I have no one to share my grief with and I find myself completely at a loss in my spare time. I have been walking about Moscow all night. This morning in all the bustle I realized that from now on I must give support and comfort to you!

VASYA. Not really?

AVENIR. You have no home. Come and stay with me. I'm a simple Soviet librarian. But I have everything beautifully laid on for suffering in dark, hopeless loneliness.

AKIM [*very angry*]. Disgraceful to suggest such a thing! When his own father is standing here, asking him to return to the house where he was born.

AVENIR [*indignant*]. Then what am I going to do?

VASYA. Turn your attention to him. [*Points at* SEVA.] At this moment he is going through a great spiritual crisis. He's just right for you.

AVENIR [*looking greedily at* SEVA]. Most, most interesting . . .

SEVA [*thrashing about on the divan*].This room is over-crowded. Stop this outrage!

AUNTY [*entering*]. Vasya, I gather you're the cause of this disorder. It seems many of our neighbours saw you break the drainpipe. Thank you very much for the flowers but you must pay the ten rouble fine.

VASYA [*hurt*]. I'm cruelly punished. [*Hands her a ten rouble note.*] Where's your Valentinov? I don't see him.

AUNTY. You may never see him. That fool Valentinov has left me. Left me for ever.

VALENTINOV [*entering*]. They were again talking – about you, that you'd gone out visiting. No, you can't be left alone any more. There's something fascinating about you. It makes me nervous. You win, Sasha. Let's get married again.

AUNTY. Oh, how nice of you!

VALENTINOV. It isn't a bit nice of me. I simply want to live in peace. I'm not young any more and I've had enough. We'll take the two kilos of best butter and go to my remarkable House. We can lend your flat temporarily to Listikov.

AKIM [*again angry*]. What is this? More liberties with my son? I'm telling you all, he's going to live in his nursery!

VALENTINOV [*to* AUNTY SASHA]. Never mind about that. Sasha, come and live in the Writers House or you'll drive me mad.

SEVA. If you don't all stop over-crowding this room, I'll call the police!

[*In great haste and hand in hand* SERGEY SERGEYEVICH *and* DARLING 3 *come running in.*]

VASYA [*indignant*]. What? You here? I told you never to come near me.

SERGEY. Quite right. But important and constructive changes have just taken place . . .

DARLING 3. Yes, yes . . . Daddy and I have decided to give away the holiday home and to say goodbye to the car. We are above suspicion now.

VASYA. Extraordinary!

DARLING 3. We're giving the car to Daddy's wife's sister. She's a very famous mountaineer.

SERGEY. You mustn't worry about the holiday home. We handed it over to my nephew. He's still young. He has strong nerves.

VASYA [*goes on shaking hands with him*]. You have behaved like a true Sergey Sergeyevich! It's good to know there are people like you living all round us.

SERGEY. No, no, we are not heroes . . . Any Soviet citizen would do the same. In short, the doors of our house are open to you.

AKIM [*exploding*]. What are you all up to? Are you in collusion? I protest! If a woman wants to join her fate with his, she can come and live in the nursery.

DARLING 3. I'd love the nursery! I accept. But let's hurry!

SERGEY. Pull yourself together, my child!

AVENIR. How absurd! He needs a friend, a friend who will always suffer by his side!

SEVA [*clutching at his heart*]. Will you all please stop coming here!

ALICIA [*to* SEVA]. At eleven we're going to Morozov. His new thing is telepathy. Last Saturday I was very surprised.

GENNADY [*to* VASYA]. Look, old man, it's going on too long. Pack your things and let's go home.

[*But apart from the dying* SEVA *and* ALICIA, *who's very interested in him, they all crowd round* VASYA, *insisting that he should immediately come and stay with them.*]

VASYA [*happily*]. Thank you! But I can't accept your invitations. This morning I was ordered to take a plane to Ustegorsk, our furthest outpost. [*With significance.*] He has been ordered west!

AVENIR. But I made up your camp bed!

SERGEY. What is this? My nephew is on his way to take over the holiday home. He can't be far from Moscow.

AKIM. My advice is fly to the outpost! You're a Listikov. It's your only way out!

DARLING 2 [*running in*]. Comrade Romanov has cancelled your transfer! You're to go on working on your new method of accountancy. They'll find another dare-devil for Ustegorsk!

AKIM. That's disgraceful!

[*But all the others shout happily because* VASYA's *staying with them.*]

SEVA [*half-rising on his divan*]. Let's stop quarrelling. Everything's turning out extraordinarily well.

VASYA. I don't want to see you!

SERGEY. I'm so glad you're staying. My nephew's journey won't be for nothing!

AVENIR. Remember my camp bed! I'm your friend who will be happy to suffer alone with you.

[VALOIS *appears in the door, looking so exultant that there is immediate silence.*]

VALOIS. Well, Listikov, it's goodbye for a long time! Here's your ticket. Hurry up and pack. You'll be airborne in two hours.

AKIM [*happy*]. Fly away, Vasya!

DARLING 2. Allow me, Comrade Romanov cancelled Listikov's flight. He is not going anywhere ever.

VASYA. No? I feel I must spread my wings and I shall fly like an eagle. To Ustegorsk! Its joys and sorrows await me. I'm now part of it. You can all stay as you were. Only don't despair, don't torment yourselves, or I shall be very sorry for you.

DARLING 2 [*in tears*]. Vasya, I'm sorry . . . Look how dirty Seva's shoes are but I don't want to clean them. And I don't want to give him tea or sausage.

SEVA [*put out*]. But why ever not?

[*There should be some very sad music at this point.*]

DARLING 2 [*to* **VASYA**]. Because, Vasya, I very much want you.

VASYA [*looking fondly at* **DARLING 2**, *speaking quietly*]. No. no, Darling . . . I still love you, but one can never bring anything back, never.

DARLING 3. Vasya . . . Oh, please, let me be part of your historic flight. I'll follow you everywhere until you finally fall in love with me.

VASYA [*looking fondly at this* **DARLING**]. You're so lovely to look at, Darling, I may not be able to control myself . . . But that will come later. In the meantime, go on with your useful studies. Just now we badly need experts in ancient Greek.

VALOIS. You have surprised me very much, Listikov. You're a splendid young man. Fly away! Keep well!

[*The sad music ends and the gay gallop is heard once more. They all step back and* **VASYA**, *dancing to the music, quickly packs his bag.*]

VASYA [*puts his cap on*]. Well, I'm off on my way! What makes our life wonderful? There are still discoveries and decisions to be made, things to be found and arranged on the shelves. We too have our part to play in deciding and arranging this and that. In our own way. And with these opportunities, can we be anything but happy!

> You're alive, so what's the fuss?
> Life's a pleasure you enjoy.
> See the people going past,
> Surely some of them are nice!
> No, don't fuss, old man, don't sulk.
> Look, it's lov'ly weather now.
> Even if it were to rain,
> Leaping puddles can be fun.

[*Dancing merrily, suitcase in hand, he recedes. The others, inspired by his example, either go rushing after him like* **DARLING 3** *or dance merrily singing his song.*]

FINAL CURTAIN

Lovely to Look At!

In an interview with I. Vishnevskaya published in Moscow's *Literary Gazette* on 11 April 1969, Arbuzov said he had decided to go in for a form of training, like an athlete or a musician. *Lovely to Look At!* was his exercise to write a play about the "ideal" hero. He followed the recommended line; unexpectedly he had created a comic character.

The play has not been produced in the West. It has not had much success in the Soviet Union. The rehearsals in Moscow's Malaya Bronnaya Theatre were dropped. Whenever the play has been produced, critics and audiences were confused.

My text is mostly based on Arbuzov's revised version in *Vybor*, 1976. I had to translate the name of a character who never appeared — Polosatikov, meaning striped, therefore Stripikov in English. But that was hardly a problem. Incidentally, Arbuzov uses other names for comic effect including a version of his own surname.

The difficulty was his mixture of bureaucratic and lyrical dialogue. This is satire, highly stylized and also good-natured. Theatrically it is very skilled – I mean, everything echoes to a conclusion and builds up hilariously. Arbuzov thinks that *Lovely to Look At!* is his most successful comedy.

ONCE UPON A TIME

(Tales of Old Arbat)

A Comedy in Two Parts

Once Upon a Time was first performed at the Little Theatre of the Bristol Old Vic on 23 March 1976 with the following cast:

Fedya Balyasnikov	Michael Hordern
Khristofor Blokhin	John Cater
Kuzma	Robert O'Mahoney
Viktosha	Felicity Kendal
Fatty	Anthony O'Donell
Levushka	Miles Anderson
Directed by	David Horlock
Designed by	Fiona Mathers

Skazki Starogo Arbata (*Tales of Old Arbat/Once Upon a Time*) was first performed in Moscow at the Malaya Bronnaya Theatre on New Year's Eve 1971 with the following cast:

Balyasnikov	B. Tenin
Blokhin	L. Bronevoy
Kuzma	V. Smirnitsky
Viktosha	O. Yakovleva
Tolstyachek	L. Kanevsky
Levushka	V. Lakirev
Directed by	A. Efros
Designed by	D. Borovsky

Skazki Starogo Arbata (*Tales of Old Arbat/Once Upon a Time*) was first performed in Leningrad on 12 May 1971 at the Pushkin Theatre with the following cast:

Balyasnikov	B. Freindlikh
Blokhin	Y. Tolubeyev
Kuzma	V. Semenovsky
Viktosha	N. Maksimova
Tolstyachek	A. Borisov
Levushka	E. Romanov and S. Sytnik
Directed by	A. Muzil'
Designed by	M. Kitayev

CHARACTERS

FYODOR KUZMICH BALYASNIKOV (FEDYA), master puppeteer, a splendid man of sixty

KUZMA (KUZYA), his son, a student, twenty-two, he looks like his father

KHRISTOFOR BLOKHIN, Balyasnikov's assistant and quiet and devoted friend, well over sixty

VIKTOSHA, a dear visitor from Leningrad, twenty and bound to be famous

LEVUSHKA, engaged to Viktosha, a personality, already nineteen

FATTY, of uncertain age

The action takes place in the sixties in Balyasnikov's fantastic studio in old Arbat, a district of small streets in Moscow.
The weather is wonderful throughout,
except that it rains in Act Two, Scene Two.

[The play should be taken at a good pace and even the sentimental parts should be played with a certain dash.]

272

ACT ONE

Scene One

Late morning in the early autumn. The weather is good. A distinct roaring comes from the next room. Then **FEDYA BALYASNIKOV,** *responsible for the singing, appears in his studio. He's a young sixty. He has obviously just woken up. He stands out from the majority of his contemporaries by his good nature and dash, his powerful build and a gay streak of laziness. His dressing-gown hanging loose, he crosses the room to the writing-table, where he finds the remains of yesterday's sandwich. This pleases him and he eats it. Luckily the beer bottle by the ink-well turns out to be half full and he washes down the remains of the sandwich with the remains of the beer. This satisfies him, and smacking his belly, he momentarily bursts into song again. The puppets and toy animals sitting and standing on numerous shelves appear to listen to his performance in a happy state of excitement. However,* **FEDYA** *picks up a toy pistol and walks on. He stops by a multicoloured and gay giraffe.*

FEDYA [*disapproving*]. You've got a cheek! [*Fires at him twice.*]

[*Finally he reaches the telephone, drops into an armchair and dials.*]

[*Into the phone.*] Irina Fyodorovna? Erasmus of Rotterdam speaking. Your father says you're going to be twenty in twenty days. Go down to the caretaker. She has a crate of champagne for you. I repeat, I'm speaking from Rotterdam. Now run down and see the caretaker.

[*He hangs up and dials another number.*]

[*In a deep voice.*] Comrade Burkov? It's Simonne Signoret – you know the 100 roubles you owe that nice man Balyasnikov. He's leaving for the Volga. You must give it back toot sweet and the tooter the sweeter. If you don't, my Yves will come and box your ears. Freundschaft!

[*He hangs up. There's a noise in the hall followed by the appearance of* **KHRISTOFOR BLOKHIN,** *laden with a couple of shopping bags full of nice eats.* **KHRISTOFOR** *looks most disreputable and is nowhere as handsome as* **FEDYA.**]

KHRISTOFOR. I got a lot of sausage.

FEDYA. Why?

KHRISTOFOR. It's nice. [*Takes out the shopping.*]

FEDYA. Have you left the champage for Irina?

KHRISTOFOR. I left it with the caretaker. Why haven't you tidied the place up? It's your turn.

FEDYA. Don't you see . . . It's the first day of our leave. I thought I'd celebrate and do absolutely nothing. We'll see where we go from there.

KHRISTOFOR [*looking fondly at him*]. Oh, all right.

FEDYA. I've put the kettle on.

KHRISTOFOR [*happily*]. Well done! [*Goes into the kitchen.*]

FEDYA. That's quite enough.

> [*FEDYA in the meantime eats. A long piece of business follows. FEDYA tastes everything. Some things meet with his lively approval. He clicks his tongue and mumbles with pleasure. Other things he finds disappointing and he shrugs in surprise, sadly condoling and heaving bitter sighs. The tasting ends when KHRISTOFOR returns with a very hot teapot.*]

KHRISTOFOR. Better not eat with your fingers. And you should wait for me.

FEDYA [*deep in thought*]. Khristofor!

KHRISTOFOR [*pouring out the tea*]. Well?

FEDYA. Somehow I'm worried. I keep listening in to myself and trying to find out how I feel. Do I feel well or do I feel ill? Yes, something's wrong.

> [*Phone rings.*]

[*Into the phone.*] Cyrano de Bergerac. [*Somewhat put out.*] What number do you want? . . . It is not the laundry. [*Puts the receiver down.*]

KHRISTOFOR [*like a teacher*]. You see, how silly that is – it's not funny.

FEDYA [*looking suspiciously at the phone*]. It hasn't rung all morning. When it does ring – the laundry, if you please! It's all very peculiar. Suddenly nobody needs me. I don't know why.

KHRISTOFOR. Relax and drink your tea. Have some sausage.

> [*The morning act begins. They eat without putting anything out on a plate, straight out of the wrapping paper.*]

FEDYA. Why doesn't someone phone me? It's ominous.

KHRISTOFOR. At the toy factory they know you're on holiday. Don't you see, dear boy, they don't want to disturb you. And your marionette theatre is on tour.

FEDYA. I shouldn't have taken a holiday. [*Eats sausage with great anxiety.*] I'm listening in to myself and ... I'm afraid of this holiday. Well, what am I going to do?

KHRISTOFOR. Tomorrow we take the boat to Astrakhan. We've booked a wonderful cabin. And when we get there we'll come back to Moscow.

FEDYA. Don't you think it's funny to go from Moscow to Moscow?

KHRISTOFOR [*patiently*]. No, because on the way we'll see some lovely scenery. Ask anyone you like. A trip on the Volga leaves a lasting impression on you.

FEDYA. Not any more! I'm sixty. I've been everywhere and I've seen everything.

KHRISTOFOR. You haven't been everywhere.

FEDYA. Well, all right, but very nearly. I swear it. Sometimes I think centuries have unrolled before my eyes. I saw Nicholas, the second, driving along Nevsky in his carriage. From a tree in the Aleksandrovsk Garden I watched, fascinated, the storming of Winter Palace. I was an actor in Meyerhold's company. I nearly got beaten up by Yessenin. And I was playing billiards with Mayakovsky the night he broke his cue ... I've been to Turksib, Magnitka, Dneprostroy! My first marionettes aroused Lunacharsky's enthusiasm. "Balyasnikov's satirical puppets are fantastic", wrote the Paris newspapers before the war. Finally, May forty-five, concussed and deafened, I entered Berlin. I had tonsilitis. I was in a state of collapse and I fainted at the sight of the Brandenburg Gate. Furthermore, I've had several unsuccessful marriages. I have talked with the Pope in the Vatican. I have often despaired. And for many years I couldn't forget the new record of the high jump. Why have you decided to put me away in a ship's cabin for three weeks? What new impressions can you possibly offer me now?

KHRISTOFOR [*pouring him a second glass of tea, putting in the sugar and stirring it*]. You see, you must concentrate. I'm told, the banks of the Volga are astonishingly conducive to concentration.

FEDYA [*swallowing a very large piece of ham*]. I must work! The artist concentrates when he works.

KHRISTOFOR. All right! But you're sixty. Why don't you retire?

FEDYA [*fiercely chewing some cheese*]. Never!

KHRISTOFOR. As before, we'll go on making marionettes for our darling theatre. You'll go on creating your extraordinary toys. But to spend every morning at the toy-factory, sitting in the office pretending to be top dog ... Believe me, it's a mad waste of time.

FEDYA. Now shut up! Or I shan't have any breakfast! Goethe said, in his old age man must do more than in his youth. You know perfectly well, I can't imagine working on my own. I must be surrounded by people. I love cranks, fantasticks, puppeteers, virtuosos — all with the imagination of children and all so helpless, so naive when faced with bureaucrats and red tape. I've got to be in the thick of the fight, pushing, advising, helping. I can't imagine life without this diabolic fuss and bother.

KHRISTOFOR. Now relax. You'd better think about the past.

FEDYA [*sticking a piece of roll in his mouth*]. Never! The past is out of my control. Only the future is under my control. We've argued enough! You've already committed a felony! Booking this holiday! I haven't sunk so low for years.

KHRISTOFOR. You're unreasonable and noisy. [*Sighs bitterly.*] You can't imagine how tired you make me.

FEDYA [*delighted*]. That's right! Man is born to be tired. Only it's disgraceful to be tired doing nothing! [*With inspiration.*] You know what? We'll work in our cabin. Our Maestro's had a brilliant idea. He wants to do "Helen of Troy" with puppets. What scope for fantasy! Paris, Meneleus, Agammemnon . . . What characters! What masks! Beautiful Helen? All enchantment and magic. Everything I'd hoped for from women which I never got. I shall put it all into this marionette.

KHRISTOFOR. You haven't been offered a contract. Our divine Maestro hasn't said a thing.

FEDYA. Who else is there? Be sensible, don't make me laugh. [*Wipes his mouth with a napkin and gets up.*]

KHRISTOFOR [*anxious*]. I hope you've had enough to eat?

FEDYA. More than enough. As I ate, there were moments when I was almost happy.

[*Doorbell.*]

The bell . . .

KHRISTOFOR [*listening*]. No doubt about that.

FEDYA. Go and open the door. But don't let in the nasties, only the niceties.

KHRISTOFOR. I'll try. [*Goes out.*]

FEDYA [*giving himself up to contemplation*]. I'm glad about the door bell. I haven't been forgotten. But is my time going to be wasted by the right person?

KHRISTOFOR [*returning*]. It's Kuzya.

[**KUZYA BALYASNIKOV** *runs in. He is a young man with a contemporary exterior but very like* **BALYASNIKOV** *Senior. In any case, their temperaments are extraordinarily alike.*]

KUZYA [*aggressively*]. Hullo!

FEDYA [*cautiously*]. Greetings. [*After a pause.*] How are you?

KUZYA [*slinging his Italian plastic mac into a distant armchair*]. All right.

FEDYA [*enquiringly*]. Would you like some tea?

KUZYA [*having glanced at the food with interest*]. No, I wouldn't. [*Paces up and down the room in silence.*]

KHRISTOFOR. Kuzya, sit down in the armchair. You keep walking about all the time.

KUZYA. Explain how you put up with him all the time.

FEDYA. Now, don't go too far.

KUZYA [*furious*]. You can talk!

[*He eats a large piece of sausage without realizing it.*]

Hypocrite!

FEDYA [*unexpectedly gentle*]. Try the liver sausage.

KUZYA. Certainly not!

[*He thumps the table with his fist but most awkwardly for himself.*]

Damn!

KHRISTOFOR. My dear Kuzya, swearing is old-fashioned. I keep telling you.

KUZYA [*blows on his fist*]. Something cracked.

FEDYA [*boyishly*]. Serves you right!

KHRISTOFOR. Fedya, keep quiet . . . [*To* **KUZYA.**] You pipe down too. I can cope with each of you separately, but both together in one room is too much.

FEDYA [*to* **KUZYA**]. What's happened now?

KUZYA [*aggressively*]. I was called this morning by Nikolayev of Multifilms, he offered me work on his cartoon. Of course, I accepted. Then I had my doubts. I asked him why his choice fell on me, a fourth year student? Do you know what he said: "Your father's recommendation is an order. He is most insistent in recommending you." I ask you! It's bad enough your recommending me. Do you have to insist as well!

[*Automatically and with a gesture very like* BALYASNIKOV *Senior he eats a large piece of ham.*]

And yesterday I got a money transfer. [*Suddenly smiles happily.*] Fifty roubles, damn it! Of course, I wanted to know who sent it. I read the name at the back – Robinson Crusoe! [*To* KHRISTOFOR.] Now, tell me who gave him the right to jeer at me and play the benefactor? Well, who is he?

FEDYA. I'm your father.

KUZYA. You? The arrogance of the man!

FEDYA. Anyway, up to a point.

KUZYA. Sounds wonderful – "up to a point!" My aunt was so right. I love her passionately. When mother died she took me in and refused to let you within a mile of me. All your life you've laughed at people and made fools of them. With your phone calls, your bright ideas, your little games! What do you mean by it? You won't let my sister have a moment's peace. Damn you, why do you go and pester the people you deserted and discarded?

FEDYA. You're wrong again. All my wives deserted me.

KUZYA. But you drove them to it, with your inattention, your thoughtlessness, your endless jokes . . . Good you've calmed down lately and stopped making these poor irrational women fall in love with you. [*With renewed despair.*] You've never needed anyone. For you your puppets take the place of the living! Or you've got people and puppets muddled up and you play with them all.

FEDYA [*losing his temper*]. Splendid, I'm no good! What about you? You haven't even the imagination to choose your own profession. You follow in my tracks like a slave! You're a copy-cat!

KUZYA. Oh no, not that! But I've had only one dream from childhood – to surpass you! To prove myself! For everyone to see! You know why? Because you never loved me . . .

KHRISTOFOR. Kuzya, stop it at once . . . I simply can't bear it.

KUZYA [*furious*]. There's only one thing I owe this man – he persuaded my mother to call me Kuzma, to the astonishment of all my future friends.

FEDYA [*angry*]. You should be ashamed of yourself! I called you Kuzma in honour of your grandfather, Kuzma Balyasnikov, the greatest craftsman of pipes and reeds in outer Moscow!

KUZYA [*still heated*]. You've always wanted one thing in life – to astonish everyone. Now you're sixty and you haven't astonished anyone.

FEDYA. Who says so? The scruffy generation? Conjurors without tricks? When we go, there will be no one left!

KUZYA. What do you know about us? You're so in love with your own magnificence, you never noticed that your time was over. Finito! Even the marionette theatre has passed you by.

FEDYA. That's a lie! [*Anxious.*] What do you mean?

KUZYA. Well, to do the marionettes for "Helen of Troy" they asked . . . They asked Lepyoshkin.

FEDYA. That's not true! [*Pause.*] Who told you?

KUZYA. They all know in the theatre.

FEDYA [*after a slight pause*]. Well, so what? It's perfectly natural. Balyasnikov is too good for all their frolics. After all, I recommended this Lepyoshkin. Who else? Do you think it was easy to persuade the theatre to take him on?

KUZYA [*looks at him for a long time*]. I'm sorry for you, Papa. [*Goes to the door and turns.*] The 50 roubles will be sent back to Robinson Crusoe by post.

FEDYA [*shouting after him*]. Oh, you . . . You were always impossible. You couldn't sound your r's till you were five!

KUZYA [*pausing on the threshold*]. Is that why you left us? Now I can sound my r's. Without your help. Which makes me fr-r-r-rightfully pr-r-r-roud! [*Goes out.*]

FEDYA [*after thought*]. Well . . . Who says the problem of fathers and sons doesn't exist? I suppose that is the problem.

KHRISTOFOR. He grows more and more like you.

FEDYA [*weakly*]. Do you think so? [*Thinking it over.*] Well, yes, he isn't all that hopeless. [*Quietly.*] You know, don't you . . . The thing I'd like most in the world is that he should live here . . . With me.

KHRISTOFOR. I know, old thing.

FEDYA. It's disgusting that I let myself go like this . . . Attacking the young generation . . . I am a nonentity, Khristofor!

KHRISTOFOR [*going to him cautiously*]. What's the matter, Fedya?

FEDYA [*in despair*]. Lepyoshkin! Lepyoshkin! [*Frightened.*] It's old age! I'm out of the swim. Finished as an artist. And why not? Sooner or later it happens to us all. Finito!

KHRISTOFOR. What rubbish! We really must concentrate. I'm sure we'll see things differently in the sunny open spaces of the Volga. Since nature makes man grow aware of himself.

FEDYA [*jumping up*]. No doubt!

[*He goes to a shelf and takes down an unfinished animal.*]

Look! This morning at dawn I found the solution. Now she can swing her tail in several directions . . . This way and that way . . . [*He demonstrates.*] Clever, isn't it? She bats her ears too — now up, now down, in surprise, as it were. [*Winks.*] How's that?

KHRISTOFOR. Astonishing! This way and that way . . . You have a great talent. I'm going home now.

FEDYA. Why? I simply don't understand, why do you have to go home all the time? Why can't you stay for a moment?

KHRISTOFOR. You see, I think that I ought to sweep my flat occasionally. I don't like being there since Masha died. Haven't you noticed? But I have to look after Masha's fur coat and her two spring coats. They always have to be cleaned. Also aired. One coat we bought together the day we moved into the flat. An astonishingly happy day. I remember, she and I drank some wine and we got a little tipsy too. We had a very good time, you know. [*Pause.*] I think I'll go now.

FEDYA. Don't go!

KHRISTOFOR. Why not?

FEDYA. It's the first day of my holiday. You thought this nonsense up! Don't leave me. We'll go and wander. I'll show you places in Moscow where I spent my youth. We'll have a wonderful day! [*Looks at him.*] The only thing wrong is — you look so shapeless, it's awful. You haven't shaved, your hair grows in all directions, somehow . . . What's that suit? You don't look interesting!

KHRISTOFOR. Do you mean me or my suit?

FEDYA. Not a single young woman would look at you!

KHRISTOFOR. What fun do I get out of her looking at my suit?

FEDYA. Don't argue . . . Now put on my jacket.

[*He puts his jacket on him.*]

There now . . . That's better.

KHRISTOFOR [*looking at himself helplessly*]. Don't you think, it looks funny?

FEDYA. Nonsense! We'll pin it up here and there with safety pins . . .

KHRISTOFOR. I'll look awfully funny, won't I?

FEDYA. It's the fear of looking funny that's funny! Come on! I'll show you places where I was happy once upon a time! . . .

Scene Two

Late evening of the same day. The windows of the studio are wide open. Here and there the starry sky is visible above the roof-tops. The soothing sounds of evening radio programmes can be heard coming from many sets outside.
 The studio is empty. Then there is the sound of a commotion in the corridor. The door opens and FEDYA *and* KHRISTOFOR *enter, accompanied by* FATTY, *obviously a provincial in his white Cossack felt hat. They've had plenty to eat and drink but they behave well, either concentrating grimly or happy like children.*

FEDYA. Well now, I think we've arrived somewhere.

KHRISTOFOR. We have. No doubt about that. But where?

FEDYA. This dressing-gown reminds me of someone . . . Khristofor, I rather think we've come home.

KHRISTOFOR. You know, I think so too.

 [FATTY *makes himself comfortable in an armchair and goes to sleep at once.*]

Look, I think we have visitors.

FEDYA. Don't give it a thought. [*Looks at him fondly.*] Today you're very handsome.

KHRISTOFOR. I think so. I've had a remarkable haircut.

FEDYA. I'm only sorry I never managed to show you the places where I was happy once upon a time. Shrubberies, benches, gateways – all gone. Instead we have isotopic emporiums. Alas, these vast new buildings destroy our memories, our past.

KHRISTOFOR. Well, God bless! We've had a marvellous time. We had refreshments. I feel refreshed.

FEDYA. I had no luck. All day I expected something extraordinary to happen. It hasn't happened.

KHRISTOFOR. That's the way it is, sometimes.

[FATTY *wakes up, takes down the giraffe from the shelf and kisses it.*]

FEDYA [*pointing to* FATTY]. Look, who is that?

KHRISTOFOR [*surprised*]. I don't know.

FEDYA [*astonished*]. Nor do I. [*Thinks.*] You think he's been here long?

KHRISTOFOR. I don't think so.

FATTY [*kissing the giraffe again*]. There are no happy faces in the shops. He's the best. He's nice.

KHRISTOFOR. Who are you?

FATTY [*concentrating*]. I'll have to try and remember.

KHRISTOFOR [*to* FEDYA]. He doesn't remember.

FEDYA. Then let him play the guitar.

KHRISTOFOR. I don't suppose he can.

FEDYA. Well, why did he come here?

KHRISTOFOR. Well, he came, don't you know. He just came, that's all.

FEDYA. He's sitting down now.

KHRISTOFOR. There you are.

FATTY [*pleased*]. I remember!

KHRISTOFOR. There, you see, he remembers!

FATTY. I got a telegram. My wife had a boy.

FEDYA. That's marvellous.

FATTY. No.

KHRISTOFOR. Why not?

FATTY. I divorced her five years ago.

FEDYA. Funny. Why did it take her so long?

FATTY. She got married. [*Excusing himself.*] I'm from the town of Gdov.

[*Pause.*]

FEDYA. I don't suppose he will play the guitar.

KHRISTOFOR. Of course he won't.

FATTY. I'm terribly glad she had a boy. She always wanted one. He's a nice man too. Very sociable. We have an exceptionally good relationship.

FEDYA. He's a romantic. No doubt of that. How did he get here?

KHRISTOFOR. He probably had refreshments somewhere with us. We've been having refreshments all evening. I expect he joined us. [*To* FATTY.] Have you had any refreshments?

FATTY. I don't touch it as a rule. But today I let myself go. I couldn't do without.

FEDYA. He's a splendid man.

KHRISTOFOR. He's fine. I understand him. Do you?

FEDYA. Me too. Even though he doesn't want to play the guitar.

KHRISTOFOR [*explaining it*]. He can't.

FATTY [*taking a photograph out of his wallet*]. You see, that's her. And we got divorced. We went and got divorced. She's very nice.

FEDYA. We'll enlarge her.

KHRISTOFOR [*climbing up on the wall somewhere*]. Then we'll hang her right here.

FATTY. Thanks. [*Kisses the giraffe.*] He's nice too.

FEDYA. He's got a cheek!

FATTY. Why not? I'm very fond of him. I spent all day shopping today. No nice faces. This one's the nicest.

FEDYA. He's a reject.

FATTY [*affectionately hugging the giraffe*]. Why?

FEDYA. He isn't typical.

FATTY [*happily*]. Who cares? [*Cautiously.*] Can I have him? Thanks. They'll be very very pleased. [*Sadly.*] Out there in Gdov.

KHRISTOFOR. There you are, he's from Gdov.

[FATTY *picks up the guitar lying on the sofa.*]

FEDYA. Incredible! He's going to play the guitar.

KHRISTOFOR. I never counted on that!

FATTY [*singing fairly well and accompanying himself*].

> Dearest love,
> Will you listen to me;
> Near your window I stand,
> Me and my guitar.

So
One glance cast on me,
Only one, only one;
Brighter day than in May
Wondrous shines from your eyes.

So
One glance cast on me,
Only one, only one;
Brighter day than in May
Wondrous shines from your eyes.

Many trials have I known;
I'd be glad of them all,
Only warm me my heart
With your tenderest glance.

So
One glance cast on me
Only one, only one;
Brighter day than in May
Wondrous shines from your eyes.

So
One glance cast on me,
Only one, only one;
Brighter day than in May
Wondrous shines from your eyes.

Dearest love,
Will you listen to me;
Near your window I stand,
Me and my guitar.

FEDYA. Unbelievable! He's a romantic.

KHRISTOFOR. He's super.

FEDYA. Don't let's give him back. Let's keep him.

KHRISTOFOR. It might be difficult. He's from the town of Gdov.

FATTY [*stops singing and looks round*]. Where am I?

KHRISTOFOR. Here.

FATTY. Surely not! How did I get here?

FEDYA. You joined us.

FATTY. Quite right. It isn't any fun alone. [*Points to the giraffe.*] Wrap him up. Where's your cash desk?

FEDYA [*wraps the giraffe in newspaper*]. You have already paid.

FATTY. Oh yes. [*Looks at the other puppets.*] I'd buy some more, but my money's run out. [*Clutches the giraffe tightly.*] It doesn't matter. This one's the best.

KHRISTOFOR. Please give our greetings to the newly born.

FATTY [*thinks*]. What if they don't show him to me? [*Smiles shyly.*] Goodbye.

[*He goes to the door, sits down on a chair and remains absolutely still.*]

FEDYA [*looks at him*]. He's in a bad way.

KHRISTOFOR. Not good. Not at all.

FEDYA. He plays the guitar well. That's when I sobered up.

KHRISTOFOR [*sadly*]. I sobered up later, when he said, what if they didn't show it to him.

FEDYA. I sobered up for the second time then.

FATTY [*active again*]. Thank you for your kindness. [*Explaining it.*] I've been thinking.

FEDYA. Put him in a taxi. [*To* **FATTY.**] My friend will accompany you.

FATTY. You're right. One very much wants to be accompanied. By anyone at all. [*Turns back in the door.*] It isn't any fun alone.

[*He leaves the room accompanied by* **KHRISTOFOR.** **FEDYA** *takes the guitar and sings the song, which has just been performed. The door from the corridor opens quietly and* **VIKTOSHA** *appears. She's fun and beautiful and worthy of interest. The suitcases she carries are obviously heavy and she puts them down quietly on the floor. Either out of politeness or interest she waits till* **FEDYA** *ends the song which he does on a stormy note.*]

VIKTOSHA. Good evening . . .

FEDYA [*looks at her for a long time*]. How interesting! All day I was quite sure that something surprising would happen. And when it hadn't happened by the evening, I was upset. Now you've appeared. Thank you.

VIKTOSHA. I haven't appeared. I . . .

FEDYA. Don't deny it. You have appeared. I'm sorry that I don't know you. Are you a nymph?

VIKTOSHA. No, no, I don't think so. It's just that two people came out of your flat and they were concentrating so hard, they were so preoccupied, they didn't answer me. [*Explaining.*] You see, I'm looking for your neighbour, Natasha Kretova. Perhaps you know where she is. Do you?

FEDYA. I don't know where she is now. The night before last, all night I heard from her flat shouts of jollity punctuated with single shots. Towards morning everything was quiet. It was obvious they'd shot each other and I fell fast asleep.

VIKTOSHA. I see you're just like the two men, helping each other down the stairs.

FEDYA. Please don't think too badly of us. We simply tried celebrating the start of my utterly futile holiday.

VIKTOSHA. Funny. I started my holiday today.

FEDYA. This coincidence brings us closer together to some extent. Are you quite sure you aren't a nymph?

VIKTOSHA. No, no, of course not.

FEDYA. Pity. At my age nymphs are less unsettling.

VIKTOSHA [*smiles*]. Are you very old?

FEDYA. I'd rather not think so. Of course, at my age it's stupid to pretend to be young. But to give way to old age is twice as stupid.

VIKTOSHA. That's very sound.

FEDYA. The approach of old age is nothing. It's the passing of youth that hurts.

[KHRISTOFOR *returns.*]

However, here's this quite remarkable man back again. Come closer. Don't be afraid. At first, I also thought she was a nymph, but it's all right. Fortunately.

[KHRISTOFOR *bows shyly to* VIKTOSHA. *He is very embarrassed.*]

VIKTOSHA [*looking round the room*]. Do you collect toys?

FEDYA. In a sense. We're quite splendid, on the whole. We'll do our very best to make you fall for us. You'll see. Now, hurry up and tell us, what's your name?

VIKTOSHA [*enjoying herself very much*]. Viktoria Nikolayevna has appeared before you.

FEDYA. She's done the right thing. I'm sure of that.

PLATE 21. Felicity Kendal as Viktosha, Michael Hordern as Balyasnikov and
Robert O'Mahoney as Kuzma, Bristol Old Vic

PLATE 22. Michael Hordern, John Cater as Khristofor and Anthony O'Donell as Fatty

PLATE 23. B. Tenin as Balyasnikov, Malaya Bronnaya Theatre, Moscow

PLATE 24. L. Bronevoy as Khristofor, V. Smirnitsky as Kuzma and B. Tenin

PLATE 25. L. Bronevoy, O. Yakovleva as Viktosha and B. Tenin

PLATE 26. B. Tenin and L. Bronevoy

VIKTOSHA. But Natasha? What do I do about her? Remember, I'm determined to find her.

FEDYA. Yes, yes. Khristofor, you know, we're all determined to find Natasha. [*To* **VIKTOSHA.**] Do you really need her?

VIKTOSHA. I should think so. I flew from Leningrad to see her. I've just arrived.

FEDYA. All right, we'll try and track her down. Khristofor! Go and find Shurik. At this time of day he's always somewhere winning at cards. [*To* **VIKTO-SHA.**] Shurik's a remarkable man! He's the trade union champion of shooting galleries. And he's always married to an actress of the Contemporary Theatre. So he's always very progressively inclined. Ask Shurik where Natasha is. He knows absolutely everything.

KHRISTOFOR. All right, I'll go and see Shurik. But, please, don't stand by that open window. It's getting cold. [*Bowing gracefully to* **VIKTOSHA** *he departs.*]

FEDYA. Dear Victoria, I must tell you that Khristofor is fantastically hard-working and enormously talented. [*Modestly.*] And he's my closest assistant.

VIKTOSHA. What does he assist you with?

FEDYA. I'm a master puppeteer. All that you see was created by me with the assistance of Khristofor Blokhin. We've been friends for twenty-five years.

VIKTOSHA. How nice of you to be master puppeteer! When I was a little girl and my parents were alive, my sister and I had lots of dolls. I sewed all their dresses. The dresses I designed! Once I created such a wedding dress for Cinderella, my youngest sister wept all night in an ecstasy of envy! Later we had to fend for ourselves. I began sewing dresses for very small little girls. I earned a bit that way. I was already sixteen, you know. My sister was only fourteen. I had to look after her. She's now a student. She even got married this spring. True, for the first time. And now I'm alone. Because my best friend Nelly also got married. [*Smiles.*] It's awful! There's only Natasha left.

FEDYA. What are you going to be?

VIKTOSHA [*delighted*]. Dressmaker!

FEDYA. Unusual! When did you decide?

VIKTOSHA. When I was three. And you know, I haven't wavered a single day in that, my first decision. That's how constant I am. I've done a two-year course of fashion design and I'm working for a trial period at the Leningrad House of Fashion. Imagine how famous I'll be when I'm mature? With a lot of luck, I may make beautiful and varied clothes for all the women of the Soviet Union. Think how marvellous, if all the famous designers of London and Paris burst with envy. That would be lovely!

FEDYA. I see, you have far-reaching plans.

VIKTOSHA. Of course. I'm extraordinarily crafty.

FEDYA. You're a show-off, that's what you are!

VIKTOSHA. One's got to bolster up one's failing strength. I'm terribly unlucky in my private life.

FEDYA. You don't speak a word of truth!

VIKTOSHA. I do sometimes. In the heat of discussion sometimes I'm forced to speak the truth.

[KHRISTOFOR *returns.*]

KHRISTOFOR. I know everything.

FEDYA. What did Shurik say? How long will Natasha be? Where is she?

KHRISTOFOR. She got married. Shurik didn't say for how long.

VIKTOSHA. Incredible! I get the impression that all the world is getting married. That's what I should have done. [*Pause.*] No wait . . . She only wrote a fortnight ago to say she finally fell out of love with her fiancé . . .

KHRISTOFOR. That's right. Shurik confirmed it. She hasn't married her fiancé but his best friend. It was a lovely wedding. They drank champagne all night and left for their honeymoon in the morning.

FEDYA. Champagne? All is clear! It explains the shots.

VIKTOSHA. How could she go on her honeymoon and get married, when she knew I had nobody to stay with in Moscow?

KHRISTOFOR [*heatedly*]. Simply amazing how that didn't stop her.

VIKTOSHA [*sadly*]. I can't go back to Leningrad.

FEDYA. Why not?

VIKTOSHA. I – I ran away.

FEDYA. Ran away? Why?

VIKTOSHA. I was getting married tomorrow.

FEDYA. Do you have to run away on your wedding day? This is something new.

KHRISTOFOR. Don't be so reactionary. You know that youth is always right. Supposing they want to be joined in matrimony in Moscow, the capital?

FEDYA. Well, I suppose there's an endearing strangeness about that. [*To* VIKTOSHA.] In that case, where's your fiancé?

VIKTOSHA. I ran away from him!

FEDYA. Were you forced to marry him?

VIKTOSHA. Not at all! It's just I'm afraid he won't be happy with me. I'm really terribly afraid of that.

FEDYA. But why?

VIKTOSHA. You know — he's too clever. He's only a year younger than me, but in his presence even I feel awfully ill-informed . . . Yes, yes, Levushka is an amazing young man. It would be absurd to expect his feelings to last.

FEDYA. But . . . You're so beautiful.

VIKTOSHA. What's the point? Well, what's the use of a beautiful wife to a clever man? He's no fool!

KHRISTOFOR. That's right, Fedya! What?

FEDYA. Keep quiet! [*To* VIKTOSHA.] How old are you?

VIKTOSHA. I'm twenty already . . . [*Sadly.*] Twenty.

FEDYA. Twenty? Ha! If I was your age!

KHRISTOFOR. You wouldn't marry again, would you?

FEDYA. You see . . . [*Turns to* VIKTOSHA.] Marriage certainly has its attractions on the one hand. Which you'd never say on the other hand.

KHRISTOFOR. I think the point is not to spend one's time getting divorced. That's the whole point.

FEDYA. You have often developed that theme. At this moment we need new ideas. Viktoria Nikolayevna, allow me to suggest you spend the night in the next room. Khristofor and I will spend the night here, in the studio. These armchairs and sofa give us great scope for all possible combinations and permutations.

VIKTOSHA. Thank you . . . It's so nice of you . . .

KHRISTOFOR [*energetically*]. Good God, what idiots we are! Why didn't we think of it at once? [*Pleased.*] Well, tomorrow we're going by boat to Astrakhan in order to concentrate. There will be our two absolutely empty flats here.

FEDYA. Are we going? [*Looks at him with interest.*] You really are an extraordinary man.

Scene Three

A week has flashed by. It has been impossible to tidy the flat,
though the presence of a woman can be felt in some things.
It is late evening again. The weather remains perfect. FEDYA
and VIKTOSHA, *happy and tired, enter the studio in semi-darkness.*

FEDYA [*switching on the light*] . Well, here you are home!

VIKTOSHA. I'm so tired! [*Sinks into an armchair.*] How can I keep up with
you? We've been charging about Moscow for five hours and you haven't
turned a hair.

FEDYA [*happy*] . I'm as tired as a dog.

VIKTOSHA [*looks round*] . Where's Khristofor Ivanovich?

FEDYA. Home and sleeping like a babe, no doubt. So I'm off too . . . I'll go and
keep him company. [*Goes to the door.*]

VIKTOSHA. Stay a bit.

FEDYA [*stops*] . Aren't you bored with me?

VIKTOSHA. Not yet. There's something entrancing about you.

FEDYA. I suppose so, in a way. [*Goes to the window.*] It's a lovely night, isn't
it?

VIKTOSHA. Moscow is a miracle of miracles. To live till twenty without having
been here. I am unique!

FEDYA. You're just a lazy bones.

VIKTOSHA. Don't scold. I had a self-willed, capricious young girl on my hands.
We hadn't much to live on, in spite of my success as dressmaker. Of course,
I could have put her in a home and gone travelling wherever I liked. But that
would be against our family tradition. Our family was simply marvellous.
My parents were awfully old-fashioned and eccentric. They died the same
year, I suppose because one without the other had nothing left to do.

FEDYA. They were lucky! I envy them.

VIKTOSHA. Yes, but it wasn't always easy when I was young. I expect I'd have
gone under if it weren't for my constant dream to provide all the women of
the Soviet Union with lovely clothes, to make them beautiful, graceful and I
might allow myself to say — seductive.

FEDYA. Do you know what a seductive woman is?

VIKTOSHA. Of course.

FEDYA. I'm sorry but how do you know?

VIKTOSHA. I have it in me.

FEDYA. You've got a cheek!

VIKTOSHA. Mother told me how one summer when I was three I had such a devastating effect on a little boy of five that he nearly had convulsions when we packed and left. You see, even as a child I was irresponsible. I had to pay for it in my youth. There was no question of travel when I was young. [*Pause.*] But I'm not sorry I haven't seen Moscow before. I was very lucky when I ran into you a week ago. You've shown me so many marvellous things. Take the Museum of the Boyars — without price. The dresses I'll design now — old Muscovite, to ravish the whole world. And the way you talk about Moscow — without compare.

FEDYA [*with a laugh*]. Moscow . . . It's absurd. Nice. Sometimes pretending suddenly to be other than it is. Sometimes so near and dear, you could weep. The decades I walked up and down these little streets, hurrying to work, enjoying myself, deep in thought, losing my temper. All sorts of things have happened to me on every street corner. Miracles sometimes. Take Tverskoy Boulevard. I died there twice. The first time I got over it. Not the second time, not yet.

VIKTOSHA. How do you mean?

FEDYA. I went and died. False, spent, pitiful, Fedya Balyasnikov. I wouldn't let him go on living. I put an end to that scoundrel. Understand?

VIKTOSHA. Vaguely.

FEDYA [*anxious*]. If man wants perfection, he must shed his skin like a snake. To be without compare — that's happiness, that's meaning. [*Delighted with the new idea.*] And suddenly to surpass everyone! That's wonderful.

VIKTOSHA [*sighing*]. To be modest. Not bad either.

FEDYA [*grumbling*]. Modest, modest . . . That will keep. When I die, you know how modestly I'll be lying down there.

VIKTOSHA. You're witty!

FEDYA [*carried away*]. To be witty is to be right. The people without a sense of humour are responsible for all our troubles. As for death, the more you think about it, the less afraid you are. You're afraid only when you forget.

VIKTOSHA. I like you most awfully.

FEDYA. More lies! Goodnight!

VIKTOSHA [*after him*] . Are you happy?

FEDYA [*turns*] . Yes.

VIKTOSHA. But you're alone.

FEDYA. So what? It's more interesting to search for happiness than to be happy. [*Pause.*] And why alone? There's my faithful Khristofor? And these kids here? [*Pointing at a shelf of puppets.*] Good company, surely?

VIKTOSHA [*picking up a puppet*] . I expect children adore you . . .

FEDYA [*mistrustfully*] . You think so? I'm awfully afraid of them. I dream of them at night. Armed with sticks and darts, always ready to do me in.

VIKTOSHA. Why?

FEDYA. Because, fool that I am, I can't make my marionettes any better. Children believe there may be better things in this world than they know of. Yes, they are the greatest of optimists.

VIKTOSHA. Meaning, the greatest pessimists are those who enjoy things?

FEDYA. Of course! The imagination's dead. They're glad because they're glad. What is there to be glad about?

VIKTOSHA. You go on and on but I still like you. Only your room is in such an awful mess. Do you ever tidy up?

FEDYA. Daily. But it always does what it wants. See this lamp? [*Mysteriously.*] Well, several times a day I put it on the table, but look — it always ends up on the floor.

VIKTOSHA. Interesting phenomenon. How do you explain that?

FEDYA. I'm a prey to conjecture. Obviously they're somehow responsible. [*Points to the puppets.*] Look, how many there are. [*Almost in a whisper.*] And they're all crafty. They're capable of anything. I assure you. Take this monkey. For a fortnight she refused to be herself. She resisted in every way. Marionettes are like people — they resist perfection and there's nothing I can do about it. True, I won her over in the end. She is not bad. But even now I think she's deceiving me. Yes, yes, I swear she could be better.

VIKTOSHA [*examining the monkey*] . Never mind, she's all right.

FEDYA. I don't know. I love them all very much, but at times I feel sad. They could be more lovely. I often wonder if by the time you've developed your skill, you haven't lost your soul? The worst of it is — the laws of beauty get clearer as you get older. It's fatal.

VIKTOSHA. Fatal? But why?

FEDYA [*sadly*]. Nothing interferes more with one's work than good taste. [*Pause. He suddenly smiles.*] You wouldn't understand yet – you're still a child in these things.

VIKTOSHA. You're right – obviously everything for me lies ahead. It makes me desperately happy!

FEDYA. I hope your seniors look after you. Do they help you with your work?

VIKTOSHA. Why? Only people with talent should get help. And we don't need it! [*Happily.*] Look, on the window sill, there's a half-empty bottle of Tokay? Let's finish it.

FEDYA. You're an alcoholic.

VIKTOSHA. Never! One sweet grape wine – that's my limit. [*Pours out the Tokay into wine glasses.*] Would you like to make a toast?

FEDYA. I would. [*Raises his glass.*] To my son!

VIKTOSHA [*surprised*]. Your son? You have a son? I'd like to see . . .

FEDYA. We're at war. It's lasted twenty-one years.

VIKTOSHA. How old is he?

FEDYA. Twenty-two. His health! [*Slight pause.*] My fondest dream has been that he should come and live with me.

VIKTOSHA. Right, we'll drink to that! [*Drinks.*] Frankly, I thought you were going to recite a panegyric in my honour. Nothing doing! Yes, obviously I must go back to Leningrad.

FEDYA. The day you leave me I shall be the most miserable of men.

[*He takes the guitar and jokily, but with a touch of seriousness, sings: "Don't leave me, my dear love . . .".*]

VIKTOSHA. You could earn your living with the guitar.

FEDYA. Well, why not, I'll try going from door to door. Though they're strict now. They might charge me with vagrancy. [*Casually.*] Are you going back to Leningrad? Are you going to marry your Levushka?

VIKTOSHA. I've changed my mind. But I'll have to be patient and try and hammer into him that he fell out of love with me some time ago. Of course, he won't believe me at first. He's going to protest an awful lot . . . Still! Driving lovers away is a hobby of mine.

FEDYA. Yes, you're a dangerous person. Poor old Levushka.

VIKTOSHA. You're wrong – he isn't poor. He's more single-minded than me, that one. And he talks his head off. Statistics, cybernetics – that's his passion. He's chock-a-block with information and extraordinarily popular with his friends. At first I was madly in love with him. But, gradually I began to cool off somehow . . . Worn out, maybe? To understand all this, he must be seen. Levushka is unique.

FEDYA [*impatiently*]. Have you really loved anyone?

VIKTOSHA. Probably that will sort of get clearer as I get older.

FEDYA. I shouldn't count on it! There's considerable confusion in these problems even at my age. There are so many people on this globe. It's most difficult to find your other half. Especially if you're busy. Saddest of all is to find her too late . . . But achieving your desire means losing it. So we'll put desire away into the most inaccessible pocket.

VIKTOSHA. You're sad all of a sudden . . . [*Pours out two more glasses.*] To optimism!

FEDYA. You're wrong if you think that's a happy toast. Optimists, as we've discovered, bravely look truth in the face. And there's no fun in that.

VIKTOSHA. It's diabolically obscure. Will you allow me to pronounce a toast?

FEDYA. Can't be helped – go ahead.

VIKTOSHA [*gets up*]. Panegyric in honour of Fyodor Balyasnikov. [*Raises her glass.*] What bliss that Natasha married her fiancé's best friend! What joy that she left with him for her honeymoon! How awful if it hadn't happened! Dear Fyodor Kuzmich – you have driven me mad. I thank you for it. When I'm a little old woman sitting by my atomic fireside, I'll tell my grandchildren about you with tears in my eyes. Please accept my assurance of my enormous regard for you. [*She empties the glass.*]

FEDYA. I'm most grateful to you.

[*He takes the guitar and plays a gipsy dance.*]

VIKTOSHA [*she gets up and stands ready to dance it*]. May I?

FEDYA. Go ahead!

[**VIKTOSHA** *dances it gaily and most dashingly.* **FEDYA** *watches her with delight and at the end of the tune tosses the guitar into the air.*]

Without precedent!

VIKOSHA. That's the woman I am! [*Collapses into an armchair.*]

[*They sit for a very long time in complete silence.*]

We mustn't wake your Shurik.

FEDYA [*not loud*]. It's twenty to one ... He isn't asleep. He's winning at cards.

VIKTOSHA. I like dancing.

FEDYA. You should be an actress.

VIKTOSHA. There are lots of actresses. Who's going to make lovely dresses for my darling women? I look about me and I see I'm their only hope!

FEDYA. Good girl! In our work we must believe everything depends on us.

VIKTOSHA. Isn't that a touch conceited?

FEDYA. Can't be helped! It's a must. If you tell the world you're a mushroom, don't pretend you're a toadstool. I know that Balyasnikov's puppets are best.

VIKTOSHA. Supermarvellous! [*Takes the bottle and looks at him gaily.*] Shall we finish it? A little at the bottom of the bottle?

FEDYA. Oho! [*Shakes his finger at her.*] You're trying to make me drunk.

VIKTOSHA. Don't be afraid. Nothing will happen to you. [*Gets up.*] And now, my son's health! For a change.

FEDYA. Ye Gods! Have you got a son?

VIKTOSHA. Not yet. But I shall. [*Raises her glass.*] To my darling! I wish him every success − and may he be just a little bit like you. I hope! To that.

[*They drink in silence.*]

FEDYA [*after a slight pause*]. You know something? I should smack you.

VIKTOSHA [*quietly*]. How silly ... Why? You shouldn't! I feel so good. [*Almost in a whisper.*] Yes, tell me, why do I feel so good? And I know. I'll tell you. Because I'm sitting in this amazing room with all these little people, all these happy animals, that little optimist of a pig, and that arrogant dog. They're all sitting here with me and listening carefully to our splendid conversation. Our conversation is quite remarkable. True isn't it? And now tell me something super-supermarvellous!

FEDYA. I'll read it to you.

VIKTOSHA. What?

FEDYA. A poem. By Tyutchev. It's my incantation. No, my prayer. I repeat it at night. [*Reads happily, exulting.*]

To new arrivals, bold young men,
I must give way, an elder sage,
Infirm and weak in my old age.

Oh, my good genius, spare me then,
From malice, jealousy and rage
At the new life of the new men.

My old desires are no great shame,
Far worse if I have not the grace
To yield my place and leave the game
To that young man who wins the race.

VIKTOSHA [*very quietly*]. How lovely . . . How good . . . What fun.

FEDYA [*goes to her, tenderly presses her to him, and kisses her on the forehead*]. Time I went. Goodnight.

[*He runs out quickly.*]

CURTAIN

ACT TWO

Scene One

Early evening the following day. Wearing a brightly coloured plastic apron, **KHRISTOFOR** *is doing the housework.* **FEDYA,** *happy and preoccupied, enters from the hall and stands in the doorway.*

FEDYA. Well, how goes it?

KHRISTOFOR. I think we can be quite sure of success.

FEDYA. Careful you don't fall flat on your face. I informed Viktosha, you were the greatest expert on meat dumplings.

KHRISTOFOR. Please don't talk so loud. She's still asleep.

FEDYA. Excellent. She must renew her energies. You know what a strenuous life she leads. [*Delighted.*] From morning to night she rushes from one fashion house to another. She visits fashion shows and clothes' factories. She meets designers and goes to exhibitions. Take today. We spent all day at the Tretyakov Gallery. The great masters we examined in silence. But I showed the pseudos no mercy – I've lost my voice, damn it! Yesterday I gave her a day to remember. We wandered about Moscow till late at night and I showed her places where I was happy once upon a time.

KHRISTOFOR. You mean, you took her round the isotopic emporiums?

FEDYA. Now, why must they be isotopic? I was happy in a lot of Moscow. [*Sighing happily.*] And do you know I feel a great upsurge of energy! I think that now I'm capable of greatness. I'm bursting with the desire to work.

KHRISTOFOR. That's excellent, of course. But I'd like to know – why are you bursting?

FEDYA. Why? [*Thinks.*] Khristofor, it is dangerous to delve in some things. [*Exulting inwardly.*] Whatever happens, tomorrow we get down to business. The marionettes for "Helen of Troy".

KHRISTOFOR. What about young Lepyoshkin? He got the contract, you know.

FEDYA [*boyish and crafty*]. Certainly! But isn't it bliss working on our own?

KHRISTOFOR. Well, you'll get no support from our thinking public if you say things like that. Do you wish to live in an ivory tower? God preserve you! Oh Fedya, you'll never keep a head on your shoulders.

297

FEDYA. Be quiet! I haven't felt so creative for ages. Lovely Helen . . . All of woman's beauty, all her perfection in a marionette . . . So far the Japanese have led the field. It'll be our turn now. [*Puts on his hat and runs to the door.*] I'll be back soon. Give your all to the meat dumplings. [*Runs out.*]

KHRISTOFOR. Well, really, the man just won't relax. He bubbles — nothing you can do about it. Being with him is like being in a pan on the boil with pepper and onions. Very hot and hopeless somehow. Though it does tone you up — you stay on the boil to keep him company.

[*Bell.*]

Now who's that?

[*He goes and rather frightened and embarrassed returns immediately with KUZYA.*]

KUZYA [*inspects him*]. Well! Interesting picture!

KHRISTOFOR [*explaining his apron*]. I'm doing the housework.

KUZYA. A week ago you were going on the Volga.

KHRISTOFOR. We changed our minds. We decided to concentrate here. On dry land.

KUZYA [*significantly*]. Is he at home?

KHRISTOFOR [*thinking it over*]. He's asleep.

KUZYA. Why? [*He makes for the other room.*]

KHRISTOFOR [*seizing hold of him*]. Don't go in, please . . . He's tired. He won't be awake for some time . . . Look us up later. Or let's meet tomorrow. Seven p.m. under the post office clock. I must go to the kitchen now.

KUZYA. Why?

KHRISTOFOR [*resourcefully*]. To cook the dumplings.

KUZYA. You've gone completely mad. [*He makes a move towards the other room.*]

KHRISTOFOR. Kuzya — stop!

KUZYA. Eh . . . Wait . . . [*Looks piercingly at KHRISTOFOR.*] Is he there alone?

KHRISTOFOR. Him? . . . He is alone . . .

KUZYA. You look rather guilty. Come on, own up — why haven't you gone on the Volga?

KHRISTOFOR [*with a backward glance*]. We decided to work. We must beat the Japs.

KUZYA. What Japs?

KHRISTOFOR. Don't you know? Well, we're making the puppets for "Helen of Troy".

KUZYA. What do you mean?

KHRISTOFOR. It's true, that damned Lepyoshkin got in our way. Never mind. We're working on it.

KUZYA [*slight pause*]. I lied to him about Lepyoshkin. The theatre didn't offer it to him.

KHRISTOFOR. Who then?

KUZYA. Me.

KHRISTOFOR. Oh! [*Clutches at his heart.*] That's a bomb! [*Looks at him.*] Come here, dear boy, let me kiss you. You've had this success! [*Hugs and kisses him.*] And now go and find our great Maestro and turn it down at once.

KUZYA. Turn it down?

KHRISTOFOR. You're young. It all lies ahead of you. In your father's case – it may be his last word. His Swan Song?

KUZYA [*after a pause*]. That's what I came to see you about. Khristofor, you've known me since I was little. You've often intervened between father and me. I've been fighting him as long as I can remember. Remember, I was five, we were having tea but father was playing everyone up ... I was eating a waffle and thinking – why's the silly fool making fun of everyone? I went and bit him as hard as I could. You saved me then. Remember how furious he was?

KHRISTOFOR. No wonder he was furious! A mite comes up – such a little angel – and sticks his teeth into his little finger.

KUZYA. I couldn't control myself. I can't forgive him anything. Especially when I meet him with women. It all flares up inside.

KHRISTOFOR [*looking at the door of the next room*]. Kuzya, my sunshine, we'd better go to the kitchen.

KUZYA. Why?

KHRISTOFOR. I'll show you how I cook dumplings.

KUZYA. No, listen to me ... I must win! I decided that when they brought me from the maternity home and he said I looked like a monkey. I must prove myself to him ... And I will. [*Hugs KHRISTOFOR.*] Are you angry?

KHRISTOFOR [*affectionately*]. You're grown up now — I can't teach you anything. Only remember one thing — your life's ahead of you but the sun shines on your father for a few years . . . Look after yourself.

KUZYA. Don't tell him I looked in. No need.

KHRISTOFOR [*relieved*]. Are you going?

KUZYA. I'll phone the institute first. [*Goes to the phone.*]

KHRISTOFOR [*happily*]. See you bang the door shut when you go.

[*Cheerfully bustles into the kitchen.* KUZYA *dials his number and at the same time* VIKTOSHA *appears in the doorway. She's wearing pyjamas and slippers.*]

KUZYA [*shaken*]. What's all this? [*Looks at her.*] How did you get here?

VIKTOSHA [*with interest*]. And you?

KUZYA. What are you doing here?

VIKTOSHA. Me? Resting.

KUZYA. How dare you?

VIKTOSHA. Dare what?

KUZYA. Well, I've got something to say to him! [*Runs into the next room and returns immediately.*] Damn, there's nobody there!

VIKTOSHA. Who did you expect? You really are so peculiar . . .

KUZYA. No, it's you that's peculiar — allowing yourself at your age . . . to walk about this room.

VIKTOSHA. Why are you making such a scene? First, I don't know you at all.

KUZYA. I've got you taped! A nice carry on, I must say! Well, you're a pretty little thing! Good-looking, almost likeable really . . . a darling.

VIKTOSHA [*at a loss*]. But this is terrible . . . He's going to start bawling any moment . . . Please don't upset yourself. [*Strokes his hair.*] Who are you?

KUZYA [*in sorrow*]. Don't talk about that.

VIKTOSHA. Well, all right. But what's your name?

KUZYA. That's the whole point. Kuzma.

VIKTOSHA. Kuzma . . . What a lovely name.

KUZYA [*astounded*]. You mean that?

VIKTOSHA. Only a loving mother would find such a rare and manly name for her son.

KUZYA. It wasn't my mother . . . It was him . . . Your Balyasnikov!

VIKTOSHA. Wait . . . Why didn't I guess. Why, you're almost him!

[*There's a knock on the door, followed by the appearance of a very serious and very young man with a small suitcase. That's* LEVUSHKA. *He's tactful, democratic and talkative. On the back of his head there's a nice, unruly bit of hair sticking up.*]

LEVUSHKA [*polite and at ease*]. Hullo, Victoria. I'm very glad I've managed to find you at last. [*To* KUZYA.] Good evening.

KUZYA [*at a loss*]. Hello . . .

VIKTOSHA. Levushka . . . [*She can't decide if she should be pleased at her fiancé's arrival.*] How did you get here?

LEVUSHKA. Natasha's neighbours with the assistance of a Shurik pointed out this flat to me. Shurik informed me that you've been living here a whole week.

KUZYA [*furious*]. Damn it! Clever!

LEVUSHKA [*to* KUZYA]. Do you think so? Of course, it's possible. [*To* VIK-TOSHA.] At first your disappearance surprised me. Say what you like but you did not choose the best day for it. Then I realized that here we were concerned with the purely elemental self-expression of the ego. You simply had to turn inside out everything deeply hidden in the crannies of your subconscious. However, I still love you, though with time the word has lost some of its glow. You see, I don't insist on anything, I don't demand anything and perhaps I don't even want anything. All the same, we shouldn't forget that for the wedding my mother bought food, some of which has already gone bad and the rest will go bad next week.

KUZYA [*to* VIKTOSHA *in a frightened whisper*]. Who's this madman?

VIKTOSHA. My fiancé . . .

KUZYA [*still depressed by* LEVUSHKA*'s speech*]. That?

LEVUSHKA. Have you lived here the whole week? Well, I suppose my love can stand this experiment too. First of all, dear friend, we must somehow classify all the available versions. [*To* KUZYA.] For instance, could you let me have your surname?

KUZYA. Balyasnikov.

LEVUSHKA [*warmly shakes him by the hand*]. That clears up a great deal. [*To* **VIKTOSHA**.] So you spent the week with him?

VIKTOSHA. Levushka, no. No, I assure you.

LEVUSHKA [*friendly but a shade above it*]. I hope you won't think I'm jealous, my dear. Let's assume, a certain intimacy has developed between you. [*To* **KUZYA**.] Let's assume, it actually took place. It's quite realizable emotionally, if one can so express oneself . . .

KUZYA. Damn you, shut up!

LEVUSHKA. I assure you, I don't bear you the slightest grudge. Of course, I'm unable to feel absolutely delighted at the news of your intimacy with my fiancée. On the other hand, isn't it time to bring into the open the emotions always suppressed by the repressive action of reason and reality.

VIKTOSHA. Now, Levushka, stop it, please. This Kuzma has absolutely nothing to do with it. The flat belongs to his father – Balyasnikov Senior.

LEVUSHKA. Aha, so, your partner isn't young. Well, can't be helped. Statistics show late marriages to be of relatively short duration. Moreover, the programme of elderly lovers is fairly limited – they twang the guitar, send baskets of flowers, sing sentimental gypsy songs and in extreme cases they declaim poetry. In short, they feel the full weight of their years.

[**FEDYA**, *dragging an enormous basket of flowers, appears on the threshold. But those present do not notice him for some time.*]

VIKTOSHA. Levushka, I assure you, you're surprisingly wrong about that too.

LEVUSHKA. One thing is certain – the claims of old men are oppressive and unfounded. Their actions, arising spontaneously from their emotions, are nearly always doomed to failure. That's why as a rule their reasonable and progressive acts are largely ineffective. [*Notices* **BALYASNIKOV** *with his basket.*] Are you from the florist? Put the flowers in the corner and go away.

[**BALYASNIKOV** *is quite taken aback by the suggestion.*]

All the same, I think old age should be respected. One can argue as much as one likes but the old have done a great deal for us. Of course, they could have done more. But we shan't reproach them with anything specific. We shan't blame your father either, Balyasnikov.

FEDYA [*furious*]. Now then, out, you scoundrel!

[*He seizes him by the collar, lifts him and carries him to the exit.*]

KHRISTOFOR [*entering the room and watching in amazement*]. Fedya, please tell me, where are you taking him?

FEDYA [*picturesquely*]. The exit.

KHRISTOFOR. Will you also please explain who he is?

FEDYA. A young man.

[*He goes out, carrying* **LEVUSHKA** *out of the room with one hand.*]

KUZYA. Damn! . . . Father's spectacular, all right – can't deny him that!

KHRISTOFOR. To think of the passions played out here! I was just throwing the dumplings into boiling water, when I heard many raised voices. Kuzya, you behaved very badly. You promised to go, I trusted you. But it appears you didn't go. You're still here.

VIKTOSHA [*to* **KUZYA**]. I see you don't like my Levushka.

KUZYA. If I'd been in his place and found you like this, I'd have shot you on the spot.

VIKTOSHA [*interested*]. Honest to God?

KUZYA. I swear it.

VIKTOSHA. You're obviously a hooligan. He's a serious, thinking young man.

FEDYA [*returns, brushing off his hands*]. From what I gather, he's your notorious fiancé?

VIKTOSHA [*sighs*]. I see, you don't like him either.

KHRISTOFOR. You know, it's quite remarkable! I've been standing here several minutes without the slightest idea of what's going on?

[**LEVUSHKA** *appears in the doorway. Tactful and imperturbable as before, he goes towards* **FEDYA**.]

LEVUSHKA. I hope you realize, I can't leave my suitcase behind. It has my clean shirt and my lunch prepared in Leningrad by my mother. Victoria, I repeat that I love you, although the egotism of possession with its animal fear of losing one's own little fortress is just as funny in our time as Freud's notorious and hopelessly outdated complexes. [*To* **KUZYA**.] I like you. I'll wait for you downstairs by the delicatessen. Why shouldn't we have another argument on another subject? [*To* **FEDYA**.] Don't let your excitement provoke you without thinking. Remember, man came into the world because the monkey went mad, once upon a time. We shall evolve backwards, you and I. [*Goes to* **KHRISTOFOR** *and introduces himself.*] Lev Hartvig, student of the Leningrad Institute of Mathematics. [*Goes to the door and pauses on the threshold.*] The world is stuffed with dynamite. We must remain quite calm so that it doesn't blow up. [*He departs worthily.*]

KHRISTOFOR. What a nice young man! Such a pity, I only wish I knew what he was talking about.

FEDYA. It's beyond me! You agreed to marry this schizo?

VIKTOSHA. Of course I did! Sometimes I'm capable of worse than that. You have no idea! But nearly always I escape in time. That's another hobby of mine.

KUZYA. Nearly always! It sounds significant.

FEDYA [*looks at* **KUZYA** *with great irritation*]. What's this person doing here? Khristofor, did you let him in?

KHRISTOFOR. You know, all this time I'm thinking, I simply don't understand what I'm doing in here when my dumplings are boiling out there. [*Goes quickly.*]

FEDYA [*to* **KUZYA**]. Well, what are you thinking? That manic-depressive is waiting for you by the delicatessen. You'll make a splendid pair, the two of you.

KUZYA. Will you begin by explaining the presence of this young woman here?

VIKTOSHA [*boiling*]. First, I'm not a young woman . . .

KUZYA. Oh, is that so?

VIKTOSHA. I mean, I am a young woman but my name's Victoria.

FEDYA [*trying to find ways of agreement*]. There, you see.

VIKTOSHA [*more gently*]. Some of my friends call me Viktosha.

KUZYA. Let us hope, I shan't have that opportunity.

VIKTOSHA. Why not? Will you please explain?

KUZYA [*he's excited in a somewhat ugly manner*]. First, I don't like your presence here at all. Unlike your fiancé, I'm rather old-fashioned. The word love hasn't lost its glow for me. I've never been in love, in spite of my twenty-two years. And if I were to fall in love, it would be . . . It would be . . .

VIKTOSHA. Why, what would it be? I'm very interested.

KUZYA. You'll see!

VIKTOSHA. But how?

KUZYA [*at a loss for a suitable answer and getting furious as a result*]. You could stop asking idiotic questions!

[*He goes noisily.*]

FEDYA. Damn it . . . I don't know why, but I was afraid he'd bite me once again.

VIKTOSHA. Yes, a most badly brought up young man. Don't you think it's partly your fault?

FEDYA. They grow so fast, one hasn't the time to realize it's one's fault.

[*Stepping heavily, unstrung in the face of calamity,* **KHRISTOFOR** *enters and sadly sinks into an armchair.*]

KHRISTOFOR. It's terrible. I'm afraid to tell you the truth.

FEDYA. Never mind, go ahead. Tell the truth always and everywhere and you'll be famous as a wit.

KHRISTOFOR. I'm quite desperate. When I was in here, it seems I should have been out there, with the dumplings. I let the right moment slip. In the last few minutes they have acquired an extraordinary appearance. On the one hand, they look like paste, and on the other, they remind me of porridge oddly enough. Incidentally, as a child I was very fond of porridge.

VIKTOSHA. Just think, he's never been in love! What an extraordinary young man, your Kuzma!

KHRISTOFOR. And you know, Fedya, what I think? We must all concentrate.

Scene Two

Ten more days have gone by. The weather has broken at last. It's raining. The evening is setting in feebly.
    Towards dusk. **KUZYA** *has just walked into the room.* **KHRISTO-FOR** *watches him reproachfully as he takes off his raincoat and shakes off the rain.*

KUZYA. I'm soaking wet. I've been nearly two hours in the rain.

KHRISTOFOR. I guessed as much . . . By the astonishing tracks you're making.

KUZYA. I dare say . . . [*Pitiful.*] I'm cold. I'm chilled through and through. And I'm so unhappy.

KHRISTOFOR. What's got into you now?

KUZYA. Don't talk about it! I feel so depressed — that's number one. [*Coming to life.*] Number two, I've handed in the models of my puppets. I burnt my boats.

KHRISTOFOR. Bother. [*Cautiously.*] I hope they're nice?

KUZYA [*meditative and sad*]. They're all right. They're smashing. [*Pause.*] Tomorrow the Maestro's due back in Moscow and all will be decided. [*Anxiously walks across the room.*] Father home?

KHRISTOFOR. First, this is not our home now. Not while Viktosha's here. That admirable young woman, you've already met. Secondly, she and your father have just gone out for a walk. Undoubtedly she has a very creative influence on him. I don't remember him working like this for a long time. With ineffable enthusiasm, volcanic! Michaelangelo, no less! An inner fire consumes him. I'm afraid for him.

KUZYA. But it doesn't prevent him from going for walks with that girl. And in the pouring rain!

KHRISTOFOR [*with insight*]. He went out with her because he finished the greater part of his work this morning. By dawn he was nearly passing out with exhaustion. That's when the clock struck five. He's hardly been out with her all week – he handed her over to my care. Look at the remarkable suit I'm wearing. We bought it so that I should make a good impression when I'm out with Viktosha. Because, you know, I go with her to all sorts of museums, where she makes sketches of every possible garment, and to fashion shows where I have to meet mannequins of astonishing agility. Look, I've even changed my hair style. They all say it's an improvement.

KUZYA [*anxiously*]. Khristofor . . . Listen, I've made up my mind! Today I'll tell him everything.

KHRISTOFOR. Tell him what?

KUZYA. Everything . . . The puppets. It would be disgusting if he suddenly heard of my victory – and not from me but someone else.

KHRISTOFOR. Wait . . . Are you sure?

KUZYA [*almost in despair*]. Well, I'm telling you, they're smashing! How will he feel when he finds out? And there's something basically unfair about the whole business. Why wasn't he commissioned to do Helen? Surely my father isn't that old? [*Seizes KHRISTOFOR and shakes him.*] Has he lost his talent?

KHRISTOFOR [*breaking away*]. Stop creasing my remarkable new suit! Viktosha will never forgive you. [*Listens.*] Quiet! They're coming. I implore you, behave yourself.

[VIKTOSHA *and* FEDYA, *both soaking wet, enter. They're enjoying themselves.*]

VIKTOSHA [*laughs*]. You're amazing and clever the way you gallop over the puddles. I've never seen it done with such zest.

FEDYA. I have a passion for galloping over the puddles. Of all natural phenomena rain is the most fun. If you are not quite sober. [*Noticing* **KUZYA.**] Oh, you here? [*With a touch of caution.*] That's very nice. Have you come to see Khristofor? You'll be going soon?

KUZYA [*losing his temper*]. How did you guess? [*Goes toward the door.*]

VIKTOSHA [*very gently*]. N-now then, stop, stop, stop . . . Why must you go? Especially in that rain? I think it would be much better if you stayed. We'll all have tea together.

KUZYA. But I . . . But we . . .

VIKTOSHA. That's lovely. You see how delighted he is to stay?

FEDYA [*to* **KUZYA**]. You know how glad I am when you appear. It's true, as a rule, it ends badly, but let's try again. Why not? Especially today because it's quite a day!

KUZYA [*worried*]. What's so special about it?

FEDYA. You'll find out soon. Now, let's go to the kitchen, Khristofor. I'll make a brew of tea without compare. [*He goes.*]

KHRISTOFOR. Now, please don't be bored. [*Followed* **FEDYA** *quickly.*]

VIKTOSHA [*after a pause*]. Well, what do you think, are we going to be bored?

KUZYA [*again losing his nerve*]. I — I don't know.

VIKTOSHA. You've completely lost your nerve . . . I can even hear your teeth chattering from here.

KUZYA. Listen, you . . . I can, you know, and — and . . .

VIKTOSHA. What?

KUZYA [*after thought*]. I can go — that's what!

VIKTOSHA. You're rivetting. But you won't go. You're a bit of a coward. For a week you've been treading on my heels, lurking in doorways. But you don't even try and talk to me. I assure you, it is not done like that nowadays.

KUZYA [*barely breathing*]. But how?

VIKTOSHA [*gently*]. Differently. I'm not going to teach you. [*Severely.*] It would be indecent. [*With interest.*] By the way, why do you appear in the evening only. Where are you during the day?

KUZYA. I study during the day.

VIKTOSHA. But you work, don't you?

KUZYA. I work at night.

VIKTOSHA. Wonderful. When do you sleep?

KUZYA. In the intervals.

VIKTOSHA. I'll have to try that. [*With unconcealed pleasure.*] Now, will you explain, why do you follow me everywhere?

KUZYA. It's just that I'm very fond of my father, and naturally I . . .

VIKTOSHA. But this last week I've been out alone or with Khristofor Ivanovich.

KUZYA. I'm very fond of Khristofor too!

VIKTOSHA. Right – you've lied yourself to a standstill. And the thing's simpler than simple. [*Friendly.*] You've fallen madly in love with me.

KUZYA [*afraid but with a touch of arrogance*]. Well, as for madly. . .

VIKTOSHA. I assure you. Everyone falls madly in love with me. Though I don't give them the slightest encouragement. [*Affectionately.*] Now aren't people peculiar, eh?

KUZYA [*unexpectedly getting it*]. Now, you know – that's enough! After all, who are you?

VIKTOSHA [*proudly*]. I'm a dressmaker!

KUZYA. Well, so what? Fancy! . . . It's disgraceful.

VIKTOSHA. Levushka, whom you know, says that my character is made of strontium. [*Affectionately.*] Perhaps that's why.

KUZYA [*exhausted*]. I'm going . . . Enough!

[*Enter* **FEDYA** *inspired. On a tray he has all that's necessary for tea. As in a procession,* **KHRISTOFOR** *follows him with various goodies.*]

FEDYA. Here we are!

KHRISTOFOR [*laying the table*]. Well, how goes it, children, were you bored without us?

KUZYA. I wouldn't say that.

VIKTOSHA. Kuzma is in smashing form today – resourceful, witty, talkative.

KHRISTOFOR. Talkative? Well, he gets that from his father.

FEDYA. Don't be rude! I go on and on because I've seen so much. I'm bursting with impressions. [*A shade sadly.*] Even alone at night I can't stop, I argue with myself. Yes, yes, I arrange meetings, I speak in debates and carry my motions . . . Children, I think I'm a little tired. Probably because the most difficult thing in art is campaigning for sensible ideas. Since proving the obvious is rather embarrassing. [*Pause.*] The one snag – it's harder to find the key to oneself than to others.

[*They start drinking tea.*]

KHRISTOFOR. I think the whole point is being kind. And being kind means being discreet. That's all there is to it. Men play with toys all their lives. When they're children, they have their toys bought for them, but later . . . It's awful to think of it.

KUZYA. Later they play with living people. Don't they?

FEDYA. Kuzya . . . Don't. [*Thoughtful.*] Perhaps I'm beginning to find out about a few things. It's funny – every year the soul grows wiser. But the body, damn it, goes on playing the fool. Kuzma, you wouldn't understand this yet – in youth body and soul are almost inseparable. But with the years the soul learns to live alone – wanting to get used to the inevitable. At night during sleep, it learns to fly out of the body. When it finally masters that . . . [*Gives a sad whistle. Pause.*] Alas, there's just one thing people shouldn't bother about – that's death.

VIKTOSHA. That's enough! I'm young, and selfish, and I hope to live a long life! Aren't you ashamed of yourself, Kuzma? We didn't ask you to stay that you should poison the atmosphere with your pessimism and disbelief.

KUZYA [*simply incapable of speech*]. Well, you know . . .

FEDYA. What's he got to do with it? [*Cheerfully.*] It was me. Suddenly I felt a twinge of sadness. But the tea's revived me. A marvellous drink – once upon a time it was my breakfast, dinner and supper! When I was young I earned so little money, it all went on living.

VIKTOSHA [*to* KHRISTOFOR]. Now, you see this man, how cheerful he is, full of the zest of life. Now look at his son – sad, depressed, empty . . .

FEDYA. Why exaggerate? The boy's a boy. [*Looks at* KUZYA.] Eh, have you got toothache? Your jaw is trembling in a funny sort of way.

VIKTOSHA [*shattering*]. His teeth are chattering. Perhaps he's got a cold? He spends an awful lot of time out of doors. In the wet too.

FEDYA [*tearing himself away from his meal*]. Talking of the wet, what's our poor Lepyoshkin doing? How's the young genius?

KUZYA. Are you interested in Lepyoshkin? Why would that be?

FEDYA [*to* KHRISTOFOR]. You hear? He thinks we're afraid of some Lepyoshkin. Ha-ha!

KHRISTOFOR. Ho-ho! [*After looking at* KUZYA.] Of course, we aren't afraid of Lepyoshkin, but . . .

KUZYA. But you envy him.

FEDYA. Envy? Why not? Only a nonentity is without envy in old age! A nonentity, whom old age has deprived of all desires. [*In a fury.*] Oh, if you knew how I envy . . . Youth, beauty, brain!

VIKTOSHA. And success?

FEDYA. Do I envy success? No, I don't know . . . You can't envy the success of others. You're either pleased or appalled by it.

KUZYA [*cheering up*]. You're right! Absolutely! My strength lies in my being me. Nobody else. To be myself is to be strong.

FEDYA. Exactly!

KHRISTOFOR. At last they've agreed about something. Lovely.

FEDYA [*most peaceably*]. Kuzma, I must tell you, I'm doing the marionettes for Helen. Yes, yes, I've always been attracted by the subject.

KUZYA [*on his guard*]. How far have you got?

FEDYA [*rapturously*]. We finished Paris and Helen at dawn today. Khristofor took them to our little tailor this morning. [*Looking at his watch.*] I expect him at any moment.

KUZYA. And will you . . . Will you show your marionettes to the theatre?

FEDYA. To hell with it! Let Lepyoshkin have his moment of triumph!

KUZYA [*suspiciously*]. Do you think your puppets are so good that when they see them, they'll kick Lepyoshkin out?

FEDYA [*pleased*]. Of course! He'll be kicked out at once!

KUZYA. What? [*Flaring up.*] That's enough! The time has come. I must tell it all. Lepyoshkin is not Lepyoshkin, but . . .

[*Doorbell.*]

FEDYA [*jumping up*]. The marionettes! I'm sure it's them! [*Rushes out into the hall.*]

KHRISTOFOR. The marionettes! They've brought Paris and Helen!

[*He hurries out after* FEDYA.]

VIKTOSHA. What else are you and your Lepyoshkin up to? You seem to have only one idea — to annoy your father.

KUZYA [*sadly*]. What's Lepyoshkin got to do with it? It's me. The theatre asked me to do Helen.

VIKTOSHA. And you had the nerve to hide that from your father?

KUZYA. I had to conquer him. I dreamt of conquest from my cradle. [*Pause.*] All the same . . . When I thought father might lose in competition with me, I suddenly felt such pain and depression! No, it wasn't pity. It was pain for him . . . His time is getting short.

VIKTOSHA. You're mad. You know why they offered you the job? Your father recommended you.

KUZYA [*at once furious*]. What? Not again?

VIKTOSHA. He was very angry with the theatre for preferring Lepyoshkin to you.

KUZYA. He hasn't recommended me again?

VIKTOSHA. Well, why not?

KUZYA. No, I'll never forgive him this humiliation. Don't you understand how desperately I love him?

VIKTOSHA. Love for him?

KUZYA. Yes.

VIKTOSHA. You're a darling!

[*Kisses him.*]

KUZYA [*desperate*]. You'll answer for this!

VIKTOSHA. With pleasure.

[*Carrying two large boxes, looking like a tom-cat with his tail up,* FEDYA *enters followed by a happy* KHRISTOFOR.]

FEDYA [*triumphant, lifting high the boxes*]. They brought them!

KHRISTOFOR [*in explanation*]. They were brought.

FEDYA [*in a thunderous voice as before*]. Our puppets — here they are!

KHRISTOFOR [*quietly*]. Here they are, here they are . . .

[*Exhausted with happiness, they look at each other and collapse into armchairs where they lie doggo for a long time.* VIKTOSHA *touches a box and* FEDYA *jumps up at once.*]

FEDYA [*his eyes blazing*]. You want to see them, don't you? Do you want to? [*Knowledgeably.*] Of course, I understand. All right, Khristofor, we shan't hide them. [*Exulting.*] Here they are! [*Removes the lid of one box and shows it to* KUZYA.] Helen! [*Opens the lid of the other box and shows the puppet to* VIKTOSHA.] Paris!

KHRISTOFOR [*quietly*]. Yes, take a good look, see what darlings they are.

VIKTOSHA [*almost in a whisper*]. Extraordinary . . . [*Turns to* FEDYA *and whispers.*] Extraordinary . . . [*Looks at the puppet intently.*] Wait . . . But it's Kuzma!

FEDYA [*smiles quietly*]. What do you mean? . . . When I was making him, I thought of my own youth.

KHRISTOFOR. Well, say something, Kuzya.

KUZYA [*he hasn't taken his eyes off Helen*]. Me? [*He goes to* FEDYA, *looks at him in amazement, shrugs and says incredulously.*] There, you see. [*Turns to Helen and again looks at* VIKTOSHA.] How beautiful you are. [*Kisses her tenderly and unsteadily goes to the door.*]

FEDYA. Hey, what do you mean by this?

KUZYA [*quietly*]. The end.

FEDYA. Where are you going?

KUZYA [*turns at the door*]. I'm going to tell Lepyoshkin, he's no damn good. [*Goes.*]

KHRISTOFOR. Kuzya! Wait . . . My dear boy . . . [*Runs out after* KUZYA.]

FEDYA [*exploding*]. What the hell! Why did he kiss you?

VIKTOSHA [*looking at Helen*]. Not me. He didn't kiss me.

FEDYA. Then who? What do you mean?

VIKTOSHA. Your Helen.

FEDYA [*pathetically*]. I don't understand . . . [*Pointing to Helen.*] Don't you like her?

VIKTOSHA. Very much. But you're wrong . . . [*Smiles.*] I'm not as beautiful as she is.

FEDYA. Stop! [*Looks at Helen and then at* VIKTOSHA.] Amazing. [*Sincerely.*] I've only just realized. [*Pause.*] Thank you.

VIKTOSHA. What for?

FEDYA [*quietly*]. I'm sure I couldn't have done it without you. You brought me luck.

KHRISTOFOR [*coming back*]. He vanished round the corner in a terrible state of confusion. [*Looks at* VIKTOSHA *and* FEDYA.] And what are you not talking about?

VIKTOSHA [*going to the window*]. I think the rain's stopped. I'm going out for a bit . . . No, I'm going alone . . . [*Goes out hurriedly*.]

FEDYA [*looking at the dolls again*]. Funny . . . I've only just realized the amazing resemblance.

KHRISTOFOR. I noticed it at once. The first day.

FEDYA [*flaring*]. Khristofor! What are we going to do when she leaves us?

KHRISTOFOR. I simply can't imagine. I don't suppose I'll ever wear this remarkable suit, which is so becoming to me. I shan't have this haircut. I shall never have my hair like this.

FEDYA. It's impossible! I keep thinking, if she goes, life goes.

KHRISTOFOR. Don't be sad. Someone else may notice our light and look us up.

FEDYA. Please, don't be astonished, but, I think . . . I love her.

KHRISTOFOR. Viktosha? Well, why not? I love her too.

FEDYA. You have no understanding. [*Significantly*.] I love her.

KHRISTOFOR [*frightened*]. What are you saying . . . No, no . . .

FEDYA. I say – yes! I'm madly in love with her. There's nothing I can do about it.

KHRISTOFOR. At your age?

FEDYA. Damn it, it is just at my age that love has a touch of madness! [*In despair*.] And think . . . In ten, fifteen years I'll have turned into nothing. She will be as hopelessly lovely!

KHRISTOFOR. Dear boy, you're awfully confused. It's not her that you love. You've only now realized, what a surprising' miracle it is: woman! At the same time, you noticed that you were alone, finally and for ever. That's all it is. [*Pause*.] And whose fault is it? [*Sighs*.] You frighten everyone away.

FEDYA. Maybe . . . [*Anxious*.] I've lived so many years, but love . . . I've never needed it so much! Maybe you're right and it has nothing to do with Viktosha. Simply I have a need to love beating away inside me and my heart rages and burns! [*Ecstatically*.] Together, reading cheerful books and sad poetry, meeting the dawn in a strange town, working to exhaustion and boasting of it to each other, keeping silent on starry evenings and dying of laughter in the rain – oh, damn, how I'd love it! It's too late, too late . . . [*Looks around.*] And our puppets? Perhaps they aren't worth a damn either? These children were just being kind and comforting to the poor little old men. Us. They comforted us and they fled! Where are they . . . Viktosha, Kuzma? Why have they gone? [*Helpless.*] Khristofor . . . No one needs me any more.

Scene Three

It is again dusk. The weather's fine again. KHRISTOFOR *is sitting in an armchair by the window, knitting something and singing to himself.* FEDYA, *brisk and cheerful, enters from the hall and stops on the threshold, amazed by* KHRISTOFOR.

FEDYA. Khristofor, pull yourself together . . . What are you doing?

KHRISTOFOR [*with quiet pleasure*]. I'm knitting. A lot of clever people say this is the best way of concentrating. We've got to concentrate. The only trouble is, I don't hold the knitting needles properly and I get very nervous.

FEDYA. The people all round you are living strenuous working lives. And you're wasting your time with a lot of damn nonsense. You do depress me.

KHRISTOFOR. Well, all right, I'm sorry. But please explain why you've cheered up. Where exactly have you been?

FEDYA [*rather pleased*]. My toy-factory.

KHRISTOFOR [*going on knitting*]. Now why go there, when you have another week of leave?

FEDYA [*cheerfully*]. I was depressed, I felt so sad! When I got there, they were awfully pleased to see me. They wanted me to be everywhere at the same time. Well, I was awfully pleased too. It's wonderful to feel you're wanted everywhere at the same time! They showed me several new toys. Some were nice. Especially the mechanical hyena – it was most amusing. Also the chimney sweep in a top-hat – I found him very moving. It's especially cheering to be missed. Do you understand? [*Walks about the room.*] Where's Viktosha?

KHRISTOFOR. She went to the House of Fashion. She has an interview there with such a famous designer, he's been invited to Paris.

FEDYA. He's going to Paris while our Helen and Paris are going nowhere at all.

KHRISTOFOR [*innocently*]. I simply can't believe you want to see them on the stage.

FEDYA. Of course I do! Living without sharing what you create! There's nothing worse. And that damned Maestro prefers a boy to me . . . No, I'm afraid there's nothing doing.

KHRISTOFOR. But you're wrong. [*Slyly.*] There's a lot doing.

FEDYA. What have you been up to? Tell me!

KHRISTOFOR. Nothing at all. Except that an hour ago I went and took your puppets to our remarkable Maestro.

FEDYA. How dare you.

KHRISTOFOR. A certain somebody advised me.

FEDYA. Who?

KHRISTOFOR. Shan't tell, not for anything. It's no good standing there looking like a goldfish and don't get excited, stop waving your arms. Better if our Maestro got all excited for once!

FEDYA [*greedily*]. Well, did he get all excited?

KHRISTOFOR. I haven't the slightest idea. I gave our marionettes to his charming wife and not to him. He'd gone out to his tailor to shorten some trousers he bought on tour. I expect he's back now. And he's admiring your marionettes.

FEDYA. What if he isn't? What if he's appalled? Or, with his wife in his arms, what if he's sniggering at them? What then?

KHRISTOFOR. Then of course, it's a bad state of affairs. But it can't be.

FEDYA. Why not?

KHRISTOFOR. Because in my opinion you're a genius.

FEDYA. Stop telling lies!

KHRISTOFOR. I don't have to tell lies. Well, Fedya, aren't you?

FEDYA [*thinking*]. On the whole, yes, of course . . .

KHRISTOFOR. There, you see.

[*Telephone rings.*]

FEDYA [*seizing the phone cheerfully*]. Captain Nemo standing by! [*Aside to* KHRISTOFOR.] Him! The Maestro! [*Listens.*] I know . . . Yes . . . [*To* KHRISTOFOR.] He's dismissed the others. He's fallen in love with Helen! [*Listens.*] Tomorrow morning at the theatre . . . Yes.

[*He hangs up the telephone.*]

KHRISTOFOR. Well?

FEDYA [*tears in his eyes*]. I'm inexhaustible.

KHRISTOFOR. You see. I told you so.

[FEDYA *thinks and goes to* KHRISTOFOR *and kisses him in silence.*]

I can't tell you how glad I am to see you happy. I've got a bottle of Czech beer in the fridge. Let's celebrate. I bought it early, early this morning.

FEDYA. Inexhaustible . . . [*Shrugs.*] Everythings's possible.

[*Goes into the kitchen with* KHRISTOFOR. *The door opens.* VIKTOSHA *and* KUZYA *appear from the hall. Their movements are slow. Without looking at each other, as though under a spell they wander about the room, quietly mumbling something. But then* VIKTOSHA *sits down on the back of an armchair and smiles to herself.* KUZYA *goes to her, looks at her in rapture and finally kisses her. Long pause.*]

KUZYA. You know – as a boy I jumped from the second floor. On my own initiative. I think of it all the time.

VIKTOSHA. I think you're going to be knocked down by the on-coming traffic. You never look when you cross the road.

[*Kiss.*]

KUZYA. I studied badly at school. Especially in the last year but one. I thought of you all the time and I made no progress.

VIKTOSHA. You shouldn't go climbing mountains. And don't get involved in fights. Why must you?

KUZYA. But I didn't get involved. It's just that I was always bored at dances. I was always waiting for you but you never came.

[*Kiss.*]

VIKTOSHA. Do you often catch cold?

KUZYA. No. But I've always wanted an aquarium.

VIKTOSHA. We'd better buy you some warm socks.

KUZYA. Before I loved you, I loved fishes. I could spend hours watching the lives they led.

VIKTOSHA. That will do. It's enough. No more.

[*Kiss.*]

KUZYA. Wait . . . Where are we going to live?

[*The rhythm of the scene changes as though they've woken up.*]

VIKTOSHA. Where are we going to live?

KUZYA [*thinks*]. At my place. [*Delighted.*] My aunt will be back from Tashkent soon. She's very complicated. I love her dearly.

VIKTOSHA. No ... [*After a pause.*] We'll live here.

KUZYA [*flaring up*]. With him? Never!

VIKTOSHA. He said it was the only thing he dreamed of – to be with you.

KUZYA. He said that?

VIKTOSHA. You know – he's so lonely.

KUZYA [*resisting it*]. It's his own fault!

VIKTOSHA. Perhaps it's their fault – those women? He turned out to be too difficult for them, and so the silly fools didn't realize the miracle of him.

KUZYA. Incredible! You're soft on him!

VIKTOSHA. Of course. And I want to be with him always.

KUZYA. What?

VIKTOSHA. In my whole life I haven't liked anybody, do you hear – not one single person, as much as I like Fedya. But for some reason or other I fell in love with you. [*She looks at him.*] Though next to him you're just a sparrow. Not a peacock, not a crow. The forest is dark. Try and sort that out. Onion tears. But please don't ever jump by parachute. [*Another kiss: quite a long one this time.*]

KUZYA [*independently*]. You know, Viktosha, I've just been thinking. Have it all your own way.

VIKTOSHA. That's what I think too. [*Affectionately.*] It's good when people agree in everything.

KUZYA. Only you talk to him ... I'm a bit scared. [*Listens.*] He's in the kitchen with Khristofor. I'll go and wander about outside.

VIKTOSHA [*craftily*]. It will sort itself out. Don't be afraid.

KUZYA [*looks at her lovingly*]. I know. [*Touches her hair, goes quickly.*]

VIKTOSHA [*going to the door of the kitchen*]. Fyodor Kuzmich!

FEDYA [*appearing at once*]. You're back? How wonderful ...

VIKTOSHA. Why are you glowing like that?

FEDYA. A decisive victory. Fedya Balyasnikov lives on! He's still in the running. He's doing the marionettes for Helen!

VIKTOSHA. What about – Lepyoshkin?

FEDYA. Out of circulation, poor thing . . . [*Smiles.*] Where have you been? On the threshold of old age, wise men seek solitude and fools seek company. I think I'm a fool . . . I missed you.

VIKTOSHA [*anxiously*]. I have news. You're not the only successful person. I'm just back from the House of Fashion. I talked with a famous man, I showed him this and that from my portfolio . . . [*Can hardly control her delight.*] Darling, they've offered me work, here in Moscow . . . And the prospects!

FEDYA. Miracle! [*Happily.*] Meaning you're splendid too – we're both all right! [*Takes her hands.*] So . . . You're a Muscovite?

VIKTOSHA [*almost in a whisper*]. Eh . . . The jokes the devil plays.

FEDYA [*triumphantly*]. Viktoria Nikolayevna of Moscow . . . Wait a moment . . . [*Amazed.*] I don't know your surname.

VIKTOSHA. Darling and remarkable Fyodor Kuzmich, I have to tell you that here in Moscow I shall have a new surname.

FEDYA [*with a tremor in his voice*]. Meaning?

VIKTOSHA [*smiling*]. It will be after your own heart . . . God knows! [*Quietly.*] Balyasnikov.

FEDYA. What?

VIKTOSHA. Viktoria Nikolayevna Balyasnikov.

FEDYA [*kisses her hands after a pause*]. No . . . No . . . Never.

[**VIKTOSHA** *suddenly understands everything and is afraid to breathe as it were.*]

What you said makes me so happy. If it isn't a joke, if you have really decided . . . It means, the young haven't overtaken me there either. [*In despair.*] Fedya Balyasnikov is still in the running! True?

VIKTOSHA [*afraid, anxious and even happy for some reason*]. True.

FEDYA. But now we'll forget about it. For ever. [*Wickedly and cheerfully.*] It's too late. Just imagine what I'll be like in fifteen years. What a laugh! But you'll be as young and beautiful as now. No – the end! Today I'm not afraid to say this. [*Fiercely.*] Today I've had a double victory. They won't overtake me now – I'm still running in front! It's funny, at this moment I feel immortal. But on this the curtain comes down. We've forgotten it all. Yes?

VIKTOSHA [*with a strange smile*]. Yes.

FEDYA [*cheerfully changing his tone of voice*]. You're moving to Moscow. We'll persuade Khristofor to move here with me and you can have his flat for the time being. [*Consoling her.*] Don't be sad. Time will pass and you'll forget me. You're sure to forget me. Some splendid young man will make you captive. It won't be easy for me when I hear of it. I shall hate him.

VIKTOSHA. You'll hate him?

FEDYA. Of course. Alas, I won't shoot him. I won't plunge a dagger in his chest. The years will pass and, finally, I'll invite him to come and drink tea with cherry jam. But I trust that is all far away. [*Joking.*] At least, let me hope so.

VIKTOSHA [*gently*]. I'll let you hope anything that will make you happy.

FEDYA. Don't be sad. It will all pass.

VIKTOSHA [*with a laugh*]. I expect so. [*Pause.*] By the way, you've always wanted Kuzma to live with you. I think, the day has come.

FEDYA [*anxious*]. You think so? Will he agree?

VIKTOSHA. Yes, I'm almost sure. So be it. It's my last request.

FEDYA. Your last?

VIKTOSHA. For today. [*Smiles.*] Another thing . . . Don't be angry with him. He was asked to do the puppets, not Lepyoshkin. He's so afraid to tell you. Forgive him. All right?

FEDYA [*getting the whole point*]. It was he who was working on the marionettes?

VIKTOSHA. He handed them in.

FEDYA. Handed them in? My Kuzya! And they turned him down? My son! How dare they? Right, my dear Maestro! I'll show you what's what! [*Dials the phone.*] Now, look here — it's me! What the hell's going on? I hear you've turned Kuzma down! The man who spurns my son spurns me!

[KHRISTOFOR *appears from the kitchen.* VIKTOSHA *stands at the door of her room for some time and then disappears.*]

FEDYA [*pause as he listens*]. Oh, is that so! Someone comes along and sticks his nose into your affairs and my son gets chucked out! . . . You can't fool me. You made a mistake. You must put it right . . . Kuzma's taken his puppets away? Right! I'm coming to take mine. So there! [*Hangs up, sees* KHRISTO-FOR.] Not bad, Khristofor? Do you know that double-dyed villain had the nerve to turn Kuzya down. He preferred somebody else. Would you believe it!

KHRISTOFOR [*unhurried*]. You know, Fedya, I don't like telling you this, but I think you've gone and lost your reason.

FEDYA. Khristofor, don't argue! [*Runs to the door.*] I'm going to get my puppets back! [*Runs out.*]

KHRISTOFOR. Well now, I must concentrate. It's like living on top of a volcano in this flat . . . Where have I put my knitting?

> [**VIKTOSHA** *enters from the next room. She wears a raincoat and carries her suitcases. Without noticing* **KHRISTOFOR***, she goes to the table, writes something and then makes for the door.*]

Viktosha?

VIKTOSHA [*turns*]. Khristofor . . .

KHRISTOFOR. Where are you off to?

VIKTOSHA [*almost in a whisper*]. It's better like this.

KHRISTOFOR. Are you leaving?

> [**VIKTOSHA** *nods without speaking.*]

For good?

VIKTOSHA. I think I've done all I can. [*Slight smile.*] Now I can go. [*Thinks.*] No, I must go.

KHRISTOFOR. Aren't you sorry for Kuzya? [*Quietly.*] I know everything.

VIKTOSHA [*quickly*]. Here . . . Give him this note. It's just a few words. [*Reads.*] "Never leave your father. Remember, you promised." [*Gives him the note.*]

KHRISTOFOR. I have grown to love you very much. And I promise you with all my heart, I'll never forget you.

VIKTOSHA. Me too.

KHRISTOFOR. Only I'm sorry for my remarkable suit. I'll never wear it again. [*Bows.*] Look after yourself.

VIKTOSHA. Thank you. [*Kisses* **KHRISTOFOR***. Listens.*]

> [*Rushes about the room. Hides behind the door curtain.* **FEDYA** *enters.*]

FEDYA [*shouts as he enters and goes into the next room*]. Khristofor, I've changed my mind.

VIKTOSHA [*urgently*]. Goodbye! [*Disappears.*]

FEDYA [*coming out of the next room*]. Where's Viktosha?

KHRISTOFOR [*not moving*]. She's gone.

FEDYA. Splendid! A walk will do her good. Wonderful weather. [*Looks at* **KHRISTOFOR** *suspiciously*.] Why are you standing there rooted? Frankly, you look awful.

KHRISTOFOR [*sadly*]. You're stupid. Be quiet.

FEDYA [*good-natured*]. Don't go too far! Besides I'm not stupid. You see, I didn't go to the Maestro. [*Delighted*.] I had an extraordinary idea! I'm surprisingly cunning and clever!

    [**KUZYA** *appears quietly from the hall. They don't notice him.*]

Today I have behaved quite splendidly, in every way.

KHRISTOFOR. In what way?

FEDYA. I shan't tell you. I don't want to boast. Except that the biggest temptation of my life suddenly rose up before me. And I resisted it. I said goodbye to hope. Now I feel sad and easy, my sorrow is surprisingly light . . . [*Pause*.] Where is Viktosha?

KHRISTOFOR [*after a slight pause*]. She's gone for good.

FEDYA. What do you mean, for good?

KHRISTOFOR [*seriously*]. Look, I've been saying for a long time that we must concentrate. I think it's more necessary than ever.

FEDYA [*getting it*]. She's gone back to Leningrad?

          [**KHRISTOFOR** *nods*.]

For good?

KHRISTOFOR. Probably. [*Pause*.] It's grown dark. We need some light.

FEDYA. Wait . . . [*Looks round and walks about the room*.] How funny . . . How funny . . . Perhaps she doesn't exist?

KUZYA [*emerging from the shadows*]. She exists, all right. I'm sure your Viktosha has a great sense of humour.

KHRISTOFOR. It would be awfully nice of you, little boy, not to say one unkind word about her. Ever. Here, take this.

          [*He gives him the note*.]

KUZYA [*reads the note, despair breaking through*]. But why?

KHRISTOFOR. Does one ever understand them. Better not think about it. [*Decides to change the subject*.] Fedya, you know, it was Kuzya who told me to show your marionettes to the Maestro.

FEDYA [*lightly hitting* **KUZYA** *with his fist*]. Kuzma, I had a wonderful idea just now! Let's work on Helen together.

KUZYA [*after a slight pause*]. In that case, I suppose I should move in with you?

FEDYA. You know, I saw him when he was two weeks old. I said he looked like a monkey – yes, yes, and at that precise moment, I proudly thought, there at last was the man who would conquer me.

KUZYA. I'm sorry I haven't done it yet.

FEDYA. Somehow I feel it in the air.

[**KHRISTOFOR** *carefully picks out on the guitar the sentimental tune recently played by provincial* **FATTY**.]

KUZYA [*looking round the shelves where the saddened puppets are holding their breath*]. All the same – why? Why has she gone away?

FEDYA [*his secret still alive within him*]. I think I can guess . . . Yes, I know why.

KHRISTOFOR [*quietly*]. If you know, keep quiet. [*Having got the tune at last, he sings quietly*.]

"Dearest love . . ."

[**FEDYA** *smiles happily*.]

FINAL CURTAIN

Once Upon a Time

Writing about his production of *Once Upon a Time*, Anotoly Efros says that Arbuzov's recent plays are a kind of parable or fairy tale.

He recounts his analysis and conversations with the cast as follows. One had to understand the serious outlook and the personal pain that had gone into the plays. When ageing preceded official classification, it was no problem. But official classification of an old-age pensioner could precede the person's subjective awareness of ageing. That is when the person might be afraid of being so classified, afraid of his next birthday, the next stage that is about to prevent him forcibly from completing his work. Holiday leave and rest could be frightening and not only to a creative artist. The fear was that the rest would be final.

The other aspect of the problem was a sudden and violent need to reassess relationships. For instance, with Fedya's approaching old age came the fear of loneliness, a need for people he had taken for granted, a yearning for the estranged son, now independent and resentful. Finally, there was the question of his work. Ones expertise gets in the way of ones inspiration, and good taste is fatal, Fedya says. Arbuzov enjoys paradoxes, continues Efros, but you only have to look at the pictures of a few elderly painters to realize they have lost their arrogance or impact. One has to keep freeing oneself of ones own professionalism and skill.

Efros talked to Tenin, who was to play Fedya, about extraordinary old men — Picasso, Hemingway, Jean Gabin. But at the same time "we need amazing airy lightness. The old psychological drama is not the new psychological drama which is comedy, fairy tale, fantasy, light, it is even light-headed while expressing the most profound and dramatic ideas and themes."

"There should be no studied characterization. The sketch of the part should be unexpected, sudden, psychologically transparent and, if you like, contradictory. Take Khristofor — he is different from moment to moment. Obviously it has all been thought out but at the same time his impact is always sudden. Apart from his being Fedya's best friend it is difficult to say how his various moments relate to each other.

"As in *The Happy Days of an Unhappy Man*, a young woman, almost a nymph, appears. In the earlier play she had been a teacher of backward children, now she was a dressmaker and quite young. All along the old man, Fedya, had been waiting for the miracle of renewal, the miracle of returning youth. The miracle occurs — the old man falls in love with the girl. The girl falls in love with his son. That's the plot. The old man becomes aware of the new and final phase of his life. Arbuzov said he had written a play about the agony of an artist. Well then, I suppose we shall have to express this agony but we'll be very controlled, grand and light as light," wrote Efros.

In Moscow, Olga Yakovleva was the nymph in both plays. In Bristol, Felicity Kendal played Viktosha. Several years earlier in Leicester she had played Lika in *The Promise*. After seeing Richard Cottrell's "symbolic production . . . all the action took place on a bridge . . . Marat's idea of the link between his youth and maturity . . .", Arbuzov wrote: "I saw a fine young actress, Felicity Kendal, who undoubtedly has a great future."

The national critics were very appreciative of Michael Hordern and mostly dismissive of the play in its Bristol production. The audiences loved both. People flocked to the Little Theatre openly challenging the critics' view of the play.

Finally, a few words about Borovsky's stage-set in Moscow: a whole floor of a small house in Arbat, an old part of Moscow, had been gutted, as it were, for Fedya's workshop. The table consisted of a door placed on trestles, half was covered with an oil-cloth where they ate out of wrapping paper, "like . . . carpenters during a meal break". There was a partition made up of doors bolted together. The walls were hung with trellis designs of the entrances of old houses, so that the workshop was somehow like a yard as well. There was a complicated arrangement of chiming door-bells by the entrances. Unfinished marionettes stuck out of a number of boxes on the floor. There was nothing pretty or cute about any of it. The effect was breath-takingly fantastic.

RUSSIAN THEATRES

The Russian theatres referred to in the Moscow productions are officially called:

Central Theatre of the Soviet Army

Moscow Arts and Academy Theatre of the USSR named M. Gorky, the Orders of Lenin and the Red Banner of Labour

Moscow Theatre named Leninsky Komsomol, the Order of the Red Banner of Labour

Moscow Theatre of Drama in Malaya Bronnaya Street

State Theatre named Y. Vakhtangov, the Order of the Red Banner of Labour

GITIS refers to the State Institute of Theatre Art named A. V. Lomonosov

In Leningrad the theatres are officially called:

Leningrad Academy Bolshoy Theatre of Drama named M. Gorky

Leningrad State Acedemy Theatre of Drama named A. S. Pushkin

Leningrad Theatre named Lensovet

LGITMIK refers to the Leningrad Research Institute of Theatre, Music and Cinema.

BIBLIOGRAPHY

Russian Publications of Arbuzov's Plays

DVENADTSATY CHAS, IRKUTSKAYA ISTORIYA (The Twelfth Hour, It Happened in Irkutsk); Ot Avtora (Author's Introduction); Iskusstvo, Moskva 1960.

TEATR (THEATRE) Sovetsky Pisatel', Moskva 1961, including *Dvenadtsaty Chas (The Twelfth Hour)*.

DRAMY (DRAMAS) Iskusstvo, Moskva 1969. Teatr Arbuzova by N. Krymova (Arbuzov's Theatre, Introduction by N. Krymova), including *Dvenadtsaty Chas (The Twelfth Hour)* and *Moy Bedny Marat (My Poor Marat/The Promise)*.

VYBOR. Sbornik Pyes (Choice. Collection of Plays) Sovetsky Pisatel', Moskva 1976, including Skazki Starogo Arbata *(Tales of Old Arbat/Once Upon a Time)* and *Moyo Zaglyadenye (Lovely to Look At!)*.

First publications

Dvenadtsaty Chas (The Twelfth Hour), *Teatr*, monthly periodical, 1959/8.

Moy Bedny Marat (My Poor Marat/The Promise), *Teatr* 1965/1.

Moyo Zaglyadenye (Lovely to Look At!), *Moskva*, monthly periodical, 1972/5.

Skazki Starogo Arbata (Tales of Old Arbat/Once Upon a Time), *Teatr* 1970/9.

Zhestokiye Igry (Cruel Games), *Teatr* 1978/4.